Unraveling the Real

Unraveling the Real

The Fantastic in Spanish-American *Ficciones*

CYNTHIA DUNCAN

Temple University Press
PHILADELPHIA

Temple University Press
Philadelphia, Pennsylvania 19122
www.temple.edu/tempress

Published 2010
Printed in the United States of America

∞ The paper used in this publication meets the requirements of the American National Standard for Information Sciences—Permanence of Paper for Printed Library Materials, ANSI Z39.48-1992

LIBRARY OF CONGRESS CATALOGING-IN-PUBLICATION DATA

Duncan, Cynthia.
Unraveling the real : the fantastic in Spanish-American ficciones / Cynthia Duncan.
p. cm.
Includes bibliographical references and index.
ISBN 978-1-4399-0240-0 (cloth : alk. paper)
ISBN 978-1-4399-0241-7 (pbk. : alk. paper)
ISBN 978-1-4399-0242-4 (e-book)
1. Fantasy fiction, Spanish American—History and criticism. 2. Spanish American fiction—20th century—History and criticism. 3. Literature and society—Latin America—History—20th century. 4. Metaphysics in literature. I. Title.
PQ7082.F35D86 2010
863'.87660998—dc22

2010008812

2 4 6 8 9 7 5 3 1

THE AMERICAN LITERATURES INITIATIVE

A book in the American Literatures Initiative (ALI), a collaborative publishing project of NYU Press, Fordham University Press, Rutgers University Press, Temple University Press, and the University of Virginia Press. The Initiative is supported by The Andrew W. Mellon Foundation. For more information, please visit www.americanliteratures.org.

Maferefún Orichas

Contents

ACKNOWLEDGMENTS

I have written journal articles about some of the authors that I discuss in this book, but my treatment of them here differs significantly from those earlier publications. Readers interested in the fantastic short story in Mexico can consult "The Fantastic as a Vehicle of Social Criticism in José Emilio Pacheco's 'La fiesta brava'" (*Chasqui: Revista de Literatura Latinoamericana* 14.2–3 [Feb.–May 1985]: 3–13); and "Carlos Fuentes' 'Chac Mool' and Todorov's Theory of the Fantastic: A Case for the Twentieth Century" (*Hispanic Journal* 8.1 [fall 1986]: 125–33). My interest in women writers of the fantastic has its roots in these articles: "'La culpa es de los tlaxcaltecas': A Reevaluation of Mexico's Past Through Myth" (*Crítica Hispánica* 7.2 [fall 1985]: 105–20); "Double or Nothing?: The Fantastic Element in Silvina Ocampo's 'La casa de azúcar'" (*Chasqui* 20.2 [Nov. 1991]: 64–72); "An Eye for an 'I': Women Writers and the Fantastic as a Challenge to Patriarchal Authority" *(Inti: Revista de Literatura Hispánica* 40–41 [fall 1994–spring 1995]: 233–46); and "Reading Power: Some Observations on the Construction of Meaning and Authority in María Luisa Bombal's *La última niebla*" (*Revista Hispánica Moderna* 51 [1998]: 304–16). I have expanded on these articles and used a different analytical focus here.

I am profoundly grateful to those people who have contributed to this book by giving me friendship, support, scholarly insights, and great advice throughout the years. Thomas C. Meehan is at the top of the list for passing on to me his love of the fantastic in Spanish America. He inspired me to become the scholar and teacher I am today. Maria Clark has been fundamental in keeping my love for the fanastic alive. Her enthusiasm for the genre as well as her brilliant analyses of it have illuminated my path. Denise DiPuccio has also been a source of inspiration and strength. She knew I would write this book long before I did, and she never stopped believing in me. Vicki Elkins, Steve Beaver, and Beth Secrist have always been willing to lend an ear and offer encouragement when I needed it. Thanks for always being there for me. I'm grateful to my parents for teaching me to love books, and to my brothers and their families, for sharing the love of books with me. The University of Tennessee provided me with a research leave, which gave me time to get started on the book. Thanks to colleagues there, especially Carl Cobb, Yulan Washburn, Bill Heflin, Michael Handelsman, and John Romeiser, who helped me find my way in life as a professor. I am grateful to Patricia Klingenberg, whose work on the fantastic has influenced me and who has generously shared her ideas with me at conferences and professional meetings. Beth Kalikoff graciously agreed to read an early version of the manuscript and provided encouraging feedback, as well as continuous moral support. Good friends in Mexico and Cuba have given me a place to work and write, and they have welcomed me into their homes and communities in a way that sustains me and keeps me firmly grounded in Latin America, no matter where I am. At Temple University Press, Emily Taber deserves my eternal thanks for overseeing the early stages of the book's progress, as does Janet Francendese for her enthusiastic support and professional guidance. I also want to thank the estate of Remedios Varo for allowing me to use her beautiful artwork on the cover. Last, but not least, I want to thank my students for embracing my fascination with the fantastic, and for being open to its magic.

Introduction: The Fantastic as a Literary Genre

The fantastic must be so close to the real that you almost have to believe in it.
—FYODOR DOSTOEVSKY

Reality is not always probable, or likely.
—JORGE LUIS BORGES

All types of fiction originate in the writer's imagination, yet some works inevitably strike the reader as more imaginary than others. Almost automatically, we tend to categorize stories and novels in terms of the reader's perception of reality; if the narrative describes a recognizable and verisimilar world, we think of it as realistic, but if the work presents a world which varies so greatly from our own that it appears more invented than familiar and true, we are apt to talk about it as a product of the writer's imagination. In Spanish America, realistic fiction has provided a particularly useful mode of expression for writers who wish to link literature to political and social causes. Nevertheless, imaginary fiction has also been an important part of Spanish American letters, and it has grown and developed parallel to the realistic vein. Nineteenth-century romanticism ushered in a taste for the bizarre and the uncanny in literature. Interest in ghost stories, strange legends, and tales of the supernatural and inexplicable came from the United States and northern Europe and comfortably settled into Spanish American drawing rooms. The spine-tingling themes of romantic writers were revived by turn-of-the-century modernists, who were strongly attracted to imaginary fiction of this kind, and in one form or another it continues to the present day. Because it was originally cultivated for bourgeois, urban readers, it took on connotations of being an elitist or escapist kind of literature, charges that still hover around it in some circles. Because it frequently played against dominant notions about the nature of reality, it also gained the reputation of being an intellectual game, not to be taken seriously or, at least, not to be taken as a serious challenge to socially committed realist fiction. These notions have been hotly contested by critics in recent years, along with the claim that the fantastic is a minor genre in Latin America. The fantastic has proven to be an enduring source of fascination for readers decade after decade, in large part because of its mysterious and still undefined relationship to our understanding of the real. Some of the most important literary figures of the past century, such as Rubén Darío, Horacio Quiroga, Jorge Luis Borges, Julio Cortázar, and Carlos Fuentes, have cultivated it, and there is a substantial and impressive body of work associated with this kind of writing. Fantastic short stories, when they are well written, are like jewels, finely polished and carefully constructed narratives that mesmerize readers through their craftsmanship. They are what Barthes called "writerly texts," stories that draw readers into the creative process and dismantle in the process long-standing assumptions about fiction and reality. Despite claims that the fantastic is unimportant, irrelevant, or even dead in other places, it continues to be a vital force in Spanish America because it provides another window onto the complex world that spawns it.

Although there is no single definition of the fantastic that stands out as absolute and final, almost all critics agree that it incorporates something into the narrative that may strike readers as supernatural or otherworldly, inexplicable or impossible, something that unsettles readers and makes them hesitate or doubt the nature of what they are reading. Some critics offer a thematic approach, focusing on the content of the fantastic story, and others look at the story from a structural and semiotic perspective, outlining strategies used by the writer to produce a fantastic effect. Some have attempted to situate it historically, linking it to a shift in thinking associated with European Enlightenment or romanticism, while others have approached it philosophically, showing how it reflects a metaphysical angst rooted in the modern world. Beyond these simple contours, it becomes very difficult to speak about the fantastic with any authority, since there is so much disagreement about the meaning of the term and how it can be used. There has also been, over the past fifty years, a tendency to conflate all kinds of imaginary fiction into a single broad category with a variety of names proposed for it, and an equally strong push to distinguish between different kinds of imaginary fiction and give each one its own clear identity. My purpose here is not to put an end to the debate, which would be an exercise in futility, but to look at the debate as emblematic of the fantastic itself. What is it about the genre that makes it so impossible to pin down?

One of the most pressing problems in any discussion of this imaginary vein of literature is what to call it. Do we highlight what it has in common, or how one type differs from another? Generic terms such as the supernatural or fantasy are somewhat misleading, since they have been appropriated by popular literature and film and sometimes refer to mass-marketed works that lack artistic merit. In contemporary criticism, fantasy is so broad a category that it is used to refer to science fiction, fairy tales, and ghost stories, along with other kinds of supernatural and magical tales, and includes authors as widely diverse as Ursula LeGuinn, Stephen King, and J.K. Rowling. The uncanny, the marvelous, the absurd, the grotesque, and gothic horror, by contrast, are terms that have been coined in reference to specific works and writers and have such a clearly defined nature that their use is restricted to those particular kinds of texts.[1] Magical realism, as the name suggests, describes works that blend the magical with the real, but the precise meaning of the term and its boundaries are far from stable entities in the world of literary criticism. The marvelous-real (*lo real maravilloso*) intersects with magical realism so often and so intimately that it is impossible to discuss one without reference to the other. For some, they are the same thing; for others, they mark different paths in the evolution of literary theory.[2] The fantastic is acknowledged as a neighboring genre to all of these types of fiction, but it has perhaps been the most difficult concept to grasp. Critics have engaged in an ongoing dialogue for the past fifty years about what the fantastic is, what function it has in a literary text, and what relationship it has to our notions of the real. Readers naturally expect critics to provide them with clear definitions that they can apply to the study of specific literary texts, but in the case of the fantastic, they are often left wanting. The slippery nature of the fantastic is part of what defines it as a genre, and any attempt to confine it to a set of marked characteristics inevitably leads to more confusion and debate. Perhaps a more productive way to approach the fantastic is to acknowledge that it can shift, slide, and transform itself over time and across cultures, and that as a literary genre it remains resistant to closure. Fortunately, there are common threads that link theoretical discussions of the fantastic together; we can identify and use them to lay down loose boundaries for the genre that prevent the fantastic from becoming a blanket term used for all kinds of fiction. At the same time, it behooves us to remember that absolute and authoritative definitions of the fantastic are little more than wishful thinking on the part of those who offer them, since they are easily dismantled and reassembled by other critics who approach the of expression never venture beyond the borders of their own culture. How appropriate it is to use critical theory borrowed from one place to study the literature of another? At the very least, we can open a dialogue about the ways that Spanish American texts illustrate theories of fantastic; at best, we can illustrate how Spanish American fiction has shaped the ways we think about the genre itself. It is absurd to suppose that Spanish American writers have written in isolation and have not been part of literary trends simply because foreign critics have neglected to mention them. Many of the Spanish American writers whose works are studied here are cosmopolitan figures, fluent in various languages, voracious readers, well aware of the latest arguments in the field of literary criticism at home and abroad. Their work can be read as a reaction and response to the ideas proposed by theorists, as well as to the literary texts on which those theories are based. Literature is defined not only by those who study it but also by those who create it. Borges, Cortázar, Bioy Casares, and Fuentes, for example, are recognized not only as masters of the fantastic short story but also rank among the foremost literary critics in Latin America. In referring to the ideas of European and North American theorists in my study, I do not mean to suggest that Latin Americans are unable to elaborate their own theories of the fantastic. They have done so, and they are included here. But their voices have too often been isolated from other discussions of the fantastic, and they have not always received the recognition they deserve in shaping the way we think about this kind of literature.[4] There has been a European or Anglo American bias in much of what has been written about the fantastic over the years, a tendency that distorts the importance of the genre in Latin America and sometimes results in accusations that it is merely an imitation of foreign models and not an authentic form of literature. The endurance of fantastic short stories in Spanish America long after the vogue in Europe had passed is sometimes cited as an example of how Spanish American literature lags behind European trends. Another way of looking at it is to see the fantastic in Spanish America as an example of postcolonial literature, a body of work that has taken on a life of its own and developed its own characteristics, appropriating foreign models and using them to delve into problems of self-representation in literature. An examination of the theories put forth by European and U.S. scholars, when interwoven into a study of fantastic literature written in Spanish America, is crucial to an understanding of how many of the assumptions we make about the genre are rooted in Western ideologies, and how those ways of thinking have been challenged by Spanish American writers. In Spanish

America, the fantastic is wedged into a space where cultural tensions come together, smoothing over surface divisions while at the same time threatening to undermine the foundations on which the culture rests. It is for this reason that so many fantastic stories from the Spanish-speaking Americas ultimately strike us as deeply subversive works.

I use the word *genre* to refer to the fantastic, although the characteristics that describe this kind of writing are far from clear-cut. Genre suggests that it is divisible from a larger body of general literature, and that it can be studied in its own context. Early scholars of the fantastic tended to look at it from the point of view of thematic concerns, but since the 1970s, critical focus has shifted to style, structure, and form. For this reason, I sometimes also call the fantastic a narrative mode, as it describes a particular way of telling a story. Whether the fantastic can appear in any kind of literary text is a much-debated question, but looking at the works that best illustrate the fantastic in Spanish America, it is clear that the short story is the ideal vehicle for this kind of writing. Because the short story can be read in a single sitting, and the economy of the form permits writers to create a compact, tightly controlled fictional world, it lends itself to the kind of tension required to bring the fantastic to life. In the short story, there are no distractions, no detours, and no motivation for readers to put the text aside and let the effects of the fantastic dissipate before reaching the story's end. If, as some critics claim, the fantastic is a brief glimpse, a temporary disorientation, or an unsettling feeling about the nature of what we are reading, it makes sense that it cannot be sustained for long periods of time. This explains why critics seldom discuss long novels as examples of the fantastic. Although a novel may have some elements we could identify as fantastic, the work in its entirety cannot maintain the same kind of tension that we find in a short story without completely exhausting its readers. The fantastic, critics tell us, must always keep a toehold in the recognizable world of the reader, and it comes and goes so quickly that it introduces a kind of vertigo into the reading experience. By contrast, magical realism, a neighboring genre to the fantastic, is much more at home in the novel, since the length, depth, and breadth of a novel allow writers to create an entire fictional world with its own frame of reference that draws readers into it at a more leisurely pace.

Critics disagree about when the fantastic came into being: some insist that the fantastic is as old as literature itself (Carillo), some find its origins in the eighteenth century, when belief in the supernatural was on the wane in Western Europe (Caillois, Todorov), and some situate it at the beginning of the nineteenth century (Bioy Casares), when romanticism was in full flower. To a large degree, our understanding of the history of the fantastic is linked to the way we conceptualize the genre, which leads back to the thorny question of what kind of literature, exactly, are we talking about? It is easier to pinpoint when writers and critics first began to argue about the fantastic. In Western Europe, "fantastic criticism develops in inverse relationship to the intensity of eighteenth-century claims for the reasonable, realistic novel, each form requiring the other for self-definition" (Sandner 286). But most of Spanish America in the eighteenth century was still under colonial rule, when censorship determined what books colonists could read and writing fiction of any kind was considered an illicit act. Literary criticism was primarily limited to the discussion of ecclesiastic texts and the works of classical Greco-Roman authors. For this reason, critical discussions of the fantastic in any form in Spanish America seem to lag behind the European mainstream, although this is not to suggest that upon entering the debate Spanish Americans did not have important new ideas to add. In fact, they were well on their way to becoming masters of the genre by the time they entered into theoretical discussions about it.

The Evolution of the Fantastic in Spanish America

Jorge Luis Borges, one of the first in Spanish America to understand the complexities of the genre and to vindicate it as an art form, wrote in his 1936 review of Adolfo Bioy Casares's book *La estatua casera*, "Sospecho que un examen general de la literatura fantástica revelaría que es muy poco fantástica" (qtd. in de la Fuente, 58). Although his statement is typically enigmatic, Borges anticipates one of the central problems of fantastic criticism in the twentieth century, that there is no common agreement or understanding about what the fantastic is; therefore, one can take up diametrically opposed positions about it in order to construct or dismantle its meaning, ultimately creating a semantic void around the word itself. A few years later, upon the publication of the *Antología de la literatura fantástica*, Borges, Bioy Casares, and Silvina Ocampo would have to confront the problem more directly in their choice of representative texts for the collection. Annick Louis has observed that some of the pieces in the anthology do not fit well within the framework of Bioy Casares's introductory remarks about the genre, but Louis claims, "El carácter ambiguo de esta antología se entiende como un rasgo constitutivo del género" (415). In other words, the selection of texts defines the genre as one characterized by contradictions and contrasts, and it teaches us how to read the fantastic as a kind of literature that is continuously pushing against its own boundaries. The appearance of the anthology in 1940 and its widespread popularity clearly suggest that there was a preexisting interest in this kind of literature on the part of a South American reading public. We can also assume that not all readers were familiar with the critical meaning of the term fantastic and that the anthology itself became their way of understanding it. Bioy Casares's introduction leads the reader through a brief theoretical discussion of the genre, where he outlines some of his views about the fantastic and illustrates them primarily with reference to European and North American works. The essay's unassuming tone, however, disguises the revolutionary approach the three editors took to the selection of texts for the work. Louis sees the anthology as "un espacio privilegiado para librar batalla en el campo literario, ya que el volumen que compilaron combate una concepción de la literatura fantástica ampliamente difundida en la cultura argentina de la época" (416). For example, the anthology omits writers like Ambrose Bierce and E.T.A. Hoffman, hitherto considered important exponents of the fantastic, and replaces them with contemporary Spanish American authors like Borges and María Luisa Bombal. In private correspondence to Victoria Ocampo, the French critic Roger Caillois complained that he found the selection in the anthology disconcerting and wrong headed.[5] Still, there can be no doubt that the anthology succeeded in generating a dialogue about the fantastic in which Spanish Americans would play a vital part. An examination of its contents reveals some important points: (1) the fantastic has strong ties to Europe, but it also exists in Spanish America; (2) it has flourished in Spanish America in places where European influence was strongest (large cities, the River Plate region, and so forth); (3) as a literary genre, it came into being in the early nineteenth century and continues to the present day; (4) the fantastic is best represented by short fictional narratives; (5) reader response to the text is one of the defining characteristics of the genre; and (6) the fantastic is not a stable entity but has been transformed over time.

Contrary to Caillois's assertion that the fantastic was born in Germany, Bioy Casares tells readers, "como género más o menos definido, la literatura fantástica aparece en el siglo XIX y en el idioma inglés" (7). This statement may reflect the editors' decision to isolate eighteenth-century gothic fiction from the fantastic, or it may simply be a product of the Argentines' intellectual ties to England. Although most of the works included in the anthology are translations from other languages, the anthology marks a significant moment in Spanish American fantastic fiction, for included along with European, North American, and oriental masters are several writers from the Southern Cone: Bombal, Borges, Dabove, Fernández, Lugones, Payrou, and Cancela. As a theorist of the fantastic, Bioy Casares perhaps makes his most important contribution when he acknowledges that the fantastic follows particular rules or laws, but they are not permanently fixed notions. He warns his reader, "Pedimos leyes para el cuento fantástico; pero ya veremos que no hay un tipo, sino muchos, de cuentos fantásticos. Habrá que indagar las leyes generales para cada tipo de cuento y las leyes especiales para cada cuento" (8). He also recognizes a symbiotic relationship between the reader, the writer, and the text that causes literature to undergo constant renovation: "Si estudiamos la sorpresa como efecto literario, o los argumentos, veremos cómo la literatura va transformando a los lectores y, en consecuencia, cómo éstos exigen una continua transformación de la literatura" (8). These observations are astute and suggest the unstable and evanescent quality of the fantastic element in any given text, an idea that other critics would take up later in more detail.

The Argentine author maintains that nineteenth-century writers often evoked feelings of fear or surprise through the creation of atmosphere, and standard subject matter such as ghosts, supernatural beings, time travel, metamorphosis, and the like provided the writer with fantastic plots. Some works allow a logical explanation of preternatural events, while others do not; Bioy Casares notes, however, that a logical explanation often weakens the effect of the narrative. He stresses the importance of the reader's reaction in his discussion of the fantastic, as later theorists would do, and he also points toward the fact that the fantastic in the twentieth century has a different nature than that of the previous century, "lo que podríamos llamar la tendencia realista en la literatura fantástica"(9), or as he puts it "la conveniencia de hacer que en un mundo plenamente creíble sucediera un solo hecho increíble; que en vidas consuetudinarias y domésticas, como las del lector, sucediera el fantasma" (8–9).

Bioy Casares sees the short story as the ideal vehicle for the fantastic but he does not pause to consider the relationship between the fantastic and short fiction. Instead, he treats it as a natural connection, explaining that "una noche de 1937 hablábamos de literatura fantástica, discutíamos los cuentos que nos parecían mejores; uno de nosotros dijo que si los reuniéramos y agregáramos los fragmentos del mismo carácter anotados en nuestros cuadernos, obtendríamos un buen libro. Compusimos este libro" (14). Although most of the texts in the anthology are short stories, the editors include a few examples of drama that they consider fantastic. Poetry, however, is conspicuously absent, which points to the implicit understanding that the fantastic effect cannot be achieved through language that encourages allegorical or metaphorical readings. This is a point that Tzvetan Todorov and later critics would also take up in their discussion of the fantastic.[6]

The publication of Todorov's *Introduction a la littérature fantastique* in 1970 is generally understood to be a turning point in fantastic criticism, for almost every scholar to discuss the subject afterward has felt a need to respond to the book, whether choosing to embrace and expand on some of Todorov's arguments or reject them adamantly in favor of another approach. Despite the apparent dearth of critical studies on the fantastic in Spanish America between 1940 and the 1970s, it is important to note that fantastic literature was at its zenith there. This period, which leads up to and overlaps with the so-called "Boom" of Latin American fiction, is a time when the writers themselves were shaping the way we think about the fantastic by producing works that signaled a new direction for this kind of writing.[7] It was, as Bioy Casares had observed, more grounded in the modern world, the recognizable and familiar world of an ideal reader, witty and urbane on the surface, but unable to feel completely at ease in his surroundings. Masterful storytellers used the fantastic to explore existential themes that related to problems of identity, both on the individual and national levels. In this way, their writing coincides with the philosophies of important European intellectuals like Jean Paul Sartre, who in turn wrote about the fantastic as an expression of his own beliefs.

The Boundaries of the Fantastic in Europe

Although Sartre does not make reference to Latin American writers, nor move his argument beyond the boundaries of Western Europe, it is clear that his conceptualization of the fantastic is in line with the thinking of writers like Borges, Bioy Casares, Ocampo, Cortázar, Fuentes, and others who were working in the genre at the time, and that together their work describes a midcentury angst prevalent on both sides of the Atlantic, rooted in different causes but with the same general effect. The possible existence of a new kind of fantastic literature intrigued the French philosopher, who claimed that it was initiated by Franz Kafka and developed in Europe during and after the two world wars. But, in essence, Sartre echoes the idea advanced by Bioy Casares a decade and a half before in the *Antología*, when he writes that "in order to achieve the fantastic, it is neither necessary nor sufficient to portray extraordinary things. The strangest event will enter into the order of the universe if it is alone in a world governed by laws" (57). Sartre posits that man is at the center of the new fantastic and that its main theme is man's abandonment in the world of his fellow man. The only fantastic object in the modern world is man himself. According to Sartre, the fantastic "seems to be stripped of all its artifices; there is nothing in its hands or pockets. We recognize the footprint on the shore as our own . . . . For contemporary man, the fantastic is only one of a hundred ways of mirroring his own image" (60). Without a doubt, these are accurate descriptions of how the Spanish American writers we have set out to study here conceive of the fantastic.

Sartre claims that man is a fantastic being living in a fantastic world; therefore, man does not perceive it as fantastic. The reader, however, must be made to observe things from a more objective point of view (as an outsider), which creates a technical problem for the writer. When seen from the outside, human activity appears reversed, and the world seems upside down or "topsy-turvy." For Sartre, this is the essence of the fantastic; it is "a world in which these absurd manifestations appear as normal behavior" (61). Whereas the absurd signals a complete absence of ends, the fantastic is "the revolt of means against ends" (61). In the fantastic, we still believe in cause and effect, we still believe that means and ends exist, but they are beyond our comprehension. They are blurred or contradictory, and we are never able to discover the ultimate end of our actions. When confronted by a fantastic situation, Sartre claims that the modern hero is never surprised, but he is angry and frustrated by the unfathomable world that envelops him. In this way, his ideas about the fantastic reveal his ties to existentialism.

Three additional European critics from the 1950s and 1960s should be mentioned here for their contributions to our modern-day understanding of the fantastic in Spanish America, although they did not speak directly about Spanish American literature. They are Caillois, Vax, and Ostrowski. Caillois and Vax were highly respected French theorists whose work was surely known in academic and literary circles in Buenos Aires and Mexico City, where writers like Cortázar, Ocampo, Fuentes, and Garro worked. Ostrowski is perhaps not so well known, but his approach to the fantastic bears examination because it challenges some of the same notions we see in Spanish American fantastic stories, specifically the tendency to understand realism in literature in too-universal terms. Caillois was clearly aware of the anthology put together by Bioy Casares, Borges, and Ocampo in Argentina, but he ignored it completely (along with Bioy Casares's introductory comments) in his 1958 essay on the fantastic. Instead, the French critic followed Sartre's lead in terms of how he conceives of the fantastic, defining it in reference to the "real" world, as most scholars of this era tended to do. Caillois characterizes the fantastic as an "almost unbearable irruption in the world of reality"(53). It represents a break in the acknowledged order of the universe, an irregularity, an intrusion of something unfamiliar into the familiar world of the reader. Caillois frames his discussion by situating the fantastic historically, as Bioy Casares had done in his 1940 essay. In its modern sense, the fantastic appeared with romanticism at the end of the eighteenth century in northern Europe as a reaction against an excess of rationalism. Caillois believes that prior to the eighteenth century, it is difficult to speak of the fantastic because we are speaking of "a universe that is still supernatural" (53), or a world where the marvelous is considered part of human experience. The masterpieces of fantastic literature, such as the works of Hoffman, Poe, Hawthorne, and Irving, appear in the first half of the nineteenth century when scientific advancements added fuel to supernatural possibilities and man's notion of reality was heightened. The themes of the fantastic are not new, Caillois claims, since "like myths, tales of the fantastic readily take up the same themes under different plot arrangement" (54). Caillois links the fantastic to the emergence of a scientifically minded society, and he believes that it reflects a certain nostalgia for the passing of an era: "The fear which is peculiar to the fantastic tale crops up only in an incredulous world in which the laws of nature are deemed to be rigid and unchanging. It appears as the nostalgia for a universe that is accessible to the powers of darkness and to the emissaries of the beyond" (55). According to Caillois, "The fantastic supposes the solidity of the real world, the better to ravage it" (51). This intrusion can be sudden or gradual, but "the essential step in the fantastic is the Apparition: what cannot happen but *does* happen, at a given moment and point in the heart of a perfectly ordered universe, from which one believed mystery to have been forever banished" (51). Caillois points out that although the writer of fantastic literature probably does not believe in the things he writes about, he plays upon our fear that these things *could* happen. In order for the fantastic to have its full effect, then, writers, readers, and characters must share a similar worldview and believe that certain inviolate laws govern the universe.

Although Caillois's remarks could apply to Spanish American metropolises like Buenos Aires and Mexico City in the late 1950s, when national projects related to industrialization and modernization were in full swing, it is problematic to talk about Spanish American culture as a singular, unified thing. In fact, much of magical realist fiction deals specifically with coexisting worldviews that contrast the "pre-scientific" or "marvelous" perception of fictional characters who live in remote regions of the Americas with that of Westernized mainstream readers who most likely adhere to the kind of laws of causality described by Caillois. Furthermore, as Kimberly Nance has astutely observed, "the timing of Latin American fantastic in itself to some extent calls into question the assertion that such literature is a direct product of a sociocultural moment when readers cease to believe in the supernatural" (8). Nance claims, "To maintain this notion in the face of the Latin American fantastic would require as a concomitant that the Latin American literary class (readers and writers who were inarguably connected to European philosophical and literary currents) relinquished its belief in the supernatural much later than its European counterpart" (8–9). Caillois's idea that readers and writers of the fantastic usually share the same worldview is an important one, along with the notion that the fantastic often feels threatening because it violates the laws that we believe govern the world we inhabit. He also rightly identifies the fantastic as a counter voice to scientific progress and projects of modernity and industrialization, regardless of when or where they occur. But the assertion that a monolithic belief system exists, and that a chronological shift moved us from a pre-scientific to a postscientific understanding of the world, is an oversimplification in the case of Latin America. As Nance argues, literary conventions often lag behind actual belief systems. To play with the idea that the supernatural might exist, and to speculate about how the reader may react to it, is not to suggest that the writer or the reader of a fantastic text actually believes in the supernatural. However, as Caillois suggests, the fantastic must rely on some vestiges of belief in the supernatural in order to make us think, even briefly, that it *could* exist. How remote those beliefs are, where they come from, and how we conceive of the supernatural may vary from culture to culture, but the fantastic always speaks from a position of absence, referring to a hypothetical moment in time when reason might fail us.

Vax's treatise on the fantastic was translated from French to Spanish in 1965 and widely circulated in Spanish American literary circles. Like Caillois, Vax makes no reference to fantastic writing by Spanish

American writers, but many of his ideas about the genre are in line with the literature that was being produced there. Vax claims that there is an inversion of cause and effect in the fantastic and that it transgresses the laws of time, space, and matter. As supernatural elements invade a world based on reason and threaten its security, ordinary men, characters, and readers are confronted by something inexplicable in their everyday lives. As he puts it, "el amante de lo fantástico no juega con la inteligencia, sino con el temor; no mira desde fuera, sino que se deja hechizar. No es otro universo el que se encuentra frente al nuestro; es nuestro propio mundo que, paradójicamente, se metamorfosea, se corrompe y se transforma en otro" (17).[8] Vax classifies the fantastic according to themes that have traditionally defined it, such as vampires, werewolves, haunted houses and abandoned gardens, alterations and perturbations of human personalities, the passage of time, and the like, but he asserts that the themes are not as important as the way in which they are used to create a sensation of fear or surprise in the reader. Vax's emphasis on the reader's role in the construction and reception of the fantastic element in the text, together with the idea that the fantastic depends on stylistic and narrative devices to produce a desired effect, are insights that open texts up to more detailed study. The fantastic must contain an element that strikes us as impossible, supernatural, or inexplicable according to the laws that govern the world we live in, but it must be presented in a way that makes us wonder if such a thing is possible. Furthermore, like Sartre, he identifies the serious metaphysical implications of the fantastic: "En las narraciones fantásticas, monstruo y víctima simbolizan esta dicotomía de nuestro ser, nuestros deseos inconfesables y el horror que ellos nos inspiran" (11). This observation suggests that the fantastic can lend itself to psychoanalytic readings as well as philosophical ones, an idea that other theorists such as Rosemary Jackson and T.E. Apter would take up in later decades. At the same time, it is perfectly descriptive of the kind of fantastic fiction being written in Spanish America at the time Vax was elaborating his theories about the genre.

A problem exists at the heart of these standard definitions of the fantastic: when it is viewed in a binary way, as something that stands in opposition to or as an inversion of reality, there must be an agreed upon understanding of what reality is. In recent decades, the notion of realism in literature has come under considerable attack by poststructuralists like Roland Barthes and Georg Lukács. They point out that a kind of subjective, middle-class European norm is presented as obvious and true in "realist" texts, but this is simply a way of upholding the dominant ideology. Ostrowski attempted to address the issue of the fantastic and the realistic as literary opposites by proposing a common-sense view of reality, which he analyzes in terms of a "matter-space-time pattern" (55). He urges us to look for a "certain pattern which is on the whole constant" (55), as a kind of prototype for reality, and then to analyze the fantastic as a rearrangement of that pattern. Anything that does not reflect the usual relations among mind, matter, space, and time can be called the fantastic. Ostrowski acknowledges that our perception of reality is a cultural construct, and that it can vary across cultures and historical periods, which is an important point to keep in mind when we are discussing the development of the fantastic in Spanish America. There is no reason that the fantastic should appear at the same time in all world literatures, or that it should take the same form everywhere it appears. For Ostrowski, the fantastic plays with consciousness, which suggests that it is not simply an essence that mysteriously permeates some texts, but rather an effect that comes from the manipulation of language. He, like most other theorists, sees the fantastic and the realistic as a dichotomy, but Ostrowski leaves room for the meaning of the terms to slip and slide relative to how we perceive them. He is one of the few critics to grasp this important point, which would later be taken up by Spanish American writers, especially women, as a way to question the solidity of dominant ideological constructs.

Spanish American Attitudes Toward the Fantastic

Prior to the 1970s, Spanish Americans understood the fantastic via three overlapping frames of reference: the *Antología de literatura fantástica* (in its original form and later in its 1965 revision); the production and consumption of fantastic texts by Spanish American writers and readers throughout the 1940s, 1950s, and 1960s; and the critical work of European scholars and critics during those same years. Defining concepts from these sources, which are still valid and shape our vision of the fantastic today, can be summarized as follows: (1) the fantastic introduces some element into the text that strikes us as potentially supernatural, impossible, or inexplicable according to logic and reason; (2) some kind of balance between the supernatural/ natural, impossible/ possible, or explicable/ inexplicable must be maintained in the text, so that one does not eliminate the other; (3) in its modern form the fantastic differs from gothic and traditional horror fiction in that it depends less on otherworldly creatures (vampires, werewolves, ghosts) and more on man's inability to understand the world he lives in; (4) readers play a role in the fantastic, in that it requires us to suspend disbelief temporarily and let ourselves be manipulated by textual strategies that may surprise or confound us; (5) the fantastic is not defined by theme or content alone, but rather by narrative techniques and stylistic devices that influence the way we read the text; (6) although the fantastic appears to set up a dichotomy between the real and the unreal, we should not confuse extratextual objective reality with the mimetic representation of reality in a literary text, and we should not assume that our perception of reality is a monolithic construct that spans all times and cultures; (7) ambiguity is one of the defining characteristics of the genre, which makes it difficult for scholars to agree on its meaning, its origins, or its relationship to other kinds of fiction writing; (8) the fantastic often strikes us as highly subversive literature because it threatens to undermine the solidity of the laws that govern our understanding of relations between matter, time, and space; (9) it is not frivolous, escapist literature, but rather one that can be used to examine important philosophical, ideological, and social constructs; (10) the fantastic has taken on a life of its own in twentieth-century Spanish America, and writers have contributed in important ways to the development of the genre, although they were largely ignored by their European contemporaries during this time. To this latter point, we can add that midcentury Spanish American critics tended to dismiss fantastic literature as something inauthentic and unrelated to national concerns, which created a long-lasting prejudice against this kind of writing as irrelevant and esoteric. The lack of scholarly interest in the fantastic in Spanish America did not prevent writers from producing fantastic fiction, nor did it turn all readers away from it, but it did mean that the fantastic would become stigmatized for some years as marginal literature while so-called realist works predominated.

Consider, for example, that in the same year Sartre's essay on the fantastic appeared, Mexican critic José Luis González wrote a strongly worded attack on fantastic fiction, claiming that the fantastic "no se trata, pues, de una manera 'distinta' y 'superior' de expresar la realidad; se trata lisa y llanamente de no expresar la realidad. La 'literatura fantástica' de nuestros días es la literatura de avestruz" (3). According to González, "En México está ahora de moda, entre una exigua pero vociferante minoría que se autodenomina la élite de la nueva generación, el universalismo literario. El universalismo de estos escritores tiene un punto de partida bien conocido: olvidarse de que México existe" (3). As late as 1967, when writers like Bombal, Borges, Cortázar, Fuentes, and

Garro had already proven otherwise, Manuel Pedro González claimed that fantastic literature in Spanish America was a "producto exótico, importado y artificial, especie de flor de invernáculo, que revisten los pocos que por acá se han escrito . . . . Es literatura para minorías ociosas, frívolas y snob, literatura exhibicionista" (qtd. in Olea Franco 124). This solid rejection of the fantastic by Spanish American critics at the very time when some of the best fantastic fiction was being produced explains to some degree the apparent hole in fantastic literary theory in Spanish America between the 1940s and the 1970s. Europeans took the lead in cataloging and theorizing the fantastic, with little or no reference to Spanish American writers, while many Latin American critics promoted "una literatura de corte realista y que tratara los problemas inmediatos de la sociedad" (Olea Franco 119). The tendency to marginalize the fantastic as "artepurista" cultivated by "la intelligenzia burguesa" (J.L. González 336) is still apparent at times, despite decades of work by scholars in intervening years to reclaim it and explain its importance. For example, Juana Porro discovered in her analysis of reading texts used in Argentine high schools in 2000 that fantastic literature was significantly underrepresented and very little critical attention was given to it in most books. She speculates that the preference for more realistic fiction in the high schools may simply be a matter of taste, but she also claims that taste is a product of ideology. She believes that "'lo fantástico' desestabliza y perturba más de la cuenta," and teachers do not want to deal with the challenge of teaching it to adolescents (176). There is an implied comparison at work, making realistic fiction normal and fantastic literature abnormal. We can read realistic fiction if we have semantic and grammatical knowledge of the language, but the fantastic requires special training in terms of how it should be read. To some degree, this harks back to the idea that the fantastic is a genre that thrives on instability and ambiguity and the lack of agreement among critics about what it is and what it means makes it difficult for educators to teach.

Todorov and His Critics

Parallel to the "Boom" of Spanish American fiction in the late 1960s and 1970s, which brought it to the attention of international readers and critics and inspired a new generation to look at works by important precursors like Borges, there was a sharp increase in critical attention given to the fantastic on both sides of the Atlantic. Much of this was inspired by Todorov's polemic book on the fantastic, which proposed severe limitations on how the term was to be used in reference to literature. Todorov's definition of the genre is so restrictive that few literary works conform to it, but he proposes a theoretical model by which texts can be measured and categorized. Despite many detractors who have aspired to prove him wrong, Todorov's influence on how we think about the fantastic today cannot be underestimated. First, he makes a good argument for why we need to come to some agreement about what words like the fantastic, the uncanny, and the marvelous mean, so that we can understand and appreciate the unique qualities of each. Second, he insists that the fantastic is a product of language, and he encourages us to pay attention not only to what the story is about but how it comes into being. Like Ostowski, he insists that in theory literary texts should be analyzed without reference to nonliterary terminology (such as reality, in the extratextual sense), but in practice he shows that it is difficult to define the genre without reference to something we recognize as our own world.

Todorov claims that the fantastic occupies the space in the text created by the reader's uncertainty. The clash between what the reader perceives as real and possible and what the reader believes to be unreal and impossible creates the fantastic effect, although it may be confined to only a brief moment in time. Todorov is particularly interested in how language is used to represent fictional truths in realistic texts, and how the fantastic manipulates and undermines the representative nature of language to produce uncertainty. His major contributions to the debate on the nature of the fantastic are both his insistence on the importance of language and the specific guidelines he offers for the analysis of fantastic texts. For him, the fantastic is defined by these obligatory conditions: the reader must consider the world of the characters to be similar to his own; he must hesitate between a natural and supernatural explanation for events in the text; and he must reject poetic and allegorical interpretations of the supernatural and be willing to maintain an attitude or doubt or uncertainty about what he has read. In addition, the reader may identify with a character in the text who experiences doubt and hesitation, and as a result, doubt and hesitation may become inscribed in the text on a thematic level (33). Todorov claims, "Fear is often linked to the fantastic, but it is not a necessary condition of the genre" (35). He defines the fantastic, instead, in terms of the reaction produced in the reader: "'*I nearly reached the point of believing*': that is the formula which sums up the spirit of the fantastic. Either total faith or total incredulity would lead us beyond the fantastic: it is hesitation which sustains its life" (31).

Once the reader resolves his doubt and ceases to feel hesitation, Todorov claims the narrative is no longer fantastic. It will pass, instead, into a neighboring category:

> The fantastic . . . lasts only as long as a certain hesitation common to reader and character, who must decide whether or not what they perceive derives from "reality" as it exists in the common opinion. At the story's end, the reader makes a decision even if the character does not; he opts for one solution or the other and thereby emerges from the fantastic. If he decides that the laws of reality remain intact and permit an explanation of the phenomenon described, we say that the work belongs to another genre: the uncanny. If, on the contrary, he decides that new laws of nature must be entertained to account for the phenomena, we enter the genre of the marvelous. (41)

Todorov illustrates his ideas with a diagram that represents a continuum on a straight line. The fantastic appears midspace on the line, flanked by two subgenres (the fantastic-uncanny and the fantastic-marvelous), which, in turn, border the uncanny at one end and the marvelous at the other end. The uncanny and the marvelous are at opposite poles, but each share some overlapping characteristics with the fantastic, which occupies a space between them. In the uncanny, shocking and extraordinary events are eventually explained with rational arguments (it was a dream; the character is insane). In the marvelous, the shocking and extraordinary are accepted as part of the narrative and elicit no hesitation on the part of the reader (as in fairy tales or myths). The pure fantastic is fleeting, since most readers will move past their initial hesitation and reach a decision: they will either accept a rational explanation, or decide that the entire story is a fantasy. In this way they close the text to multiple meanings and the fantastic ceases to exist. It will dissolve first into one of the subgenres, the fantastic-uncanny or the fantastic-marvelous, and then ultimately into one of the neighboring genres, the uncanny or the marvelous. He compares this idea to our notion of time: just as we think of the present as something that exists on a continuum between the past and the future, the fantastic inhabits a point between the marvelous and the uncanny. Todorov associates the marvelous with the future because it conjures up things not yet seen, whereas the uncanny refers to something that has already been experienced, or the past. The fantastic exists in the present, in the intersection of these two neighboring fields. Todorov defines the fantastic in terms of the *perception* of events, not the events themselves, which gives it a transitory nature and sets it apart from other genres of imaginary fiction. He also describes it as a reading experience or a textual phenomenon, rather than in terms of content. The fantastic exists only through the written word, since it has no form outside the text. It is not a preexisting essence to be captured in words; it is our reaction to words that bring it to life. While earlier critics had also spoken of the fantastic in terms of the reader's emotional response to it, Todorov insists that he is describing "no actual reader, but . . . the reader implicit in the text. . . . The perception of this implicit reader is given in the text, with the same precision as the movement of the characters" (31). His discussion of the implied reader as a textual construct rather than a real person underscores the notion that the fantastic is created through narrative strategies and language, not merely through the treatment of certain themes.[9]

Todorov's idea of a pure or theoretical genre provides a way of narrowing the field when speaking about fantastic literature and concentrating the discussion on a specific kind of writing that meets the conditions he has laid out. But it is precisely his narrow view of the genre that has caused other critics to bridle at his work. He acknowledges the problem by explaining that literary theory can exist independently of concrete works, and that "there is no necessity that a work faithfully incarnate its genre, there is only a probability that it will do so. Which comes down to saying that no observation of works can strictly confirm or invalidate a theory of genres" (22).

Many complex literary works are multilayered and open to interpretation, but not all complex narratives are fantastic. What sets the fantastic apart, according to Todorov, is the hesitation the implied reader experiences when confronted with two or more explanations for a seemingly impossible event. The idea that the fantastic exists only for the duration of the reader's hesitation is a point some critics reject, for if the fantastic is construed as a literary game, the reader can willingly choose to suspend disbelief for as long as he wants, and as many times as he likes. What is less polemic in Todorov's discussion of the fantastic is the notion that it is a direct challenge to reason. The fantastic cannot exist in a text that privileges a logical explanation over a supernatural one: both explanations must be woven into the text, and both must appear equally valid within the confines of the narrative. It is up to the implied reader to choose between them, but when faced with irreconcilable visions of the world, he experiences a momentary tearing apart at the seams that threatens to destroy established order.

It is this aspect of the fantastic that causes Rosemary Jackson to call it "the literature of subversion."

Todorov's structuralist approach to the genre did not concern itself with the social and political implications of the fantastic, but later theorists like Jackson have used his ideas as a point of departure for a broader investigation into the fantastic as it relates to culture. Jackson acknowledges the importance of Todorov's work but believes it falls short in its scope; she aims "to extend Todorov's investigation from one being limited to the *poetics* of the fantastic into one aware of the *politics* of its form" (6). But Jackson's arguments, while astute and helpful for an analysis of the modern Spanish American fantastic, are muddied by her indiscriminate use of fantasy and fantastic as interchangeable terms. This stands her in opposition to Todorov, who had called for more uniform use of terminology and who insisted that what we call things matters. If we understand that for Jackson fantasy is similar to what Todorov and others had called the fantastic, then we can see how her conceptualization of the genre has important implications for the study of the fantastic in Spanish America. She claims that "a literary fantasy is produced within, and determined by, its social context. Though it might struggle against the limits of this context, often being articulated upon that very struggle, it cannot be understood in isolation from it" (3). According to Jackson, fantasy (or the fantastic as we conceive of it here) "characteristically attempts to compensate for a lack resulting from cultural constraints; it is a literature of desire, which seeks that which is experienced as absence and loss" (3). Jackson does not define desire in psychoanalytic terms, but her discussion of it echoes Lacanian notions about desire as an indeterminate and inapprehensible element that organizes itself around that which is lacking. She finds Todorov's repudiation of Freudian theory to be a "major blind-spot of his book," because in her opinion "it is in the unconscious that social structures and 'norms' are reproduced and sustained within us, and only by redirecting attention to this area can we begin to perceive the ways in which the relations between society and the individual are fixed" (6). These ideas are particularly useful for the analysis of fantastic texts that deal with issues related to the social construction of gendered identity and psychological conflicts stemming from problems of self-identification.

Jackson locates the subversive quality of the fantastic in the ways it interrogates our notions of the real. She explains, "Fantastic literature points to or suggests the basis upon which cultural order rests, for it opens up, for a brief moment, on to disorder, on to illegality, on to that which lies outside the law, that which is outside dominant value systems. The fantastic traces the unsaid and the unseen of culture: that which has been silenced, made invisible, covered over and made 'absent'" (4). She insists that if the fantastic is to be defined as "a literature of 'unreality,'" then we must acknowledge that "fantasy has altered in character over the years in accordance with changing notions of what exactly constitutes 'reality'" (4). Like Todorov, Jackson reminds us that the discussion of how the fantastic challenges cultural notions must be approached in terms of language, not in terms of extratextual notions of the real. By drawing attention to the limits and failures of language, the fantastic makes us understand that fiction is never "real" or "true."

Todorov's and Jackson's theories about the language of the fantastic have proven extremely useful for the analysis of literary texts, but one additional problem must be addressed before we move on to a discussion of twentieth-century works from Spanish America. Just as their European predecessors were wont to do, both critics ignore writers from Spanish-speaking countries. This is particularly puzzling in light of the fact that authors like Borges, Cortázar, and Fuentes were already established in the genre and had an international reading public. Todorov declared in 1970 that the fantastic was "dead," but his comments reveal that, like Sartre, Caillois, and Vax, he is thinking primarily in terms of Europe when he discusses the fantastic as a genre. On the one hand, he suggests that modern psychiatry has replaced the fantastic, since the themes of the fantastic have become topics of psychological investigation in the twentieth century. On the other hand, following Sartre's ideas, Todorov hints that a new fantastic may have come into being with the works of Kafka. He says, "With Kafka, we are thus confronted with a generalized fantastic which swallows up the entire world of the book and the reader along with it" (174). Todorov's comments about the death of the fantastic as a genre illustrate what Jackson and others have pointed out, that the discussion of literary texts cannot be divorced from their sociohistorical context, and that the cultural norms that inform the critic's worldview are not universal. In Spanish America, for example, the fantastic continues to be used as a sophisticated vehicle for social criticism, the questioning of cultural stereotypes, and the exploration of issues related to personal and national identity. This idea, which I insist upon repeatedly here, is one of the most important unifying threads of the present study.

Spanish American Responses

Todorov's claim that the fantastic is dead strikes us now as premature and Eurocentric, but it had one important consequence: it prompted Spanish American scholars and critics to enter into the fray and carve out a space where their voices could be heard. Among the most influential in terms of advancing fantastic theory are Barrenechea, Beleván, and Cortázar, along with anthologists like Hahn and Cócaro, who have contributed greatly to the dissemination and appreciation of the genre in Spanish America in the last four decades. Barrenechea acknowledges the importance of Todorov's work as a useful guide for the analysis of Latin American literary works, but she disagrees with him on several important points. She claims, "Esta rigidez de exclusiones genéricas, buena para ciertas épocas de clases literarias muy definidas, no resulta aplicable a la literatura contemporánea que construye géneros híbridos o con carácteres más fluctuantes" (393). She defines the fantastic instead as "un sistema de tres categorías construido con dos parámetros: la existencia implícita o explícita de hechos a-normales, a-naturales o irreales y sus contrarios; y además la problematización o no problematización de este contraste" (392). It is not doubt about the nature of the narrated events but rather the *problematization* of their nature that Barrenechea singles out for study. She shifts our attention back to the text itself and to the way that the fantastic writer creates or resolves tension between two (or more) conflicting elements in the story, rather than speculate on the implied reader's response to those elements. Barrenechea feels that it is necessary to stabilize the evanescent nature of the genre prescribed by Todorov to include a broader spectrum of works, specifically those by Spanish American authors who might otherwise be excluded from discussion. Specifically, his assertion that the fantastic exists only in the instance when the reader hesitates about the nature of events described in the text is too narrow a definition of the genre. Recognizing the Eurocentric focus of Todorov's study, she insists that Spanish American writers must be included in the canon of fantastic literature. The Argentine critic lists Cortázar, Borges, Bioy Casares, Fuentes, Garro, Hernández, Anderson Imbert, Carpentier, and Arreola, among others, as writers who have cultivated the fantastic and whose works merit further study. She also provides a schema for the classification of these works: (1) "Todo lo narrado entra en el orden de lo natural"; (2) "Todo lo narrado entra en el orden de lo no-natural"; (3) "Hay mezcla de ambos órdenes" (396–97). She notes that through the problematization of what constitutes "lo natural" and "lo no-natural" in the texts, the contrast between the two orders threatens us with the idea that "quizás en este mundo de los hombres no exista ningún orden" (399). Although Barrenechea sidesteps the vexing problem of the normal and abnormal as preexisting epistemological categories, her essay takes an important leap forward in the conceptualization of the fantastic as it relates to Latin America. She claims a space for the critical discussion of Spanish American authors and asserts that the fantastic is a viable form of self-expression for them. She disagrees with Todorov and others who have suggested that the fantastic is a dying genre. She points out that although scientific discoveries and psychoanalysis have given us new insights into the nature of the universe and the workings of the human mind, there will always be something outside the realm of human knowledge that will inspire 'imaginaciones fantásticas" (402). She also notes that if the fantastic is born of language, as Todorov claims, then as literature becomes more sophisticated and complex, the fantastic can become a self-referential kind of "literaturidad pura" that turns inward on itself and interrogates the relationship between language and the world it proposes to represent (402). With specific reference to the future of fantastic literature in Latin America, she explains:

> Los preocupados por problemas sociales, tan alucinantes en nuestra época, acusan de escapista a esta literatura y anuncian su desaparición por obsoleta, por no reflejar los problemas humanos más urgentes, por ser un arte burgués. A ellos habría que recordarles que los teóricos del marxismo no rechazaron por ese motivo a lo fantástico. . . . La concepción marxista del realismo afirma que el arte debe hacer sensible la esencia. Esta posición o la de un Julio Cortázar que cifra la función revolucionaria del artista en revolucionar el ámbito de las formas o la de un Umberto Eco que asigna ese poder revolucionario a la destrucción y creación de nuevos lenguajes, abren también al género otras posibilidades bajo el signo de lo social, siempre que lo fantástico sea una puesta en cuestión de un orden viejo que debe cambiar urgentemente. (402–3)

These comments signal an important shift in thinking in Spanish American criticism in the sense that Barrenechea recognizes the fantastic as a socially relevant form of literature, and she argues that it be recognized for its power to transform our ideas about language and literature.

Like Todorov, the Chilean critic Beleván prefers to approach the fantastic from a purely theoretical viewpoint, and he coins the term "descritura" to describe the process through which the fantastic comes into being. *Descritura* plays with the notion of un-writing, or destabilizing what is written; it refers to the gap that Beleván identifies between written language and its perceived meaning, especially when linguistic signs are used to refer to something that is considered unreal outside of language. He agrees that language plays a major role in the creation of the fantastic, but believes that the fantastic does not constitute a language in and of itself. It belongs completely to what he calls "el mundo de lo imaginario" (27), which exists outside of language. The reader uses intuition and unconscious processes to decode messages in the text through the apprehension of certain signs or signals that Beleván calls "deslices textuales," or textual slippages. These linguistic signals tell the reader that the fantastic is threatening to invade reality; the implied reader's security is menaced and he feels hesitation or doubt. Like Todorov, Beleván thinks that the fantastic exists only during the moment of hesitation, but he also states emphatically that the fantastic is never explained. Presumably, then, the reader's doubt is never totally assuaged. Beleván coined his own term, "basculación," which captures the essence of the fantastic for him. It is not vacillation, but rather a seesaw effect, a scale eternally out of balance that sets in motion the destruction of one order by another, which then tips back to the other side and forces us to revise our understanding of what we are reading. For Beleván, the fantastic is a conjunction, a simultaneous occurrence, of the real and the imaginary. He observes that because the fantastic exists outside of language, the use of language to attempt to describe it creates a self-referential narrative that calls attention to its own discursive shortcomings and failures. Although Belevan's abstract theory of the fantastic does not situate itself specifically in the field of Spanish American letters, his work indicates that Spanish American literary critics are no longer willing to sit on the sidelines when the fantastic is under discussion. He advances some useful theories about how to understand the fantastic, particularly in terms of the narrative devices used by writers and the slippery nature of language.

Cortázar, who is one of Argentina's most prolific writers of the fantastic and a recognized master of the genre, offers what is perhaps the most meaningful, although perhaps at the same time most unorthodox, definition of the fantastic in Latin America. Speaking on "The Present State of Fiction in Latin America" in 1976, Cortázar claims that he is open to the possibility that fantastic worlds exist. He states that he does not write about imaginary worlds, but rather about a world he has glimpsed, often in dreams. He concedes that play is also a door to the fantastic, and that the reader must be willing to go along with the game, to accept the unacceptable and live in what Coleridge called the suspension of disbelief while engaged with the text. Cortázar suggests that there is a tacit agreement between the writer and the reader of the fantastic, as well as a shared value system and cultural heritage. The writer knows what his reader fears and is thus able to manipulate the reader's reactions by second-guessing what they will be. Before the game can begin, the ground rules about what is possible and real must be agreed upon, for without them, there can be no fantastic. What sets Cortázar's views of the fantastic apart from those of European and North American critics is his suggestion that the fantastic does not stand in opposition to reality but is simply another way of thinking about it. What is real and possible can vary from one culture to another, and from one moment in time to another, as Bioy Casares pointed out in his 1940 essay. Fear is not necessarily its defining element, nor is surprise. Cortázar suggests that the reaction produced by the fantastic is closer to puzzlement or confusion, a momentary disorientation, a realignment of thinking. In this sense, he echoes Sartre's ideas about the new fantastic, where man is at the center of a fantastic universe.

Cortázar claims that "fantastic literature is the most fictional of all literatures, given that by its own definition it consists of turning one's back on a reality universally accepted as normal, that is, as not fantastic, in order to explore other corridors of that immense house in which man lives" (522). He acknowledges that critics have not been able to agree upon a definition of the fantastic because "when it is given to us through a literary text [it is] a sensation which varies considerably throughout the course of history and from one culture to the next" (523). In terms of his own work, he describes the fantastic as an "eruption of the unknown [that] does not go beyond a terribly brief and fleeting sensation that there is a meaning, an open door toward a reality which offers itself to us but which, sadly, we are not capable of apprehending" (526). Cortázar believes that the fantastic inhabits a space he calls "interstitial, slipping in between two moments or two acts in order to allow us to catch a glimpse, in the binary mechanism which is typical of human reason, of the latent possibility of a third frontier" (526). Readers and writers who see the fantastic as merely a literary fabrication, who are not open to the possible existence of the fantastic, are "those who live satisfactorily in a binary dimension" (526). For him, the function of fantastic fiction is "taking us for a moment out of our habitual little boxes and showing us, although it might only be vicariously, that perhaps things do not end at the point where our mental habits fix them" (527). He ends his essay by urging Latin Americans of the future to construct their own basis for reality and to leave room for the fantastic in their worldview because it will save them from becoming "that obedient robot into which so many technocrats would like to convert us" (532).

Cortázar's claim that the fantastic is not constructed through binary oppositions is an important break with traditional thinking about the genre, along with the assertion that the fantastic might be a bridge to another (third) plane that we have not yet been able to see. Perhaps he refers literally to a dream world or a world governed by the unconscious, where we are suspended between the rational and the irrational, or perhaps he is speaking in metaphors, using the notion as a way to urge us to look at the familiar with fresh eyes. His assertion, that despite scientific and technological advancements the universe is larger and more complex than we know, lies at the heart of the fantastic. It is an idea that accommodates slippage and refuses to be locked in place by whatever vision we have of the real at any given moment in time. For Cortázar, the fantastic is not the opposite of the real; it is something else, unidentifiable and unknowable, always just outside our grasp. We should not be too quick to dismiss it, however, as a literary game if we want to develop our ability to think and see beyond socially constructed boundaries. If its primary function is to make us think in new ways, it has the potential to revolutionize the world we live in. This is a dramatic declaration when we remember that two decades earlier the fantastic was dismissed by many Spanish American critics as a literature of evasion.

Finding Common Threads

During the past thirty years, theorists and critics have continued to discuss the fantastic, both in general terms and in relation to specific writers and texts. Despite our efforts, we are no closer today to a uniform understanding of the term or the boundaries that govern its use. It continues to intrigue us, but it always seems to outrun our grasp.[10] As Jesús Rodero observed in 2005, "Practicamente todos los críticos parecen estar de acuerdo en una cosa: la naturaleza elusiva de lo fantástico, la dificultad de categorizarlo de forma sistemática" (86). Rodero outlines three tendencies in fantastic criticism at the beginning of the twenty-first century: a broad view that encompasses all forms of fantasy or supernatural literature (using Rabkin's model); Todorov and his followers and critics who examine the way doubt, hesitation, or uncertainty are inscribed in our reading of the fantastic text (Barrenechea, Belevan, Brooke Rose, Risco); and those who see the fantastic as a subversive kind of literature that questions dominant cultural values (Cortázar, Jackson, Bravo, Alazraki, Armitt, Rodero). As Rodero notes, the transgressive potential of the fantastic, especially in Latin America, "es una de sus tendencias más destacadas" (88). Rodero's schema is useful as a way of understanding the different approaches to fantastic criticism, and it also allows us to pick and choose, as most scholars have done in recent decades, from an elaborate buffet of ideas to elaborate our own vision of the fantastic, which we can then use as a tool for the analysis of specific Spanish American texts. Sandner reminds us that the history of fantastic theory is made up of "intractable disagreements, surprising shifts of emphasis, inadequate definitions, and immodest claims of writers and critics" (277). For this reason, any discussion about what the fantastic means cannot lead to a single, definitive answer but will instead contribute to an ongoing debate. As I attempt to summarize what the fantastic means to me and why I believe Spanish American fantastic literature, in particular, is important, I hasten to add a disclaimer (as Sander does in his essay on the fantastic) that "someone could put together a different history of the fantastic and be right" (278). We are inarguably dealing with a literature that is resistant to closure, and while there are some constants that shape our understanding of the genre, there is also an inherent ambiguity in the fantastic that cannot be too tightly pinned down.

First, it is difficult to discuss the fantastic without making reference to reality or the perception of reality. To do so requires us to problematize not only the meaning of the fantastic but to interrogate the notion that reality can be reflected in literature, and how the perception of reality might vary from one time period or one culture to another. We cannot assume that we all mean the same thing when we discuss objective reality or a realistic view of the world in a literary text. It is not within the scope of the present study to examine realism in literature, but we must bear in mind that since the fantastic is often described as a reaction to the real world, we are talking about a representation of reality (and therefore, a personal and subjective vision of reality) in a literary text, or the implied reader's perception of reality as a cultural construct. Whether the fantastic and realism are to be seen as binary forces that stand in opposition to each other, a sliding continuum, mirror images of each other, or as interstitial spaces that exist within a broader spectrum of human experience, the fantastic contests the rational limits imposed on our understanding of the real world and cannot be conceptualized without reference to that world. The fantastic is a subversive genre in that it seeks to make the reader question and doubt his understanding of the world around him. It is based on the reader's willingness to entertain the idea that the supernatural *may* exist and can invade the real world and usurp it. The fantastic does not require absolute belief in the supernatural but merely an openness to the idea that there are experiences and situations that defy logic and reason or that are beyond scientific explanation. Whether the reader feels actual fear or uncertainty about the nature of what he is reading is a point left open for debate; as Cortázar reminds us, for some it is merely a literary game played between the writer and the reader, who is expected to suspend disbelief for the time he is engaged with the text. The actual reader of a fantastic text is often encouraged to identify with the characters through an implied reader, who perceives the fantastic through linguistic signs that have ambiguous or multiple meanings. In order to encode the fantastic into the text in ways that will condition reader reaction, the writer must share the worldview and cultural norms of his readers and characters so that they conceive of reality in similar ways and will feel a similar kind of alarm when the order of their known universe is altered. The fantastic does not conform to a preestablished idea of what is possible and real. It pushes the limits of our thinking and opens doors into what Cortázar calls "the latent possibility" of other frontiers.

Second, the fantastic relies on a number of predictable themes, but it cannot be classified or understood only in terms of the themes it addresses. To speak about the fantastic in literature is to speak about more than the story's content, for, as Todorov and others have shown, the fantastic comes into being through language and should be studied as a system of linguistic signs and codes. The fantastic attempts to describe an experience, an object, an essence that challenges representational language because it has no signification outside of the text. The reaction of the reader, which is central to the functioning of the fantastic, is manipulated through language. Therefore, it seems appropriate to analyze individual texts to identify the narrative strategies used by the authors to achieve the best fantastic effect and, especially, to pay attention to the self-referential aspects of the texts to understand how they call attention to their own literariness. As literature becomes more sophisticated and readers more wary of the inherent truth quality of any fictional text, the fantastic becomes a way to deconstruct traditional reading practices and interrogate the creative process itself. As Sartre suggested, in the twentieth century fantastic literature no longer depends on vampires, werewolves, ghosts, or similar otherworldly creatures. Man, himself, has become the center of much contemporary fantastic fiction, and the fantastic has become, in turn, a way to explore philosophical and psychological issues.

Perhaps for this reason, the fantastic hero or heroine in contemporary fiction tends to be an ordinary person, men and women who are basically comfortable in their existence, albeit at times they lead a lonely, alienated, or dull life. When confronted with a fantastic situation, characters react in predictable ways simply because they are so apparently normal. The best fantastic fiction does not explain the supernatural, but instead allows the reader to form his own conclusions about the nature of what has happened in the text. In many fantastic stories, clues or other slippages in the text (*deslices textuales*) appear that point toward the existence of the fantastic before it makes a full-blown appearance in the text, but these linguistic gaps are purposely vague and polysemic so that they create hesitation or uncertainty in terms of how we are to interpret what we read. Short stories lend themselves particularly well to the fantastic because they can be read in a single sitting and the reader can experience the full cycle of the fantastic without disengaging from the text: he enters the world of the characters, encounters the unsettling effect of the fantastic, feels uncertainty about the nature of the events described, chooses how to interpret it, and emerges having reached a conclusion about what happened in the story. The emotional impact (fear, doubt, surprise, unease) is felt most strongly when the reader temporarily forgets that he is reading a fictional story and imagines, at least for a moment, that he is reading about his own world. This willingness to slip into the fictional world of the characters is what Cortázar refers to when he explains that play opens the doors to the fantastic. When we think of the fantastic as a game, it is easy to understand why readers enjoy re-reading fantastic stories. On second and third readings, our interest lies not so much in knowing what happens in the story as to uncover *how* it happens. We go down the same path, but we look for new signs that might warn us of what lies ahead, we watch for gaps that make us stumble, we are wary of tricks that mislead us. We know the characters, their blind spots, their weaknesses, their flawed thinking, and we cannot only second-guess them but our own response to them. We are drawn deeper into the text looking for the strategies that have been used against us, all the while admiring the skill with which the traps were laid. A well-constructed fantastic short story can be read many times because it opens itself up to multiple readings and may even mean different things to readers at different moments in their lives. Many elements, such as frame of mind, mood, level of physical comfort, time of day, and setting, to name only a few, can influence the actual reader's reaction to a literary text and his/her ability and willingness to identify with the implied reader or characters in the story. Because the story can be read in different ways, it is theoretically possible for a reader to reach one conclusion on a first reading, another conclusion on a second, and then on a third reading, decide that the original explanation was the correct one after all. Details that may not seem important on first reading can later suggest new scenarios on repeated readings, or the reader may simply change his mind about what he thinks. The seesaw effect (*basculación*) of the fantastic allows it to metamorphose into an endless chain of shifting signs and signifiers, always leaving something slightly beyond our comprehension. Those readers who insist on absolute closure, on knowing and understanding clearly the nature of everything they read, will not generally respond well to fantastic texts, which can leave them feeling frustrated, as if they have been tricked into a game they are not willing to play. As Porro has noted, fantastic literature perturbs readers on the psychic level, and individuals have different levels of tolerance for this kind of reading experience.

We can safely say that the fantastic has not disappeared as a genre, and that although it has its roots in Europe and the United States in the late eighteenth and nineteenth centuries, it found a home in Latin America soon afterward. It emerged as a reaction against the Age of Reason and the excesses of rationalism that marked the late eighteenth century in the Western world, and it came ashore in mid-nineteenth-century Latin America on the tide of romanticism. Although the fantastic has undergone some changes in terms of style and subject matter, its essence remains the same in the twentieth and twenty-first centuries, and many of the characteristics of the classical fantastic described by Caillois, Vax, Todorov, and others are still found in contemporary narratives. Hahn has provided a detailed study of the fantastic in the Spanish American short story of the nineteenth century and has analyzed texts by writers like Montalvo, Gorriti, Blanco, Roa Bárcena, and Darío, among others, to show that "lo fantástico, al actualizarse en una obra determinada, adquiere la forma de la tendencia literaria en boga, cuyo sistema de preferencias condiciona los temas y motivos, los personajes y el tipo de acontecimiento ruptural" (83). Hahn establishes a link between romanticism, which he dates in Latin America from 1845–89, and modernism, which overlaps with it in the 1880s and continues until about 1910, through the writers' interest in the fantastic as a literary genre. At the same time, he stresses that the fantastic is not stable and intransmutable; as society changes, so does the nature of the fantastic.

To discuss the fantastic in the context of Spanish America, we must be prepared to bend definitions of the genre as it has been construed by European and North American theorists, and we must also acknowledge that the fantastic will take different shape at different moments in time and in different countries. Spanish America, after all, is to some degree an artificial construct, a geographical marker that sets the English-speaking Americas apart from those places where Spanish is spoken. There is no reason to assume that an Argentine writer and a Mexican writer will approach the fantastic in the same way, or even share the same notions about it. Nevertheless, we cannot overlook the fact that Spanish American literature in general has been excluded from some of the most important critical discussions of the history and development of the fantastic, and that many of the important theoretical discussions about what constitutes the fantastic as a genre have overlooked Spanish American writing altogether. As a marginalized body of work, then, it can be loosely framed as a unit as a way to distinguish it from fantastic literature in other parts of the world, especially that of Europe and the United States. If we accept the notion that the fantastic in literature automatically carries with it an assumed frame of reference that we call reality, it stands to reason that the nature of the fantastic will shift and change from one cultural framework to another. This idea bears further examination and is one of the motivating factors behind the present study.

Magical Realism and the Fantastic

Although most critics, theorists, and writers who work with the fantastic argue persuasively that it is not to be confused with magical realism, a neighboring genre in Latin American fiction, the two terms have been so closely linked through decades of use and misuse that it is still difficult to untangle the complicated threads that bind them together. Just as the debate surrounding the nature of the fantastic has raged for decades, so too has the discussion of what magical realism means and what kind of literature it best describes. At the heart of the matter seems to be the attitude or tone of the inscribed narrator toward the subject matter under discussion in the text, where his allegiances lie, what worldview has shaped his thinking, what belief system he subscribes to, and how he positions himself vis-à-vis the characters he is describing and his inscribed reader. While a fantastic narrator generally aligns himself with Western logic and sees the supernatural in stark contrast to the rational and real world he inhabits, the magical realist narrator appears to embrace the magical and the real as complementary and symbiotic parts of a unified whole. The element of doubt, hesitation, unease, anxiety or fear which characterizes most fantastic texts is usually missing in a magical realist one, since the supernatural or magical is embraced by characters as something that is part of their world. In this sense, magical realism appears to have more in common with the marvelous than it does with the fantastic, as Alejo Carpentier's use of the term, "lo real maravilloso," suggests. However, the marvelous has its origins in fantasy and portrays a world that has largely been invented, whereas magical realism, or *lo real maravilloso*, claims to represent a recognizable reality. In Spanish America, magical realism has found its greatest expression in geographical areas where a strong non-European presence is felt: the Caribbean, rural Mexico and Central America, and parts of the Andes. This has led many critics to speculate that it is the conflict between European and African or indigenous worldviews that gives rise to magical realism in literature, for magical realist texts often create a space where politically, socially, and economically marginalized peoples can contest colonial discourse by reframing the notion of reality in ways that hark back to their own belief systems.

In 1949, Carpentier declared in the prologue of his short novel, *El reino de este mundo*, that the entire American continent inherently possessed a mysterious and magical essence that provided writers with a wealth of subject matter that had scarcely been touched by writers. He asked, "Pero ¿qué es la historia de América toda sino una crónica de lo real maravilloso?" (121). Carpentier's claim that the marvelous could coexist together with the real, and that in order to portray Latin America in literature the writer needed to tap into both, was an important new idea but his name for it, *lo real maravilloso*, did not appeal to critics. Instead, for reasons that are not entirely clear, they preferred a term borrowed from the world of European art, *realismo mágico*. German art critic, Franz Roh, had first used the term in 1925 as a way to describe postexpressionist painting in northern Europe. Although Roh made no reference to Latin America in his writing, his ideas resonated there because of his belief that "el misterio no desciende al mundo representado sino que se esconde y palpita tras él" (1). Roh claimed that reality could appear unreal when seen from unusual or unexpected perspectives, and that the surprises found beneath the surface of everyday life could form the basis for art. These notions coincided with Spanish American writers' fascination with their immediate, familiar surroundings in the 1930s and 1940s, and their search for a new, more authentic way of writing about the American experience. By 1948, when Uslar Pietri wrote about magical realism in his native Venezuelan literature, the term had become integrated into the lexicon of literary critics in the New World, although it appears to have no clearly defined meaning, other than "la consideración del hombre como misterio en medio de los datos realistas. Una adivinación poética o una negación poética de la realidad" (Uslar Pietri 162).

The distinguished critic Angel Flores is responsible for popularizing the term in the 1950s, but like Uslar Pietri, he used it as a general category to describe the monumental changes he perceived taking place in Spanish American literature at midcentury. Flores called attention to the importance of style, to the ability to transform "the common and the everyday into the awesome and the unreal" (190), but he did not clarify how magical realism differed from other neighboring genres like the fantastic or the absurd. Anderson Imbert described magical realism in more concrete terms in 1956 when he wrote, "Everyday objects appear enveloped in such a strange atmosphere that although recognizable, they shock us as if they were fantastic. Reality is so subjectively treated that frequently the reader seems to be following the scenes of a dream or the symbols of an allegory" (148). Two decades later, Anderson Imbert went further, adamantly rejecting Carpentier's claim that the American continent provides ethnographic subject matter that inspires magical realist writers; according to Anderson Imbert, magical realism depends on technique, not content, and is not linked to any particular geographical area. This stance opened the door to heated debate about whether magical realism is distinctly linked to Latin America or is a universal phenomenon, an issue that has yet to be resolved. In addition, Anderson Imbert's claim that the magical aspect of magical realism does not come from reality itself but from "el arte de fingir" (43) signals a reluctance on the part of Eurocentric intellectuals to embrace a non-Western or culturally hybridized view of Latin American reality. Fernando Alegría disagreed strongly with Anderson Imbert's position and urged a return to Carpentier's original conception of *lo real maravilloso* as a basis for understanding magical realism. Alegría names Carpentier and Miguel Angel Asturias as two exemplary magical realist writers; he explains that the magical elements in their work are not invented but instead based on reality, and that "ese realismo vive de una constatación de hechos históricos que se tornan leyendas en la imaginación del pueblo y actúan, luego, como mitos desde una subconsciencia colectiva" (356).

Luis Leal was among the first to suggest that magical realism is above all about the writer's attitude toward his subject matter. He states that the writer "se enfrenta a la realidad y trata de desentrañarla, de descubrir lo que hay de misterio en las cosas, en la vida, en las acciones humanas" (232). He adds, "El autor no tiene necesidad de justificar lo misterioso de los acontecimientos" (234), because the writer sees the world around him as one that is essentially true and real, albeit mysterious and magical at the same time. Like Carpentier, Leal believes that magical realism is linked to specific subject matter, and that it is content, not form, which gives unity to the genre. He says emphatically that magical realism does not distort reality, it does not rely on oneiric motifs, and it does not attempt to explain psychological motivation. This distinguishes it from neighboring genres like the fantastic, surrealism, and psychological literature. Pioneers like Flores, Anderson Imbert, Alegría, and Leal, unable to agree among themselves about the meaning and use of terms like magical realism and the fantastic, launched ensuing generations of scholars into theory-driven debates that Emir Rodríguez Monegal described as "un diálogo de sordos" (26). He noted that the lack of communication led to confusion, and he urged critics to identify key texts and offer careful analysis of them to illustrate theories about the genres they worked with. This prompted many scholars to write about magical realism in the 1970s and 1980s, and some writers associated with the genre, like Miguel Angel Asturias and Gabriel García Márquez, to discuss their ideas about it. Constant bickering and disagreement about the meaning and application of the term caused some critics to declare that magical realism was "un mero vacío teórico, un concepto ambiguo e innecesario en la crítica hispanoamericana" (Mena 395), but others fell into a tacit understanding that they would agree to disagree on some points and focus instead on common elements that they all associated with this kind of writing. Recent decades have seen a burst of activity surrounding the study of magical realism both in Latin America and world literature, much of it linking narrative discourse to social realities of specific places.

Amaryll Chanady's work in the mid-1980s provided a useful framework for a discussion of how magical realism intersects with Boom and post-Boom writing in Spanish America, colonial discursive practices, and social context. According to Chanady, magical realism is characterized by "two conflicting, but autonomously coherent, perspectives, one based on an 'enlightened' and rational view of reality, and the other on the acceptance of the supernatural as part of everyday reality" (21–22). The belief system that controls what is real and possible in the text belongs to the characters and/or the narrator, not the implied reader. The reader is invited to enter the world of the characters and temporarily adopt their worldview in order to see reality from a different perspective. Chanady explains, "In magical realism, the supernatural is not presented as problematic, he does not react to the supernatural in the text as if it were antinomious with respect to our conventional view or reality, since it is integrated within the norms of perception of the narrator and characters in the fictitious world" (23). In contrast to the fantastic, magical realism does not inspire fear, hesitation, or doubt in the reader, which is one of the fundamental differences between the two modes of expression. Chanady notes that "the absence of obvious judgments about the veracity of the events and the authenticity of the worldview expressed by characters in the text" is another important characteristic of magical realism (30). She believes that the lack of hierarchy between two mutually exclusive belief systems or logical codes in magical realism facilitates the acceptance of the mysterious, magical, or supernatural in the text.

Wendy Faris points out that many magical realist texts are set in rural spaces and rely on a Jungian perspective that grounds magical and mysterious elements in a collective experience rather than in individual memory, dreams, or visions. She also notes that magical realism lends itself to an extravagant, carnivalesque style that creates a sense of the outrageous, best represented by *Cien años de soledad*, which is often held up as the most representative work of magical realist fiction in Spanish America (185). Theo D'haen considers magical realism to be "the cutting edge of postmodernism" in that it subverts earlier literary conventions and the metanarratives and ideologies that those earlier conventions upheld (201). When seen as the flip side of the kind of literary realism so popular in Spanish America in the late nineteenth and early twentieth centuries, magical realism indeed turns the notion of what is real and possible on its head. It also privileges the worldview of those who had previously been marginalized, ignored, or portrayed as the literary "Other" who could be observed but not allowed to speak from any perspective other than the one embraced by the educated implied reader.

Another fundamental difference between the fantastic and magical realism is that the former finds its best expression in works of short fiction, whereas the latter is most often associated with the novel. The fantastic effect, born of doubt and hesitation, cannot easily be sustained for long periods of time, since a break from the text disrupts the reader's response to it and encourages him to reach conclusions about the nature of events described in the text. They are fantastic only so long as he is willing to admit the possibility that they may be fantastic; once he puts aside the text, he will most likely reach a conclusion about the nature of what he has been reading and the fantastic will slide into a neighboring category like the marvelous or the uncanny. Magical realism, by contrast, does not depend on the reader's doubt and hesitation and, instead, seduces the reader into entering the world of the characters through lengthy, complex, and elaborate narrative threads that prop up their worldview. Novels like *El reino de este mundo* by Carpentier, *Hombres de maíz* by Asturias, *Cien años de soledad* by García Márquez, *Pedro Páramo* by Juan Rulfo, *Siete lunas y siete serpientes* by Demetrio Aguilera Malta, and *La casa de los espíritus* by Isabel Allende stand out as examples of magical realism in Spanish America; for this reason, it has intersected in more obvious ways with so-called Boom of Spanish American literature. From the late 1940s through the 1980s, magical realism became almost synonymous with the Spanish American literature on the international (and commercial) level. The fantastic short story, however, has been somewhat relegated to the margins in critical discourse, perhaps because few of the works have had "best-seller" status. The simple equation of magical realism with the primeval jungles, isolated rural communities, flamboyant and eccentric characters, or the turbulent and dramatic history of Spanish America makes the genre appealing to audiences who enjoy a taste of the exotic. It also conforms to some readers' notions about "primitive peoples" and the effect of economic underdevelopment on certain regions of the world, which allows them to establish and maintain an emotional distance from the text and ultimately relegate the mysterious and magical to realms other than their own.

Putting Theories into Practice

In Spanish America, the fantastic generally reflects the modern urban experience, with the strongest and most enduring tradition in fantastic literature found in the Southern Cone, especially in Argentina and Uruguay. Cortázar addresses the link between the fantastic and the River Plate by stating:

> Many times critics have looked for the answer to this question; they have spoken of the cultural polymorphism of Argentina and Uruguay resulting from the multiple waves of immigrants; they have

> alluded to our immense geography as a factor of isolation, monotony and tedium, with the consequent refuge in the startling, the exceptional, in the search for an anywhere, out-of-the-world type of literature. As a participant in that literary current, I feel these explanations to be only partial; and in the end, instead of a rational explanation, the only thing that I can see is once more a mechanism of chance, that same chance which once, and in infinitely greater proportions, concentrated a creative explosion in Renaissance Italy and in Elizabethan England, which made possible the Pléiade in seventeenth-century France, and in Spanish the generation of the Golden Age or the poets of the Spanish Republic in the 1930s. Suddenly, and without logical and convincing reasons, a culture produces in a few years a series of creators who spiritually fertilize each other, who emulate and challenge and surpass each other. (527)

In acknowledgement of the importance of writers from the Southern Cone in the development of fantastic literature in Spanish America, more than half of the authors included in the present study are from that region: Adolfo Bioy Casares (Argentina, 1914–99); María Luisa Bombal (Chile, 1910–80); Jorge Luis Borges (Argentina, 1899–1986); Julio Cortázar (Argentina, 1914–84); Leopoldo Lugones (Argentina, 1874–1938); Silvina Ocampo (Argentina, 1903–93); Elvira Orphée (Argentina, 1930–); and Horacio Quiroga (Uruguay, 1878–1937). Another significant group of writers comes from Mexico: Elena Garro (1920–98); Carlos Fuentes (1928–); and José Emilio Pacheco (1939–). In the 1950s, Luis Leal described the fantastic as a "género poco adaptado a la psicología del mexicano, hombre realista por naturaleza" (129). Nevertheless, Mexico has also been a breeding ground for the fantastic, perhaps because writers there have been especially effective at using the fantastic to explore Mexican issues. Leal's assessment of the Mexican as a person who is by nature realistic does not exclude the possibility of looking at reality through the lens of the fantastic. As Cortázar suggests, there is an element of chance behind the fact that these texts come in large proportion from specific regions of the world and appear at specific moments in time. When we look at the ways writers and texts coincide and overlap in approaches and concerns, it becomes apparent that they do not exist in isolation from one another. Those who cultivate the fantastic in the Spanish language "spiritually fertilize each other," as Cortázar claims (527), both within and beyond national borders. As he points out, one of the characteristics of the modern world is "a growing consciousness that not only is no man an island, but that countries are not islands either" (531). This cross-fertilization may be due, in part, to a shared preoccupation among Latin Americans that Cortázar identifies as "the anguished search for our identity, for our necessary and irreplaceable reality" (532). Although that reality may vary from country to country, what binds Latin Americans together is the search for an autonomous identity, both on a national and personal level, and it is this notion of identity as a cultural construct that is at the heart of many of the fantastic narratives examined here.

If we accept as a point of departure Jackson's observation that "the fantastic cannot exist independently of that "real" world that it seems to find so frustratingly finite" (20), it seems appropriate to organize the study of individual stories according to the ways in which they challenge the implied reader's perception of reality. It is, of course, problematic to make claims about what a culture is like, or what human beings are like, based on situations and characters presented in works of literature. However, since one of the functions of the fantastic is to problematize the representational ability of language and literature in general, the study of fantastic narratives allows us to look at the way reality is culturally constructed in a text, the better to understand where the flaws in that construction lie and where the truth of the fiction begins to come apart at the seams. In this sense, it is as appropriate to discuss the social function of fantastic literature as it is to talk about realistic fiction in those terms. Jackson explains, "The fantastic exists as the inside, or underside of realism, opposing the novel's closed, monological forms with open, dialogical structures. . . . The fantastic gives utterance to precisely those elements which are known only through their absence within a dominant 'realistic' order" (25). The fantastic expresses unconscious drives, desires, fears and obsessions and shows "in graphic forms a tension between the 'laws of human society' and the resistance of the unconscious mind to those laws" (Jackson 6–7). We know, of course, that literature is not the same as reality, but literary texts do reveal something about the culture in which they originate, even when their aim is to undermine and subvert some of the basic premises that culture holds true. The fantastic provides us with rich territory to explore in Spanish America, not only in terms of its artistic merit but also as a literature that concerns itself with human beings and the world they inhabit. The present study is not a general history of the fantastic short story in Spanish America, although it does attempt to show, through representative texts and writers, how the fantastic has developed there over the course of the past century. At the same time, each chapter offers an in-depth analysis of the narrative strategies used by the writers as a means of linking thematic concerns to the use of language that generates a fantastic effect.

Chapter 1 situates the modernist fantastic story as a counterdiscourse to positivism, the prevailing philosophy of the late nineteenth and early twentieth century in much of Latin America. These stories, far from being examples of escapist literature, directly interrogate and challenge the dominant ideology of the times. They call attention to the limitations of language, to the inability of words to express certain experiences or to accurately describe situations that fall outside of normal bounds. They suggest that scientific truth is not absolute and, in fact, can often be manipulated to reach false conclusions. The reader is called on to fill in gaps in the texts, and ambiguity leads to multiple levels of meaning that allow readers to interpret facts in different ways. The fantastic in the hands of modernist writers becomes a subversive genre, one that questions the value of progress at all costs. It is an excellent point of departure for our discussion of the genre in Spanish America because it shows that Spanish American authors have reached a level of sophistication that puts them on a par with European and North American writers of the fantastic, and it also points to some of the thematic concerns later writers will take up in their fiction.

Chapter 2 focuses on stories that explore the relationship among readers, writers, and texts. Specifically, these stories address questions such as who is the ideal reader of the fantastic? Is it possible to create an original work of literature? How can the text convincingly represent something that has no reality outside the written word? The stories explore the role of the literary critic in the construction (and imposition) of meaning and also encode multiple ways of reading the text into the narrative structure through different kinds of implied readers (the naive reader versus the sophisticated reader, for example). As examples of self-referential literature, the stories have as their central preoccupation the process of writing and reading; ultimately, in one way or another, they ask us to think about what literature is and what role it has in our lives. They question the authority of the author, the power of the written word to shape our perception of reality, and the possibility of literature as an escape from reality. They suggest that literature is a game or a construction, not a mirror of truth, and call for an examination of how the interpretative process functions (and sometimes breaks down or goes awry) in the production and reception of literary texts. This is a preoccupation that

European and North American poststructuralists would express several decades later, although usually without reference to Spanish American literature.

Chapter 3 concerns itself with the intersection of the fantastic and history, particularly in terms of how the interpretation of historical events shape personal and national identity. Time travel, which is a common theme in traditional fantastic fiction, has a more complex function here. It is a structural device that brings together different moments in time so that characters can understand more clearly their relationship to the past and its influence on the present. Space becomes symbolic because it splits along lines that reflect historical conflicts. Mexico City is the scene of three of the stories because it is a physical and geographical metaphor for the imposition of one culture on another. Characters can live in both the pre-Hispanic and modern world at the same time because they are one in the same, separated only by time, which proves to be an unstable entity. In a similar way, the dichotomy between civilization and barbarism, the predominant theme of Argentine literature in the nineteenth century, allows Buenos Aires and "El Sur," or the vast plains of the pampas region, to function as a reminder that the conflict has not been resolved in the twentieth century, although history has apparently relegated it to the margins. Characters in these stories come face to face with the Other, the historical shadow of the person they once were, or a representative of the culture they have forgotten and pushed to the side. The stories speak of "the anguished search for our identity, for our necessary and irreplaceable reality," which Cortázar identifies as a major preoccupation in Latin American fiction (532).

Chapter 4 examines the connection between the fantastic and psychoanalytic theory, especially as it relates to the concept of the gendered subject. It takes as its point of departure stories that express themes of the double, but explores how the fantastic treatment of the theme illustrates the workings of the unconscious. In the stories, male narrators position the female characters as mirror images of themselves, but at the same time, they struggle with the need to acknowledge sexual difference in order to take their rightful place in a patriarchal culture. The female metamorphoses from the double into a mysterious Other, a metaphor for longing and repressed desire, and the male, if he is unable to recover the illusion that they are two halves of a single whole, resorts to the fantastic as a mechanism for dealing with the rupture. Women are disappeared from the text or swept aside, leaving only the male narrator's reconstructed idea of them in their place. The males, who recognize themselves as victims of the fantastic, explain away the bothersome aspects of the female Other through supernatural events. These stories illustrate that the fantastic, like unconscious desire, cannot be contained in language. The fantastic calls attention to insufficiencies in the linguistic system we use to represent ourselves. They bring to the surface the unconscious fear that there is no solid core to the "I" who speaks, and the position from which we articulate our personal identity is an arbitrarily assumed one. At the same time, they undermine societal values that prop up male authority by suggesting that power relations are largely a matter of habit and custom, and not inherently prescribed by gender.

Chapter 5 explores the connections between gothic romance and the fantastic, particularly as it relates to the treatment of the female body and problematizes the nature of feminine desire. In the two novellas studied here, the question of a lover's identity is brought to the fore by a narrator who may or may not be mad. The narratives play off the conventions of gothic romance as a way to explore some of our assumptions about romantic love and sexual desire, and they point to the ways in which narrators establish or lose authority over the texts because of culturally constructed notions about gendered identity. The "real" world of the characters is dull and monotonous, and the possibility of an "impossible" love offers them an escape. But the aging female body becomes the site of resistance in the texts, and her claim to desire, which seems so transgressive in the texts, is the element that opens the door to the fantastic in the narrative. The no longer desirable female who steps outside conventional behavior to act out her sexual fantasies and obsessions positions the male lover as the object of her longing, but this inversion of roles is dangerous, since it changes the way we think about romantic love. The lover in the texts, whether real, imaginary, or supernatural, allows us to explore some of our preconceived notions about gender, sexuality, and the body. The aging female, traditionally cast as the madwoman or monster of gothic fiction, is also portrayed in a more ambiguous light as a human being driven to desperate acts through unsatisfied desire. The novellas challenge us to think about the reader's role in creating meaning based on conjecture and preconceived notions and to think about how we respond to language that is not transparent.

Chapter 6 looks at the fantastic short story in the hands of women writers. The stories examined here establish that the way a writer chooses to frame discourse is an ideological statement. What we think of as natural patterns in language are, in fact, merely the result of dominant practices, and when women break these patterns in an attempt to create a reverse discourse, we become more aware of the subversive potential of language. The fantastic is a particularly useful tool for women writers because it undermines patriarchal authority by suggesting alternate visions of the real world. The question of who speaks, who sees, and who controls our access to information in the narrative is central to these stories. They make us aware that when we grant (or deny) authority and reliability to a narrator, these reactions are culturally conditioned, and that our perceptions of what is real and possible in a text are never entirely our own but are, instead, encoded into language. Women writers of the fantastic turn narrative practices inside out, creating a space for those who are normally denied a voice. Some of the stories foreground their own enunciation practices by using language that is purposely elliptical, perhaps as a way to reflect the ambiguity of women in male-dominated discourse. They undermine the assumption that language has fixed meaning and that the same narrative strategies are appropriate for everyone. As a feminist practice, the fantastic does not attempt to replace one hierarchical structure with another but merely to extend our perceptions as a way of opening a space for those who have been marginalized.

Chapter 7 frames the discussion of the fantastic in cinematic terms, looking at the way film directors create a fantastic effect in a medium that is primarily visual. The fantastic, which is normally articulated through language and is most often associated with written texts, presents a particular challenge in film. If it resists representation and remains invisible or unnamed, how can viewers perceive that it exists? If the supernatural takes concrete form on screen, most viewers will quickly perceive it as a cinematic device and relegate it to the realm of fantasy or the marvelous. The hesitation or doubt that gives rise to the fantastic in literature requires that the supernatural be suggested but not made explicit. Films most successful at achieving the fantastic effect are those that rely on ambiguity and inference, but this is difficult to accomplish without tipping the scales in one direction or another. The films examined here lend themselves to two or more explanations, one always pointing in the direction of the supernatural and the other(s) suggesting a natural explanation such as madness, delusion, chicanery, allegory, or tongue-in-cheek irony. The fantastic is simultaneously visible and invisible because it takes human form, and there is nothing otherworldly about the characters except in terms of how they perceive themselves. In this sense, it is closest to what Sartre described when he wrote, "For contemporary man, the fantastic is only one of a hundred ways of mirroring his own image" (60).

The epigraphs that appear at the beginning of this introduction open a dialogue about the relationship between reality and the fantastic, and they also suggest that the critical debate about the nature of the fantastic cannot be one-sided. Spanish America has produced some of the most important fantastic literature of the twentieth century, but it has seldom been included in international discussions of critical theory. What I want to do here, then, is to bring the dialogue into the open and look more specifically at how the fantastic manifests itself in Spanish America, both theoretically and in specific texts that illustrate the techniques used by fantastic authors. The stories and films I have chosen for analysis are outstanding examples of the fantastic, in terms of style as well as substance. They illustrate the thematic concerns of Spanish American writers, along with the mastery of their craft. As we know, the fantastic explores the relationship between language and the thing it claims to represent. As Bioy Casares pointed out in his discussion of the fantastic, it is a literature that calls attention to the relationships among the writer/ reader/ narrator/ text. It is also an evanescent genre, one that permutes and transforms itself over time and across cultures. These ideas are woven into my textual analyses, since the fantastic is a genre that is characterized, at least in part, by the reader's response to it, particularly in the way that it interrogates notions of the real. Because fantastic texts are multilayered and language is polysemic, they are usually open-ended and much is left to the reader's imagination. The tendency that leads toward what Barrenechea called "literaturidad pura," or a self-referential kind of writing that interrogates the nature of literature in general, is another idea that ties together the texts chosen for analysis here. I find that the concept can be extended to apply to fantastic films as well as short stories, in the sense that the viewer is called upon to make decisions about the nature of what he sees. Cortázar hinted at the subversive nature of the fantastic when he referred to it as a genre that inhabits an intersticial space, one that breaks down binary oppositions between real and unreal and posits that there are other ways of perceiving and describing human experience that do not fit neatly into any known category. Beleván's emphasis on *descritura*, or the unraveling of the discursive power of language to represent the real, shows us how the fantastic traces the invisible and unknown and inserts it into an epistemological system where it otherwise has no form. Both of these notions provide us with a useful way to approach the analysis of fantastic texts, for they make us look not only at the words used to tell the story but also at the omissions and gaps in the texts where the fantastic can take root. In Latin America, the fantastic clearly is not dead, as Todorov proclaimed it to be. It has taken on the task of addressing social problems, especially those related to the search for national and personal identity, which makes it as relevant today as it was a hundred years ago. It has also inspired some of the most fascinating narratives in the Spanish language, narratives that deserve more recognition on the international level as exemplary works in the fantastic genre.

While it is difficult to say what direction the fantastic will take as it moves through the twenty-first century, in the concluding chapter I turn to Carlos Fuentes's work, *Inquieta compañía* (2004), for a glimpse of what the future might hold for this kind of literature. It is telling that Fuentes, who began his career as a writer of fantastic short stories, returns to the genre fifty years later as a way to close a cycle in his life. The stories in *Inquieta compañía* are not throwbacks to an earlier era, but rather stories that clearly situate themselves in the contemporary world. They address themes such as globalization, immigration, racism, class conflicts, social injustice, and cultural and economic imperialism, while at the same time they explore what it means to be Mexican or, for that matter, simply a human being in a new millennium. The fantastic is an ideal tool with which to carry out this investigation because it allows the past, present, and future to exist on the same plane and brings together different physical spaces to show us that no country, no person, exits in a vacuum. The contemporary world portrayed by Fuentes in these stories is characterized by fusion, but also scarred by the inability to reconcile difference in a constructive way. This links his work to a long tradition of socially conscious literature in Latin America and shows that the fantastic continues to be a viable genre today.

It is easier to pose questions than to answer them, but when dealing with a literature that is forever in the process of transforming itself, turning back on itself, and opening up new dialogues about its meaning, it is foolhardy to impose a monolithic reading of it. The questions that motivate this study are clear: Does the fantastic have a different nature in Spanish America that sets it apart for special study? Why has it flourished there when critics in other parts of the world have declared it dead? Why are writers like Fuentes, Borges, Cortázar, Garro, and others studied here so attracted to it as a literary genre? What purpose does this kind of literature serve? In my attempt to address these questions, I hope to encourage a new generation of readers and scholars to engage with the texts, so that they, too, may fall under the spell of the fantastic in Spanish American literature.

1 / Modernist Short Stories and the Fantastic

Critics and readers who insist on a strong dose of "reality" in literature have often dismissed the fantastic in Latin America as an evasion and an irresponsible disregard for the many political and social problems that confront people on a daily basis in many parts of the New World. Even in the context of *modernismo*, a movement that elevated art and artifice to a new level in Latin America in the closing decades of the nineteenth century, the fantastic has not occupied a central place.[1] José Olivio Jiménez has written that the fantastic short story is "una de las más importantes contribuciones del modernismo" (10); nevertheless, scholars of modernism have seldom examined in depth the presence of the fantastic within that movement. Literary historians tend to think of the nineteenth- and early twentieth-century fantastic as a genre consumed by a romantic fascination with the gothic and the horrific, often lacking in artistic merit. On the surface, if we identify it with its early incarnations in Latin America, the fantastic seems out of sync with modernism, whose goal it was to overcome the linguistic stodginess and worn out clichés of romanticism.[2] Critics usually categorize modernism's interest in supernatural themes as a holdover from earlier decades, or dismissed it as imitative of foreign models.[3] Such prejudices have no basis when we begin to examine some of the fantastic short stories of the modernist period in detail; in fact, we find in them some of the same narrative strategies and structures that Borges and other masters of the genre would use in later years. José Javier Fuente de Pilar explains, for example, that modernist writers working in the fantastic vein "integraron en sus cuentos la máxima libertad creativa con la poesía, con la imaginación subvertida, con lo oculto e invisible . . . para inventar un continente literario donde lo antiguo y lo nuevo, la superstición y la ciencia, caminaba con absoluta naturalidad bajo un firmamento lleno de posibilidades" (iii). Being one of the first narrative forms to call attention to itself as literature, that is, to acknowledge itself as a literary creation and not a faithful reproduction of our surrounding world, the modernist fantastic short story opens a space from which to question the limitations words have as linguistic signifiers and their ability to stand in for the real. From this perspective, the fantastic in the hands of the modernists acquires a strong ideological connotation that belies its escapist character. It obliges us to reconsider the ways in which the fantastic works to deconstruct and challenge the teachings of positivism, the philosophical movement that dominated the modernist era.[4]

As theorists of the fantastic have observed, it is impossible to discuss the fantastic as a genre or a narrative mode without establishing its relationship to the real. Although fantastic texts permit—we could even say require—the eruption of the supernatural, the inexplicable, or the impossible in a world we recognize as our own, they achieve the fantastic effect precisely through the juxtaposition of the real and the unreal. According to Rosemary Jackson, the fantastic "recombines and inverts the real, but it does not escape it: it exists in a parasitical or symbiotic relation to the real" (20). In other words, the fantastic text "takes the real and breaks it" (Jackson 20). By violating the dominant belief system of a culture, by challenging accepted literary conventions, and by ignoring the laws and boundaries that govern what readers consider real and possible, the written word can achieve a subversive nature. It can plant doubt and hesitancy in readers' minds, it can eat away at the security they feel in regard to their own knowledge, and it can threaten to undermine the norms that prop up their view of the world. The fantastic text questions the category of the real and challenges the power of those who attempt to determine for us what that reality will be. William Plank tells us that "it is the political, technological power of a culture that defines what is real and what is fantastic. Reality therefore becomes an exercise in politics, and the fantastic is the realm of the powerless and the disaffected. Power, whether military, political, academic, scientific, or something else, validates itself through its claim to being real, true, and right" (80). Jackson takes a similar stance when she says, "Realism, as an artistic practice, confirms the dominant ideas of what constitutes this outside reality, by pulling it into place, organizing and framing it through the unities of the text. It presents its practice as a neutral, innocent and natural one, erasing its own artifice and construction of the 'real'" (83). The fantastic, by contrast, brings to the forefront its mechanisms of enunciation in order to stress the difficulties inherent in the process of representation. It plays with its readers, teasing them with the possibility that reality is not as stable as they would like it to be, and in this way, it eats away at the firmness of their beliefs by creating a space in the text for them to doubt their own perceptions. Wolfgang Iser believes that this is the task of all good literature; more than simply reinforcing the perceptions of the world that we already have, literature should violate or transgress normative ways of seeing and show us new ways of understanding.[5] In this manner, the written text can create a deeper awareness, forcing us to examine more critically the philosophy and scientific knowledge that has shaped our concept of the world.

Irmtrud König finds in Spanish American modernist literature "un intento de compensar el vacío espiritual que genera el pensamiento cientificista y su pretensión de reducir el universo a las leyes de la razón" (80). It is not surprising, therefore, that at the end of the nineteenth century and at the beginning of the twentieth we find what König calls, "la aparición de características tales como la propensión hacia lo irracional y lo misterioso, cierta deliberada ambigüedad en el mensaje artístico, la predilección por lo extraño, lo anómalo y lo exorbitante, la exploración literaria de experiencias oníricas y hipnóticas" (82). In this sense, she explains, "la literatura fantástica constituye en cierto modo una categoría en que se extrema esta 'ambigüedad' del escritor frente a los fenómenos sociales, culturales y científicos de la Modernidad" (92). Rather than thinking of fantastic stories as a return to the worn-out themes of romanticism, it is possible to see them, instead, as a projection toward the future, an acknowledgment of the unresolved issues of modernity. Fantastic writers of the modernist period not only explore the limits of scientific knowledge but also delve into the existential themes and psychological aspects of the genre that theorists would later identify as typical of the genre at mid-twentieth century.

There is no doubt that the creators of the modernist fantastic short story lived in a world that was in a state of rapid transformation. That which was for previous generations fantastic, inconceivable, or impossible came to be common and widespread: the railway system, steamships, and automobiles made it possible to travel across great distances in a relatively short amount of time; advances in the postal service, the transatlantic telegraph, telephone, and radio sped up communication and allowed news to spread quickly; refrigeration, electric light, and gas transformed households and made domestic life easier; and photography and x-rays revealed the mysteries of the human body from within and without. In spite of the marked scientific character of the era, popular imagination saw these new inventions as something like miracles, and the frontiers between the real and the unreal began to blur and blend together. As is to be expected, the fantastic short story, a literary form that expresses the spiritual unease of those years, found in the gap that separated the known from the unknown a space where seeds of doubt could be sown. In these unexplored territories, the literature of the fantastic could grow and bear fruit.

Rubén Darío

Ilán Stavans reminds us that Rubén Darío, "the indisputable leader of the Modernista movement," was a man who "witnessed the arrival of modernity in every aspect of life on this side of the Atlantic: from education to religion, from politics and the arts to science and technology" (xvii). Darío is principally known as a poet; his verses have attracted the attention of countless scholars in the past hundred years, and Stavans claims that Darío's book, *Azul*, published in 1888, "vies with Borges's *Ficciones* as the single most influential book-length publication ever to appear in Latin America" (xxv). Stavans notes, however, that "in comparison with Darío's poetry, his stories have commanded limited attention" (xxviii). The dearth of serious work dealing with Darío as a fantastic writer confirms this statement, and it is one of the reasons his work is under consideration here.

In "El caso de la señorita Amelia," the protagonist-narrator of the story confronts the tenets of positivism, observing that the foundations of knowledge are totally arbitrary and depend on the power of the individual who is speaking. He asks, "¿Quién es el sabio que se atreve a decir esto es así? Nada se sabe. Ignoramus et ignorabimus. . . . Va la ciencia a tanteo, caminando como una ciega, y juzga a veces que ha vencido cuando logra advertir un vago reflejo de la luz verdadera" (44–45). According to this character, a famous doctor and metaphysical researcher, "la inmensidad y la eternidad del misterio forman la única y pavorosa verdad" (45). His words seem almost heretical in the mouth of a man of science, a member of the intellectual elite and representative of *La ciudad letrada*, who uses his formidable discursive power to shape the way others understand the world they live in.[6] His claim, that mankind is destined to live in a world of mystery where absolute truths do not exist, goes against the grain of what most Spanish American intellectuals at the end of the nineteenth century would hold true. He tells us unequivocally that if there is a single truth (which he doubts), then we can never penetrate it, and that which we call truth is nothing more than "un vago reflejo" of something that will always be outside of our grasp. The doctor's theory expresses a concern that cultural theorists and postmodernists will take up many decades later: How does knowledge come into being, and on what basis does it acquire truth value in a society?

His story, narrated in the form of a monologue to a group of listeners gathered around him at a party on New Year's Eve, deals with his own personal experience with the fantastic. He tells them that twenty-three years ago, he lived in Buenos Aires and knew the Revall family there. For reasons the doctor claims to not understand, he was strongly attracted to the youngest daughter, Amelia, and as he tells the story, he emphasizes his inability to put his feelings into words: "el por qué de mi apego a aquella muchachita de vestido a media pierna y de ojos lindos, no os lo podré explicar" (46). The disturbing, vaguely erotic reference to a prepubescent child is repeated when the doctor describes a later scene when he said farewell to the girl. He recalls, "en la frente de Amelia incrusté un beso, el más puro y el más encendido, el más casto y el más ardiente ¡qué sé yo! de todos los que he dado en mi vida" (47). His acknowledgment that a kiss could be at the same time pure and passionate or chaste and burning with desire hints at a conflicted sexual pathology, but the use of powerful antonyms also emphasizes that language is being pushed to the outer limits here. The exclamation of "¡qué sé yo!" abruptly halts his efforts to tell the story, perhaps signaling that he is wading into murky waters he would rather avoid, but also literally dismantling what has been said thus far by suggesting he does not know what he is talking about. This rather lengthy introduction serves to build tension in the narrative and to prepare his listeners (and readers) for what follows, an incursion of the fantastic. Before he reveals the story's end, he assures everyone, "Juro, señores, que lo que estoy refiriendo es de una absoluta verdad" (48).

Given the fact that the doctor has already informed us that truth always lies beyond our grasp and that any attempt to penetrate the unknowable is bound to fail, it is not surprising that he equates "una absoluta verdad" with his own personal experience. His truth is the only truth he acknowledges, but it becomes immediately apparent that his listeners (and perhaps readers, too) will have some difficulty accepting his words at face value; as a result, the whole concept of truth will be problematized in the text. After an extended absence, the doctor returns to the Revall home and finds Amelia's sisters have become middle-aged spinsters (just as he, himself, has aged and physically changed with the passing of time). Amelia, however, has inexplicably remained a twelve-year-old girl. The narrator's immediate reaction to seeing the child is silence, again emphasizing the limitations of language to describe his experience. As he tells his audience, "Yo no hallé qué decir" (49). His first conclusion is perhaps the most logical one: he assumes that the girl is Amelia's daughter, "fruto de un amor culpable" (49). It is the shattering of his image of the chaste, innocent, and childlike Amelia that forces him out of the house "como perseguido por algún soplo extraño" (49), because he cannot reconcile his memory of her as a pure young girl with the idea of her as a mother or a sexualized woman. Ironically, a fantastic explanation is more agreeable to him than one based on ordinary possibilities because it preserves intact his illusion of the pure Amelia. Therefore, he quickly erases his first impression and substitutes it with another interpretation of events, which strikes us as impossible but which he relates with authority and conviction: "Luego, lo he sabido todo. La niña que yo creía fruto de un amor culpable es Amelia, la misma que yo dejé hace veintitrés años, la cual se ha quedado en la infancia, ha contenido su carrera vital. Se ha detenido para ella el reloj del Tiempo" (49). His conclusion that time has literally stood still for Amelia may astound his readers, but it does not cause him to wonder or doubt his perceptions. He dismisses the how and the why of his discovery, exclaiming only, "¡quién sabe con qué designio del desconocido Dios!" (49).

The doctor's refusal to explain further brings the story to an abrupt ending and leaves us with a number of questions unanswered. How did the doctor discover the "truth" that he presents to us? What is the foundation of his knowledge? What proof do we have that his truth is the absolute one? And, what reasons do we have to believe him? Although the doctor claims that he has set out to tell his audience a story about the impossibility of understanding abstract concepts like time and space, he has in fact delivered a practical lesson in the way truth and power interact. The second narrator of the story, one of the young men listening to the doctor's tale, has attributed great authority to the doctor in the opening pages of the text. He speaks of "sus sabias palabras" (44), and characterizes him as "ilustre, elocuente"(43). The doctor describes himself as a man of great knowledge and stresses how he has devoted his life to study and research. He does not, however, encourage blind acceptance of prefabricated and predigested truths. He warns the young man that he and others of his generation "ya estáis muertos, es decir, muertos del alma, sin fe, sin enthusiasmo, sin ideales, canosos por dentro; que no sois sino máscaras de vida, nada más"(44). The way in which he tells his story, emphasizing points that seem true to him and leaving out others that may be of more interest to his listeners, confirms the power he has as narrator. His discourse literally shapes the way others receive and react to information. The fact that they willingly give him the authority to do so is proof that they do not question the mechanisms that create truth for them.

The doctor's young listener misunderstands the criticism and reacts by telling the older man, "Creo . . . en Dios y su Iglesia. Creo en los milagros. Creo en lo sobrenatural" (44). It is this pat answer that inspires the doctor to tell his tale and to end it with a reference to God and the miracles that the young man had mentioned. The doctor seems to be saying that neither God nor science provides us with all the answers. His use of the word "desconocido" in relationship to God's plan is purposely vague: Does he mean that God is an unknown entity to him, or does he mean that the unknowable is part of God's plan? In either case, he is clearly not looking for blind faith in the supernatural, such as the young man's belief in miracles. Instead, he asserts that it is mankind's fate to be eternally confused. He has already told us that science is limited by the ability of human beings to penetrate the "impenetrable bruma" that blurs our vision (47). Those like the young man of the story who believe without knowing and who know without experiencing are living only half-truths. Whether the doctor is pulling the young man's leg, testing the limits of his credulity, illustrating a moral, or telling a story he believes to be true, we are left without a convincing explanation for Amelia's eternal youth, and we may doubt that Amelia exists at all outside the doctor's imagination. It is in this precise moment of hesitation in the story that the fantastic emerges and the power of the doctor's discourse is called into question, thereby undermining the authority on which the text has been built.

In terms of content, the story resembles a tall tale or fable, but it is Darío's way of telling the story that places it firmly in the realm of the fantastic. He mimics romantic narrative conventions, such as exclamations by the diegetic narrator to heighten suspense, but he uses them in a self-conscious way that calls attention to the limits of the narrator's knowledge and the shortcomings of his language ("¡qué sé yo!" and "Yo no hallé qué decir"). They are not cries of fear, but expressions of frustration by a narrator who finds it difficult to tell his story. Because the doctor is an educated man and a skilled orator, it is unsettling when words fail him. Readers are left wondering exactly what *does* the doctor know? When he faces an audience willing to accept almost anything he says, why does he insist on pointing out the gaps in his own narrative? The story explores metaphysical concerns, such as the meaning of time, the relationship between faith and knowledge, and the ability of the human mind to understand the mysteries of the universe. In this sense, it is typical of the *fin-del-siglo* anxiety experienced by modernist writers like Darío, who were attracted to esoteric and spiritual themes in some of their work. It is not content alone, however, that makes a short story fantastic; what makes "El caso de la señorita Amelia" fantastic is structure and form. The supernatural element (Amelia's eternal youth) exists in the text only through the doctor's words, and readers are given conflicting indications of how those words should be read. The reader must decide if the doctor is the authority he seems to be, or if he is a liar, madman, or practical joker. It is not a simple case of an unreliable narrator, however, for to dismiss his authority as narrator threatens to bring down the entire system he represents: human knowledge, language, and the power of official discourse to shape our notions about reality. The function of the diegetic audience in the story and the story's second narrator, the young man who struggles to make sense of the doctor's tale, effectively dramatizes this dilemma for the implied reader of the text, setting in motion the seesaw effect of doubt and hesitation that brings the fantastic into being.

Darío again examines the impact of science on human beings in the short story "Verónica," where he stresses the incompatibility between knowledge and faith. It restates the message found in "El caso de la señorita Amelia," that there are some things beyond the scope of human comprehension, and the pursuit of scientific proof for something that is essentially unknowable is a foolhardy endeavor. Darío constructs this fantastic tale on the premise that faith requires us to believe in things we cannot see, whereas science permits us to see things that may challenge our beliefs. The protagonist of the story is Fray Tomás, "un espíritu perturbado por el demonio de la ciencia" in whose soul "estaba el mal de la curiosidad" (51). The story is not told from the friar's point of view, but instead filtered through an omniscient narrator who tells the priest's story to convey a particular moral to his readers. Again, the story seems romantic at first glance, both in terms of content and narrative form, but a closer reading shows that it departs from romantic formulas in important ways. The first thing that stands out in the narrator's description of the friar is the unexpected use of words with negative connotations ("perturbado," "demonio," "mal") to describe concepts that were generally regarded as desirable qualities under the influence of positivism ("ciencia," "curiosidad"). Fray Tomás, unlike his romantic counterparts, is not haunted by a ghost or called upon to work miracles. The demons that plague him are technology and scientific discovery, emblems of modernity that Latin America was eager to adopt in the closing decades of the nineteenth century. While the narrator is not an actual character in the story (like the doctor in "Señorita Amelia"), he makes his presence felt through interjections and opinions, and other narrative strategies that reinforce the illusion he is speaking directly to his readers, as if they were seated around the room listening to him. We see he is an erudite man through his polished vocabulary and eloquent style of speech, so it is particularly difficult to understand his negative attitude toward learning and research. Nothing in the story overtly suggests that he is speaking ironically. Therefore, his anti-intellectual tone becomes a device that draws readers into the story, in hopes of hearing an explanation of what brought him to this state of mind. It is through the story of Fray Tomás that readers come to understand why the narrator thinks that knowledge is a dangerous thing. This notion, so at odds with the dominant ideology of the positivist age, appears to be a throwback to a prescientific era, when mankind turned to religion to understand the nature of the universe. At the same time, it provides a frame of reference against which Fray Tomás's modern soul rebels, and it is through the juxtaposition of old and new ways of thinking about the world that the fantastic comes into play.

According to the narrator, Fray Tomás became obsessed with the idea of inventing a machine similar to an x-ray that would allow him to prove in scientific terms the existence of God. Fray Tomás believes, "Si se fotografiaba ya lo interior de nuestro cuerpo, bien podía pronto el hombre llegar a descubrir visiblemente la naturaleza y orígen del alma" (53). To position Fray Tomás as a scientist is an unexpected twist in the story, for if anyone were to claim that faith alone could guide man, we could expect it to be the priest, rather than the omniscient narrator. The friar's claim that science can be used as a tool to explore the divine seems to conflate contradictory ideas in a way that deeply disturbs the narrator, who passes on his own doubts to the implied reader. Fray Tomás appears naive and foolish, in comparison with the erudite narrator. His interjection

("¿por qué no?") in response to the skepticism of his listener(s) becomes the driving force in the story. It is the flip side to Darwinist theory, for rather than question God's role in the creation of human life, Fray Tomás wonders if human science can be used to prove God's existence?

The narrator undermines Fray Tomás's credibility, asserting that it is the nature of faith to believe in concepts that cannot be proven. He criticizes mankind's attraction to science as "[la] obra del pecado, y añagaza del Bajísimo para impedirle de esa manera su consagración absoluta a la adoración del Eterno Padre" (52). The narrator reminds his listeners of "el pecado bíblico de la curiosidad, el pecado de Adán junto al árbol de la ciencia del bien y del mal" (53), and he refers to Fray Tomás's experiments as a product of "su enferma imaginación" (53). Fray Tomás, by contrast, speaks of "los maravillosos ensayos que abrían una nueva era a la sabiduría humana" (53), and he exclaims with enthusiasm, "Si en los momentos en que Jesús o su Madre Santa favorecen con su presencia corporal a señalados fieles, se aplicase la cámara obscura. . . . ¡Oh, cómo se convencerían entonces los impíos! ¡Cómo triunfaría la religión!" (54). Such a debate is not out of place between intellectuals at the end of the nineteenth century in Latin America, but the roles played by Fray Tomás and the narrator appear reversed. The priest embraces modern technology, while the narrator condemns it as a sin. What lies behind the narrator's extremely conservative point of view, and what feeds his fiery condemnation of scientific progress? These questions remain unanswered during most of the story, creating a gap that lays the groundwork for a fantastic denouement.

Most of the story consists of a philosophical discussion of the conflict between faith and knowledge, or religion and science, and plot development is minimal. At times, "Verónica" resembles a Borges story in the way it uses metaphysics as a red herring, to divert the readers' attention from a fantastic element about to make its way into the text. The narrator explains that Fray Tomás neglected his religious duties and immersed himself in the world of science, until one night he mysteriously died in his cell. According to one of the priests who found the corpse, Tomás's death was from natural causes, the lamentable effect of too much study. The narrator, whom we would expect to concur with this theory, suddenly shifts gears and decides that Fray Tomás was the victim of supernatural forces. He tells us that the friar received a visit in his cell from the Devil, who gave him the very instrument he had been hoping to invent. Fray Tomás, unable to resist temptation, used the machine to photograph the Host, which he stole from the tabernacle in the church.

This part of the narrative focuses closely on Fray Tomás and is purely descriptive, outlining his actions in a matter-of-fact way. The narrator seems to disappear from the story at this crucial juncture; he no longer steps in to explain or express his own views, and the frequent exclamations that signaled his presence are gone. The sentences become shorter, language is less precious, and a more objective tone takes hold in the text. A sudden break on the page marks the death of Fray Tomás (which is not described in the story) and the outcome of his photographic experiment remains unknown, since he died without speaking of it and the narrator apparently refuses to discuss it further.

What seems to be the fantastic element in the story, the appearance of the Devil, is told in a way that leaves little room for doubt or hesitation in the reader. It relies too heavily on romantic conventions, like those used in Zorilla's *Don Juan Tenorio* or Goethe's *Faust,* for contemporaries of Fray Tomás (like the implied readers of the story) to accept it at face value. At this point in the narrative, "Verónica" appears to go off in the direction of legend or fantasy because the priest is so distracted with his "misterioso regalo" that he fails to notice "que bajo el hábito se habían mostrado, en el momento de la desaparición, dos patas de chivo" (54). He expresses no surprise or concern at the Devil's presence, nor does he express fear. To him, the machine is simply a wonderful scientific discovery and its origin has no importance. The easy portrayal of supernatural events at this point in the narrative suggests to readers that they are dealing with a *leyenda*, a genre associated with romanticism in Latin America, but it misleads them about what is happening in the text.[7] It is not until the story's conclusion that the fantastic appears in its true form, taking readers by surprise. As it turns out, the most troubling aspect of the narration is not who gave the machine to Fray Tomás, but what the machine was able to do. This information is introduced incidentally, without explanation or elaboration. The archbishop discovers a photographic plate on the floor of Fray Tomás's cell "en la cual se hallaba, con los brazos desclavados y una terrible mirada en los divinos ojos, la imagen de Nuestro Señor Jesucristo" (55).[8] How this image came to be engraved on the plate is never revealed, but it seems to endorse the improbable theory put forth by Fray Tomás in the early pages of the text that science can be used to prove the existence of God. The narrator is apparently at a loss as to how to present the information, for he makes no attempt to expand on it. The image is left hanging in a linguistic void, confined by the narrator's silence and the story's end, and we cannot see how the fantastic process occurred. If, as the narrator suggests, Fray

Tomás's death is linked to the pursuit of forbidden knowledge, then the desire to know what cannot be known and to prove what cannot be proven is indeed the dangerous thing that the narrator warned us about in the beginning pages of the story. In retrospect, it becomes clear that his ranting against the pursuit of knowledge stems from his belief that the friar's "sickly obsession" with science and technology caused his death. The supernatural aspect of the story (the miraculous machine and the photographic image of Christ) is all the more disturbing because it is not centrally highlighted in the telling of the tale. It is treated as a casual aside, a negative consequence of the friar's unwise behavior. The ultimate irony of Darío's tale is that both men, so initially different in their thinking, are shown to be equally correct in their beliefs. We may choose one perspective over the other, but both are equally ingrained in the text. Tomás's death proves the point of the narrator (science is dangerous), just as Tomás's scientific achievement proves his hypothesis (science can prove God exists). As in "El caso de la señorita Amelia," truth is shown to be an arbitrary and highly subjective thing, depending on the point of view from which it is articulated.

The fantastic stories examined here are what Stavans calls "a form of writing obsessed with style" (xxix), in the sense that language and narrative strategies are purposefully manipulated to produce a fantastic effect. At the same time, they explore the preoccupations of an intellectual elite, characters or narrators who are grounded in the rational discourse of positivism but who reject it because they find it too finite and limiting. Darío's fantastic stories do not prop up the established order, but rather reveal it to be highly flawed. Metaphysical debates in the texts give way to irrational anxieties, to the sensation that mysterious, unfathomable elements in the universe control us more than we know. Morality, as a code of social conduct, becomes irrelevant because humans cannot foresee the outcome of their actions. Regardless of the choices they make, they have little determination over their own lives. The characters do not reject conventional morality; they simply ignore it because it has no bearing on their stories. Human existence does not get better with the passing of time, nor do technology and scientific discovery improve the conditions in which man lives. This gives the stories a decadent air and a subversive power because they dismantle the assumption so typical of the late nineteenth century, that adherence to bourgeois morality leads to human progress and social stability. In Darío's stories, such a premise does not hold true.

Leopoldo Lugones

In a number of modernist fantastic texts, especially those that we have set out to examine here, binary oppositions are erased or blurred and replaced by ambiguity. It becomes increasingly difficult to know what is true or untrue, smart or foolish, good or bad because characters do not behave in predictable ways and the outcome of their actions is surrounded by doubt. Obvious distinctions between man/ animal/ plant, between the living and the dead, the powerful and the powerless, the sane and the insane, love and hatred, or kindness and cruelty disappear. Or, the elements are inverted, turned inside out, and mixed until they become one in the same thing. In "Yzur" by Leopoldo Lugones, for example, scientific experimentation becomes a form of torture and the scientist is transformed into a sadist. Written in a dry prose style with scholarly references to anthropological, biological, and linguistic theories, the story outlines the attempt of the narrator-protagonist to teach a chimpanzee to talk. He has no particular training in this field and no real reason for undertaking the project; it begins merely as a whim and it stems from the casual discovery of an article in which he claims to have read, "no sé donde, que los naturales de Java atribuían la falta de lenguaje articulado en los monos a la abstención, no a la incapacidad. No hablan, decían, para que no los hagan trabajar" (17). The source of the information does not matter to the narrator, nor does he bother to verify it in any way. Instead, he becomes obsessed with the notion of reverse evolution and decides that monkeys were once men who returned to a more primitive state as a way to avoid responsibility. Driven by a need to prove his theory at any cost, the narrator works for five years to dissolve differences between himself and the chimpanzee named Yzur. Ultimately, Yzur does become more human, but the narrator becomes more like an animal, without a conscience and without guilt for inflicting pain on a weaker creature.

He acknowledges that his readers might not accept his "en apariencia disparatada teoría," but to justify his scholarly stance, he compiles a bibliography of references to prove "que no hay ninguna razón científica para que el mono no hable" (18). The fact that he finds nothing to prove his theory wrong does not necessarily mean that his theory is correct; it may simply show that his theory is so far-fetched that no scientist has thought to explore it. But the narrator knows that information (or the lack of it) can be manipulated in many ways, and he cites the intense effort he has put into looking for scientific records that do not exist as a means of confirming his own authority on the subject. For three years, he conducts daily experiments and carries out exercises with Yzur, a former circus chimp. Although Yzur is young, intelligent, good-natured, quick to learn, and devoted to his owner, he cannot produce the sounds the narrator wants to hear. Gradually, the narrator loses patience with the chimpanzee and begins to force the experiment to go his way, regardless of the pain it inflicts on Yzur. In his frustration with the lack of progress, he becomes convinced that Yzur's "mutismo rebelde" is intentional and is designed to sabotage the experiment. This in turn causes him to act more violently toward the monkey, and he admits, "aquello había llegado a convertirse en una obsesión dolorosa, y poco a poco sentíame inclinado a emplear la fuerza. Mi carácter iba agriándose con el fracaso, hasta asumir una sorda animosidad contra Yzur" (23).

At this point in the story, it seems that the narrator is losing touch with reality and his reliability comes into question; however, the introduction of a secondary character, the cook, adds an unexpected twist. He tells the narrator that he heard Yzur "hablando verdaderas palabras" in the garden one night (23), although "el terror le impedía recordar lo esencial de esto, es decir, las palabras. Sólo creía retener dos: cama y pipa" (23). Taking this vague and inarticulate report as proof that Yzur is intentionally withholding speech from him, the narrator steps up his campaign with such force and aggression that the chimpanzee falls ill and dies from the abuse. Ironically, Yzur's demise marks the triumph of the narrator because according to the latter, the monkey finally spoke to him before dying. He delivers this information to us in all seriousness, as if it were the only logical conclusion to his years of experimentation, but it is impossible for him to prove what occurred since there are no witnesses and the subject of the experiment has died. Furthermore, he mentions that he had been sleeping shortly before he heard Yzur speak, which introduces the possibility into the text that he may only have dreamed Yzur's words. They may also be a projection of his own thoughts onto the subject of his experiment, stemming from an intense desire to hear Yzur talk. Regardless of how readers choose to interpret the ending of the story, there remains an element of hesitation and doubt about the information they have been told. Perhaps the narrator is mad or delusional, but the use of scientific discourse and the tone of authority with which he speaks are designed to give the readers pause. At what point, exactly, does scientific inquiry turn into madness in the text? Is it madness, or is it the pursuit of science and knowledge? What prompted the narrator to conduct the experiment in the first place is also problematic. It displaces the notion that science is carried out in an objective, rational way and presents the idea that scientific conclusions can be distorted to tell us what we want to hear instead of conveying some kind of universal truth.

Central to the creation of the fantastic effect in "Yzur" is the presentation of the narrator as an increasingly unsympathetic person. This technique allows readers to gradually transfer their allegiance to Yzur as a character, making it possible for them to identify with the chimpanzee more than with the man by the story's end. The narrator represents a late nineteenth-century literary type immediately recognizable as the gentleman-scientist, a dilettante with superficial knowledge of the subject he has set out to study, who uses procedures borrowed from science without fully understanding the principles behind them. He is the personification of the ivory-tower intellectual, the man who has shut himself away from a world he finds too ordinary, in order to devote himself to the study of the esoteric. He is economically independent, which means he can dedicate himself completely to his project with Yzur, and he has servants who take care of his needs, so he need not concern himself with the mundane. His intellectual pursuits consume him, but because he works in isolation, no one holds him accountable for the quality of his research. He imitates scholarly writing, careful to include enough allusions to scientific study to show that he has, in fact, done his homework. But he uses the information in a random way to substantiate ideas that are only tangential to the work he cites. When attempting to force his experiments to confirm what he has read in books, he resorts to methods that have no scientific basis at all: for example, he reports, "Los labios dieron más trabajo, pues hasta hubo que estirárselos con pinzas" (136). The juxtaposition of scholarly discourse with descriptions of senseless, cruel actions carried out in the name of science produce a disquieting effect that makes readers aware that the narrator is not exactly the distinguished person he claims to be. As in the case of Darío's fantastic short stories, "Yzur" suggests that scientific progress is not moving humankind forward, at least not in a way that contributes to a better society. The narrator's abuse of power and privilege, both on a physical and a discursive level in the text, reflects a world marred by social injustice, where modernity is not the civilizing influence it claims to be.

In "Yzur," Lugones suggests that it is not intelligence that separates man from animal, but rather compassion. When a human being is carried away by the desire to know, to understand everything, and to prove theories, he loses something of his humanity. In this case, the narrator-protagonist of the story is more of a beast than the innocent victim of his experimentation, the chimpanzee. The animalized-man, seeing himself reflected in the eyes of the humanized-monkey, experiences a feeling of profound anxiety when he realizes that his dominance over the other is based on brute force, not intelligence or the ability to speak and use language, as he had originally thought. He who regarded himself as the master of words ultimately discovers that words fail him when he most needs them. The moment of truth for him remains outside language, and his question, "¿Cómo explicar el tono de una voz que ha permanecido sin hablar diez mil siglos!" (26), stands in as a linguistic marker for the absence of language, since it raises a question that can only be answered with silence. The failure of language compromises the narrator's authority over the subject he has set out to relate and creates a disorienting effect in the text. Readers must determine if and when he crossed the line from sane and reasonable to insane and irrational, and they must rethink the claims on which his scientific discovery is based. By the time the story ends, Yzur has become so sympathetic to readers and so human in his suffering, the fantastic denouement possesses an internal logic that makes it almost believable: Yzur takes narrative control of a story that rightfully belongs to him and effectively silences the person who previously claimed to represent him in the text. His dying words, "Amo, agua, amo, mi amo" (144) add poignancy to the story, momentarily distracting readers from the improbability of the action. Readers are positioned in this way between the uncanny and the marvelous, precisely in that state of indeterminacy that is one of the hallmarks of the fantastic.

In "Viola acherontia," also by Lugones, a similar situation arises when a gardener becomes obsessed with the creation of a new type of flower that will have human characteristics. His horticultural experiment is successful–he manages to create a black violet that moans and cries with a human voice–but it is successful at an inconceivable price. The gardener has taught the black violets to cry by torturing children in front of the plants and encouraging the flowers to imitate the human sounds they hear. In order to produce the sound on a repeated basis, the plants must be nourished with the children's blood, which the gardener provides for them. He justifies his actions by claiming they are necessary for the success of his experiment, but there is no triumph in Lugones's stories of scientific discovery. In "Viola acherontia," science creates monsters, and man's obsessive desire to control nature has become a corrupting force.

The story is narrated by a diegetic witness-narrator who describes the experiments of "aquel extraño jardinero," who devoted ten years of his life to the cultivation of "la flor de la muerte" (121). The narrator invites readers to look through his eyes by using the inclusive first-person plural, calling the character "nuestro jardinero" (121), and he brings readers into the story-telling process by addressing them directly from time to time. At first, he carefully distinguishes between his own observations and information that comes from the gardener by prefacing some statements with markers like "Según él . . . " (121). This strategy serves to establish a distance between the narrator and "el extraordinario jardinero," making it clear that the gardener is not like other people, whereas the narrator takes pains to show that he is an educated, rational man. He relies on academic language to show that he has studied theories related to the topic under discussion, and he cites the work of scientists to illustrate his main points. For example, he lists numerous discoveries in the field of science that initially seemed absurd but eventually proved true, including work by Charles Darwin, Jacques Henri Bernardin de Saint-Pierre, and Francis Bacon. But compared with the ideas of these distinguished men of science, the narrator stresses that the gardener's experiment with plants "permaneció siempre misterioso para mí" (125). In part, this is due to the gardener's tendency to personify plants, which strikes the narrator as problematic. It may also be due to the fact that the narrator identifies himself as "un conocedor" of botanical science, whereas the gardener is merely "un anciano de porte sencillo" (125) who lacks the same degree of knowledge as the narrator. The two men come together, not as social and intellectual equals, but as a scholar and a gardener who are equally interested in experimentation. In the early pages of the story, it is the witness-narrator's role to point out the shortcomings of the gardener's theories and undermine the validity of his ideas.

Focalization shifts abruptly about midway through the text, however, when the gardener begins to explain in his own words how he created the black violet that his companion finds so fascinating. Here, he establishes that his understanding of science is more complete than the scholar initially thought. His language becomes more erudite, and his tone more authoritative: for example, he tells his listener, "el origen de los colores que llamamos añilinas, es una combinación de hidrógeno y carbono; el trabajo químico posterior, se reduce a fijar oxígeno y nitrógeno, produciendo los álcalis artificiales cuyo tipo es la añilina, y obteniendo derivados después" (125). His lengthy and detailed explanation of the experiment seem to substantiate his knowledge as a scientist, elevating the narrator's opinion of him. He is no longer a simple gardener, but a potential scientific genius: the narrator acknowledges that a shift in power is taking place between them when he says, "Mis labios rebosaban de objeciones; pero callé, por ver hasta dónde iba a llevarnos el desarrollo de tan singular teoría" (126). The gardener's references to Shakespeare confirm that the two men have more in common than the witness-narrator first thought, and there is a distinct warming of relations between them: "Aquel recuerdo que tendía a halagrar visiblemente mis inclinaciones literarias, me conmovió" (127). This gradual erasing of difference between the men is important for the incursion of the fantastic in the text, for as the narrator moves closer to the gardener in mind-set, so too does reader identification begin to slide toward the character who was initially kept at a distance.

At the end of the story, when the witness-narrator tries to take control again, asserting that "la locura de mi personaje se me presentó evidente" (127), he is at the same time obliged to narrate the fantastic element of the story because he has been drawn into the world of that character. The gardener tells him, "Pero aproxímese, juzque por usted mismo" (128), handing the conclusion of the story back to the other man. The witness-narrator confirms, "Aquellas flores se quejaban en efecto, y de sus corolas obscuras surgía una pululación de pequeños ayes muy semejantes a un niño" (128). It is up to the narrator to find an explanation for such a remarkable occurrence, and he does, this time relying, however, on legends associated with witchcraft rather than scientific theory: "Recordé que al decir de las leyendas de hechicería, la mandrágora llora también cuando se la ha regado con la sangre de un niño" (128). This explanation is confirmed by the gardener, and the narrator concludes by saying, "Pero mi convicción de ahora es que se trata de . . . un perfecto hechicero de otros tiempos, con sus venenos y sus flores de crimen" (129). What had previously seemed impossible has come to pass, and the witness-narrator, who had seemed initially to be a man of reason, has completely changed his frame of reference, asserting that magic and witchcraft provide explanations for things that science does not. His final question ("¿Debo entregar su nombre maldito a la publicidad?") goes unanswered (129), but it serves its purpose as a textual marker for readers, to show that the narrator believes what he tells them is true. The moral component of the story–the torture and murder of children, which creates the special flowers–becomes the central focus, shifting attention away from the fantastic element itself, the claim that flowers can talk. This is an effective strategy for creating doubt and hesitation in the readers because readers have been encouraged to identify with the witness-narrator throughout the story. His solid understanding of science assured them that his version of events would be based on fact, not fantasy. When he suddenly embraces a supernatural explanation as the most natural one at the end of the story, it leaves readers without a ground to the world they had identified as their own.

Horacio Quiroga

Quiroga, appearing on the scene as a fiction writer, not a poet, just as modernism was beginning to wane, is not always associated with that literary movement, but in some of his early short stories, like "El almohadón de plumas," there is a clear modernist sensibility that bears examination. Because his stories are often tinged with horror, critics have compared him to Edgar Allan Poe, but at the same time, he is generally recognized as the first truly modern short story writer in Spanish America and his influence on later generations cannot be underestimated.[9] In his guide to good writing, the *El manual del perfecto cuentista*, Quiroga insists that short fiction, like poetry, needs its own economy of language and controlled style. Although he does not comment directly on the fantastic, his awareness that particular effects are achieved through language and structure is a key point that later theorists would take up and apply to the genre. He urges readers and writers to think not only about the theme of a story but also about the way the story is told. This encourages a close-reading analysis of texts, which, in turn, challenges writers to pay more attention to how they construct their stories.

"El almohadón de plumas" is an interesting case in point, for it manipulates reader reaction in a very skillful way. Initially, it appears be almost a literary cliché, a throwback to romanticism and the cultivation of gothic horror tales. Readers, familiar with this kind of writing, may expect monsters and ghouls to appear in the text, but they do not. Instead, there is a growing sense of dread, a fear that something terrible may be happening, but the nature of that thing remains unclear. The story illustrates well what Todorov meant when he talked about the possible existence of a new kind of fantastic writing in the twentieth century. Todorov asserts that in this kind of fiction, "the narrative movement consists in obliging us to see how close these apparently marvelous elements are to us, to what degree they are present in our life" (172). Quiroga's story contains no truly supernatural elements, but presents normal things that have inexplicably taken on bewildering and frightening possibilities. What troubles readers is the idea that something real, something that is part of their recognizable world, is capable of carrying out a fantastic function.

In "El almohadón de plumas," Alicia dies as a result of what appears to be vampirism; the form the vampire takes, however, is not one associated with traditional horror fiction. The blood-sucking killer is not a reanimated corpse with unearthly powers, but instead a common parasite that has for unknown reasons reached incredible proportions. The first description of it in the text comes as a shock, since the omniscient narrator has carefully kept the cause of Alicia's death a secret until the final paragraphs of the story. Then, by encouraging a momentary identification between the reader and the servant who has been sent into Alicia's room to strip the bed after Alicia's death, the narrator dramatically presents the scene as it unfolds. We see through the servant's eyes and feel her emotion as she lifts the pillow and feels its extraordinary weight. We realize what she is seeing at the same moment she does, and our reactions may echo hers as we see what she sees: "La sirvienta dio un grito de horror con toda la boca abierta, llevándose las manos crispadas a los bandós: —sobre el fondo, entre las plumas, moviendo lentamente las patas velludas, había un animal monstruoso, una bola viviente y viscosa. Estaba tan hinchado que apenas se le pronunciaba la boca" (58). Following this grotesque and frightening description of a seemingly impossible *monstruo* that has been living unbeknownst to anyone in Alicia's bed, the narrator steps in again to inform us of the details surrounding Alicia's death. The cool and objective tone of his narration stands in stark contrast to the horror experienced by the servant (and by extension most readers). It diminishes the supernatural aspects of the *monstruo* and situates it firmly in the real world. He tells us:

> Noche a noche, desde que Alicia había caído en cama, había aplicado sigilosamente su boca–su trompa, mejor dicho–a las sienes de aquélla, chupándole la sangre. Las picadura era casi imperceptible. La remoción diaria del almohadón había impedido sin duda su desarrollo, pero desde que la joven no pudo moverse, la succión fue vertiginosa. En cinco días, en cinco noches, había vaciado a Alicia. (58)

In case readers are still in doubt about the existence of such a creature, the narrator goes on to explain, "Estos parásitos de las aves, diminutos en el medio habitual, llegan a adquirir en ciertas condiciones proporciones enormes. La sangre humana parece serles particularmente favorable, y no es raro hallarlos en los almohadones de pluma" (58–59).

In contrast to the other modernist fantastic short stories examined here, the language of Quiroga's narrator is crisp and precise. At no moment does he lack words to describe what the characters see and experience. Nor does he express doubt about the nature of the events that he describes. The final two paragraphs of the story, those which follow the terrible revelation of the monster in Alicia's bed, are presented in an objective, matter-of-fact style, bereft of exclamations, interjections, and personal observations that so clearly marked the speaking voice of the other narrators. The absolute authority and lack of hesitation on the part of the narrator to explain in clear terms what has happened do nothing to calm readers' nerves. In fact, it is his assurance that everything is real and normal that sets their nerves on edge. Any feeling of terror that readers experience while engaged with the text comes from the realization that everything is a potential source of danger to them: those things which they normally think of as harmless and inoffensive or that are so unimportant to them that they scarcely notice them have the power to turn against them and destroy them. Ironically, the only information the narrator withholds is the very piece readers need to understand the story and Alicia's death: What are the "ciertas condiciones" that cause the parasite to reach gigantic proportions? In a paragraph so full of concrete detail, the narrator's reluctance to give the information readers most want to know is troublesome and produces the uneasy sensation that the world is a dangerous, threatening place.

In an era when medicine was making rapid strides toward finding cures for illness and disease, "El almohadón de plumas" suggests the failure of modern science to prolong life and combat human suffering. The first clue to the breakdown of medical expertise in the text is a reference to a common illness that in Alicia's case does not respond to treatment: "Tuvo un ligero ataque de influenza que se arrastró insidiosamente días y días; Alicia no se reponía nunca" (55). The use of the verb, *arrastrarse*, coupled with the word *insidiosamente* attract our attention because they humanize the disease and make it appear evil. Followed by the announcement that "Alicia no se reponía *nunca*," we realize that Alicia's light attack of flu must be something else, but that "something else" becomes a linguistic void in the text. The doctor who examines her cannot explain her illness: "No sé . . . Tiene una gran debilidad que no me explico" (56). Further consultation reveals "una anemia de marcha agudísima, completamente inexplicable" (56). The narrator informs us, "Los médicos volvieron inútilmente. Había allí delante de ellos una vida que se acababa, desangrándose día a día, sin saber absolutamente cómo" (57). Finally, the doctor dismisses the entire matter, telling Alicia's husband, "Es un caso serio . . . poco hay que hacer . . . " (57).

Ironically, as we learn at the end of the story, there is a very simple solution to Alicia's problem. The cause of her illness was literally under the nose of the doctors, hidden in her feather pillow. Their inability to diagnose the illness is due to their unwillingness to look and their inability to see what the servant discovers immediately by merely lifting Alicia's pillow from the bed. The simplest solution is the one that escapes the doctors because it is *too* simple: it requires no knowledge of medicine, no training, and no special skills to cure Alicia. It only requires action, which they do not take. The narrator offers us numerous clues throughout the text to show us what is happening to Alicia, but like the doctors, we do not know how to interpret them. When the doctors order "calma y descanso absolutos" for Alicia, we are told "Al otro día Alicia seguía peor" and "se iba visiblemente a la muerte" (56). Obviously, the doctors' orders are wrong, yet they are never questioned. The fact that Alicia does not respond more positively to them is dismissed in the text as "completamente inexplicable" (56). The narrator tells us, "Durante el día no avanzaba su enfermedad, pero cada mañana amanecía lívida, en síncope casi. Parecía que únicamente de noche se le fuera la vida en nuevas olas de sangre. Tenía siempre al despertar la sensación de estar desplomada en la cama con un millón de kilos encima" (57). Despite these clues that something is happening to Alicia while she rests in her bed, she is encouraged by the doctors to do the very thing that seems to be making her so ill, to remain in bed and rest. She experiences hallucinations that subconsciously link her physical symptoms to the real cause of her illness and tell us what is killing her. However, like the doctors, we do not know what to make of them and thus we hesitate to take them seriously. For example, the narrator tells us, "Sus terrores crepusculares avanzaron en forma de monstruos que se arrastraban hasta la cama y trepaban dificultosamente por la colcha" (57). This image clearly prefigures the description we have later in the text of the *monstruo* that has been sucking her blood, but it is dismissed by Alicia's husband and the doctors as "alucinaciones" (56) and "delirio" (57). Only after Alicia's death, when the servant finds bloodstains on the pillow, does Alicia's husband think to investigate the matter on his own. When he cuts open the pillow and discovers the *animal monstruoso* that has been sucking his wife's blood, the narrative focus of the story abruptly shifts away from him, the story ends, and we are left in the same position as Alicia's husband, wondering why the obvious has escaped everyone's attention until it is too late.

Whereas "El almohadón de plumas" evokes the mysterious and haunting atmosphere of late nineteenth-century romanticism, "El vampiro" is set in the modern, urban world. It deals with the power of cinema to transform our notions of the real and with the fascination man has with technology. As was the case in Lugones's "Viola acherontia," the story is presented by a witness-narrator who becomes increasingly drawn into the strange world of an acquaintance. Initially, the two men seem very different from each other, and the implied reader is encouraged to identify with the narrator, who strikes us as more reasonable and sane. Over the course of time, however, the two characters' lives become intertwined and the narrator is confronted with a fantastic event for which he has no logical explanation. According to the narrator, his friend found a means of transferring the image of a silent movie star he admired on screen into "el espectro sonriente, escotado y traslúcido de una mujer" who could act as his companion in "real" life (193). While the narrator at first expresses shock and disbelief at such a possibility, his friend convinces him that it is the natural result of a scientific process: "Una película inmóvil es la impresión de un instante de vida, y esto lo sabe cualquiera. Pero desde el momento en que la cinta empieza a correr bajo la excitación de la luz, del voltaje y de los rayos N^{1}, toda ella se transforma en un vibrante trazo de vida, más vivo que la realidad fugitiva y que los más vivos recuerdos que guían hasta la muerte misma nuestra carrera terrenal" (196). Because the narrator himself has some scientific knowledge of the so-called "rayos N^{1}" and, in fact, had authored a paper about it, his acquaintance insists on involving him in the experiment he wants to undertake. The seriousness of the enterprise is called into question, however, by the strange behavior of the man and by the narrator's confession that he, himself, is merely a "vago diletante de las ciencias" (184). Neither man has real scientific training. Yet, drunk with the enthusiasm of the modern age they are living in, they dive into the unknown with the conviction that they can unravel its mystery.

The narrator tells the story in flashback from a sanatorium, where he has been hospitalized due to a nervous breakdown. By the time he speaks about his experiences, his friend is dead and there are no other witnesses to confirm or deny what he relates. Certainly, his unstable mental condition casts doubt on his story, but at the same time, he uses logic, reason, and science to explain events, and his tone remains carefully neutral and guarded. There is something off-kilter about the way he narrates the story: although he occasionally expresses doubt, surprise, and even fear at the supernatural events he describes, his reactions are often delayed, misdirected, or dismissed without much reflection on his part. For example, when he first sees the specter of the woman, he is startled, but his friend acts as if it were "normal y corriente," which encourages him to adopt the same attitude (193). He engages in a conversation with the woman as if she were an ordinary dinner guest, ignoring his own trepidation: "En cualquier otra circunstancia distinta de aquélla, la fina lluvia del espanto me hubiera erizado y calado hasta los huesos. Pero ante el *parti-pris* de vida normal ya anotado, me deslicé en el vago estupor que parecía flotar sobre todo" (194). His easy acceptance of the supernatural creates a gap in the text, allowing the implied reader to begin to doubt his reliability. At the same time, it is clear that the narrator's apparent ease is feigned and that he is making an almost superhuman effort to behave calmly so that he will not offend his dinner companions. The "vago estupor" that surrounds him may be the psychological effect of dealing with such stress, or it may be the hypnotic pull of the other man's theories about science. Ultimately, the fear that he might appear unworldly or uncouth is stronger than his fear of the supernatural. He feels compelled to accept the presence of the specter as a natural phenomenon, simply because it seems bad manners to question it.

He sets aside the problem of whether the screen image of a film star can take on a life independent of the actual person who lives thousands of miles away and focuses, instead, on a new issue introduced by his friend of how to sustain the elusive image and breathe real life into it. Once again, the men engage in lengthy dialogue about the scientific possibilities of animating a projected image, diverting attention away from the monstrous crime "required" as part of the experiment. According to the friend, he must murder the film star so that her life can be transferred to the specter. For him, murder is a small price to pay in the name of scientific achievement, and he justifies the crime by claiming that his inspiration is divine. The narrator's conviction that his friend has murdered the woman provokes a nervous collapse, but this knowledge comes to him only in the form of a psychic vision. At no time does he question the possibility that the information may be untrue. Instead, he seems to feel extreme remorse for his role (albeit a passive one) in taking the woman's life. Too late, he has come to understand that experimentation can lead to regrettable results and the unknown is not only seductive but also dangerous.

The equation of scientific experimentation with divine creation is at the heart of the story and calls into question modern man's absolute faith in logic and reason. The outcome of the experiment is not what the men expected, despite their apparent grasp of the mechanics of the situation. Contrary to what they had supposed, the specter cannot exist without a living person to project life into her. The image exists only when it is tied to the person or thing it represents. The death of the real woman reduces her shadowy image to a skeleton who, according to the narrator and his friend, haunts them daily. By this point in the story, the narrator has evidently assumed the point of view of his "strange" acquaintance, and the two men embrace the supernatural as another problem that science must tackle. When the friend decides that he will use film, light, and a projector to transfer his own life into the skeleton, the narrator relates it as fact and expresses concern that it will lead to his friend's death. Indeed, at the end of the story, when the friend dies, there are two possible explanations: a fire, produced by the projector, caused the man to die of cardiac arrest; or the skeleton drained him of life and has disappeared back into the "real" world from whence she came. The narrator prefers the second version and closes the story with the affirmation: "Estoy seguro de que en lo más hondo de las venas no le quedaba una gota de sangre" (207). Nevertheless, the fact that he delivers this opinion while confined to a mental hospital plants more than a few seeds of doubt in the implied reader's mind.

"El vampiro" follows the classical structure of a fantastic short story in that it allows both a natural and supernatural explanation for events described. We can accept the narrator's story at face value and embrace the idea that human life can be projected via film and light, or we can assume that he suffered a nervous breakdown as a result of his friend's death and that the story he tells is a hallucination. The idea of an avenging ghost is suggested, but there is no way to confirm that it was more than the product of a feverish dream. There is no way to know if the film star was murdered, for the disappearance of the specter at the end of the tale suggests that she returned to the "real" world fueled by the blood of the man who killed her. At the same time, the lack of evidence that a specter or skeleton ever existed makes the story of the murder more doubtful. What makes "El vampiro" particularly interesting is that it uses an established literary motif, the vampire, and gives it new meaning by linking it to modern technology. Life, it suggests, can be drained from someone in a less conventional way. In an age when cinema was still a relatively new and magical phenomenon, the story would have engaged the imagination of readers on a level that escapes those of us firmly situated in the twenty-first century. Technological advances, born of scientific inquiry, seemed to portend marvels in the early decades of the twentieth century. Things that had previously been impossible, such as the projection of an image on a screen representing someone who was not physically present, pushed the limits of what spectators were willing to think of as real. Images that could stand in for the actual person or thing presented new possibilities, and, like other modernist writers examined here, Quiroga seems to be asking what happens when we use logic and reason to explain things that have no apparent connection to the real? When actions are cloaked in scientific (or pseudoscientific) discourse, who among us is in a position to judge what is normal behavior? And, when science is presented as an act of divine inspiration, does man take the place of God? As the narrator of "El vampiro" learns, traditional belief systems are easily toppled and replaced by new ideas that lead in unexpected directions. The story creates layers of discomfort and unease by attempting to erase difference between the natural and the supernatural in ways that end in moral bankruptcy. The focus is no longer on whether ghosts exist, but whether man has the right to control life and death. In this way, "El vampiro" functions as a modern kind of fantastic story, putting man at the center of an unfathomable world.

Conclusions

Adam Sharman claims, "The *modernistas*' ambition was to build their own tradition–a kind of antimodern modernism–by laying waste to the dominant positivist legacy that exerted a huge influence on Spanish-American intellectual life at the end of the nineteenth century" (70). "El almohadón de plumas," "El vampiro," and the other stories examined here show clearly that modernism "does not betoken the full and complete arrival of modernity" in Latin America (Sharman 39). Modernist stories are not political in the same way that turn-of-the-century regionalist or *criollista* fiction could sometimes be, but they nevertheless have important ideological implications. Néstor García Canclini explains, for example, that although modernism as a literary form coincided with many outward signs of development in Latin American cities, the majority of the population continued to live with high rates of illiteracy and "premodern" economic and political systems that positioned them as workers for the oligarchy (87). Latin America at the end of the nineteenth century represented a kind of intersection, where the new and the traditional met on contested ground. Modernism was certainly not a direct call for political action, but neither did modernist writers feel obliged to prop up the ruling class and their agenda of order and progress. Edmundo Paz Soldán and Debra A. Castillo remind us that "the nineteenth-century scholar possessed control over the social and political order because he also controlled, among other powers, the authority of scriptographic technology in a mostly illiterate society. He, thus, had few competitors–certainly no female ones–in his ambitious effort to organize the new republics according to the power of the word" (3). This is the intellectual elite that Angel Rama critiqued in *La ciudad letrada,* the philosophers and scientists who protected the power of the oligarchy and determined the way others would think about Latin America through their writing. Under the influence of positivism, governments "supported those works that represented a boost to official nationalism and its ideology of modernization, and which were written using a realist code of language" (Corona 195). The fantastic short story became one way that modernist writers could challenge the dominant discursive practices of the time by calling attention to the fact that "a realist code of language" does not guarantee that what we read on the page is real or true. The narrators of the stories are educated men who speak with authority, yet they ask readers to believe things that go against the grain of common sense. The stories also question what concepts like progress and science mean, or what comfort comes from the acquisition of material possessions when humans cannot control their own destinies. Intellectuals "found themselves confronted by a different Latin America, one in the midst of a profound modernization, whose most visible markers were urbanization, technological progress, and the changing customs of urban masses in the great cities" (Paz Soldán and Castillo 3). This is the world portrayed in the fantastic stories examined here, but rather than embrace it, they prompt readers to ask how profound the modernization really is. What lies behind the visible markers of technological progress? The modern world exists side by side with a premodern one, and it is precisely in this conjunction where the fantastic takes root. It captures the anxiety of an age where people feel they are moving toward the unknown, where the familiar has become strange, and the conflict between faith and knowledge is still unresolved.

The interpretation of a fantastic story is never an easy task because ambiguity and uncertainty are written into the text. Although the narrator or character might offer an explanation of events, it is never the only one. Regardless of the conclusions readers fabricate for themselves, there are loose threads and unresolved mysteries in the narrative. Any attempt to untangle the mystery leads us back into a labyrinth of ambiguity and inexplicable elements. Ambiguity, which gives life to the fantastic short story, is born from language and from gaps in the text that readers are encouraged to fill. The narrators, whether they are omniscient or the protagonists of their own tales, are conscious of the limitations on language, and they employ a number of strategies to call our attention to what they have not said or what they are not able to say. The small silences in the text, the lacuna where the narrator abandons readers, engender multiple possibilities that cannot easily be conflated into a single and absolute truth. Textual gaps emerge through the use of ellipsis, questions without answers, incomplete sentences that trail off into silence, and exclamations marking frustration. These rhetorical devices act to deconstruct the story being told rather than build a solid foundation of knowledge for us. The insistence on narrating that which cannot be expressed, or that which cannot be named, and the inability of words to relate certain feelings and experiences show how words sometimes fail us. These narrators are very conscious of their discursive shortcomings. When they lack words, they become silent and they leave the readers to make what they will of the text. In this way, they call attention to the fact that literature is an unstable entity and that interpretation of meaning in a text is sometimes arbitrary, depending to a large extent on the belief system that readers bring to the texts.

By one means or another, the narrators who guide us through modernist fantastic short stories discover that it is pointless to look for clear connections between the written word and the reality that it supposedly represents. They also insinuate that it is hardly worth their time to worry about the problem because as the narrator of "Yzur" tells us, "el demonio del análisis . . . no es sino una forma del espíritu de perversidad" (34–35). This attitude, so unsettling in the cultural context of positivism, reveals the subversive character of the fantastic as a literary genre. It is a literature that turns on its readers. It tears away the solidity of their world in a way that mimetic fiction seldom does. The indeterminate quality of the fantastic text opens the doors to dialogue between the reader and the written word that can be repeated an infinite number of times. It does not facilitate an escape from reality, but rather a constant return to and interrogation of the concept of the real. The modernist fantastic short story is one of the first narrative forms that calls attention to the gaps in the text and to the ambiguity of the relationship between words and the objects or experiences they represent. Rodero observes, "El cuestionamiento del empirismo racionalista iniciado por los modernistas lleva al relativismo radical que culmina con Borges y su escepticismo irónico que transgrede toda explicación, racional o sobrenatural, filosófica o mítico-religioso del universo" (35). Certainly, we have the beginnings of a new kind of fantastic in Spanish American modernism, for these stories emphasize the idea that all systems of representation are problematic. They question and subvert monolithic forms of discourse that are based on the claim that they possess a single, cohesive truth. They ask readers to question the source of their knowledge, to examine the manner in which they attribute authority to a character or narrator in a text, to acknowledge the limitations of science and other forms of technological progress, and to regard the teachings of positivism as the ideological constructions they are. In this sense, the modernist fantastic short story is a truly modern form of literature, and it signals the beginning of a new phase in Spanish American literature.

2 / The Fantastic as an Interrogation of Literary Practices

The fantastic, born as it is of ambiguity and contradiction, takes an equally indeterminate stance about its own position as literature. On the one hand, it draws readers into a situation in which the willing suspension of disbelief is an essential part of the reading strategy: they must be willing to entertain the notion that certain things, although inexplicable, are possible so that they do not dismiss the fantastic too rapidly, before some degree of doubt has taken root in their minds. On the other hand, they must hold onto the idea that there are certain laws that govern their universe and that cannot be violated without evoking chaos, so that they do not accept the fantastic too casually, before they have given it careful thought. It is, in large part, the reader's hesitancy that brings the fantastic into being, but it is this same hesitancy that creates the greatest problem for readers. If they are to experience the text to the fullest, they must temporarily forget that they are reading a literary construction and enter into the world of the characters, accepting it as their own. It is this deliberately naive reading of the text, however, that leads them into trouble. Just as they erase the boundaries between the written page and the world that they inhabit, the fantastic erupts, forcing them to confront an image, an object, or an experience that has no existence in their recognizable world. They are asked to make a space for it in their imaginations, allowing for the possibility that if it can be conjured up through language, it might materialize before their eyes. This aspect of the fantastic makes readers associate the unknown, the unseen, or the unspeakable with something to be feared, for it gives form to something that lies outside of their lived experience and makes them confront the limits of reality as a set of arbitrarily drawn lines.

As we know, there is more than one way to read a fantastic story, just as there is more than one kind of reader. For this reason, the notion of an implied reader is so important in any discussion of a fantastic text. Iser defines the term as a hypothetical reader who possesses the qualities necessary for a literary work to have its desired effect. These qualities are not constructed through empirical outside reality but by the text itself, through language, structure, point of view, and narrative strategies that create the conditions necessary for the implied reader to do his or her work. The implied reader is not a real person but a literary construct who acts like an anchor to ground the work to a specific time, place, and mind-set. Frequently, in fantastic fiction the role of the implied reader is entrusted to a character or narrator, who listens to or reads a story and reacts to it on a diegetic level, thereby illustrating for actual readers what kind of response is appropriate in a given situation. In the absence of such a character or narrator, the text creates a map for reading that the implied reader can follow, using linguistic markers to indicate which direction to take so that the story will have its full effect. Naturally, there is no way to predict how actual readers will respond to a text; they may or may not follow in the footsteps of the implied reader and share the same reactions. Real readers bring to any text their outside experiences, beliefs, and values that shape how they read and understand things. In a genre like the fantastic, where reader reaction at least partially defines the genre, the implied reader is a guide who shows others how the fantastic comes into being. Real readers can identify so closely with implied readers that they experience the same sensations and reach the same conclusions; they may keep an intellectual distance and enjoy the fantastic as a literary game without ever questioning its relationship to the real; or they may reject the implied reader's response altogether and dismiss the fantastic as nonsense. The level of involvement is variable when we talk about real readers, but the implied reader of a fantastic story will always have the same response, one that hovers between the uncanny and the marvelous in the moment of hesitation or doubt. It is through the implied reader that the fantastic takes hold in the text.

Modern readers, especially those well versed in literary theory, will know that that they should never confuse a literary construction with real life, nor should they believe that everything they read is true. They will be alert to potential traps from the opening sentence of a story, for they have been trained to look for the ways in which language manipulates meaning. They know they should not trust narrators, who are infamously unreliable, and they bring with them to any text background knowledge that informs the way they read. For example, anyone today who has heard of Borges will know that the Argentine writer created elaborate labyrinths and stories of parallel worlds that challenge our perception of time and space. Anyone who has read Cortázar will know that his texts are sometimes like a gallery of mirrors, where ideas and images double back on themselves in curious ways, erasing clear boundaries between objects and people and leading readers in many directions at once. Still, real readers do not always have this prior knowledge about the authors and their work, nor do they always possess a postmodern frame of reference for literary analysis. The implied reader often plays the role of a naive reader, one who can fall under the spell of the fantastic and experience it to its fullest extent. In a genre like the fantastic, a naive reading does not mean a poor reading; to the contrary, the adoption of a naive perspective, even momentarily, allows one to be open to a text, willing to look at it with fresh eyes and to respond emotionally as well as intellectually to it. It can be layered against a sophisticated, critical reading not only to determine what happens in the story but to understand how it happens. All readers carry within them residues of naive reading practices, carried over from childhood and associated with books they read for pleasure, "mindless" diversions that allow them to put aside their analytical skills and lose themselves in the pages of a book. The fantastic relies on its ability to tap into that feeling by lulling the implied reader into a sense of complacency and hoping that real readers will follow, at least for the time they are caught up in the spell of the story.

The counterpart to the implied reader is, of course, the implied author. In the early 1960s, North American literary critic Wayne Booth proposed the notion of the implied author as a way to discuss authorly intention without relying on extratextual sources, such as biographical details of a particular writer's life. This important rhetorical device was already deeply embedded in much of Borges's fiction by the 1940s, and it is particularly useful in the analysis of the fantastic effect in them.[1] Like the implied reader, the implied author exists as a hypothetical entity, a literary construct prompted by the text itself and reconstructed through the act of reading, not to be confused with an actual flesh-and-blood person who is the real author of the work. The implied author establishes the norms and values that are expressed in the story, sometimes directly through the words of characters or narrators, and sometimes indirectly through the implied author's choice of language and tone. The norms and values in the text are not necessarily those of the real author; they function, instead, as literary constructions that arbitrate relations among the implied reader, the narrator, and the characters in the text, and they help the implied reader know how to make sense of the fictional world he is reading about. The implied author has an even more significant role in fantastic stories, where narrators so often prove unreliable and characters become unstable. The implied reader can reject what a narrator or character says by aligning himself with the implied author, who provides distance from narrators and characters and offers a steadying hand that keeps the text from moving into the realm of the marvelous. The contrasting perspectives of narrators, characters, the implied author, and the implied reader create the kind of interstitial spaces that Cortázar spoke of when he defined the modern fantastic in Latin American fiction.

In the stories to be examined here, "Pierre Menard, autor del *Quijote*," "El milagro secreto," and "Tlön, Uqbar, Orbis Tertius" by Jorge Luis Borges, "Continuidad de los parques" by Julio Cortázar, and "La fiesta brava" by José Emilio Pacheco, the act of reading or writing is foregrounded and plays an integral part in creation of the fantastic effect. These stories interrogate the relationship among reader, writer, and text, and question whether it is possible for any form of literature, regardless of its apparent nature, to be either a mirror image of or an escape from reality. They also look critically at the concepts of great literature, artistic genius, the authority of the author, the role of the reader, the possibility of originality, and the power of the written word to shape reality. Moreover, each story reveals, by drawing attention to its own textuality, that literature is always an ideological construct, that it is never a neutral, innocent practice, and that it can strike at the reader in subtle, unexpected ways. These ideas are not new to modern sophisticated readers, but as a way of understanding the radical shift that would take place in Spanish American fiction writing during the famous Boom years of the 1960s and 1970s, the fantastic stories examined here illustrate and even foresee some of the important changes that would occur in reader-writer relations. They show how (not) to read fiction and how to think about the creative process in a more complex way. Compared to the realist novel that predominated in Latin America in the first half of the twentieth century, fantastic stories seem remarkably fresh and new. In the past four decades, countless scholars have looked at the work of Borges and

Cortázar, analyzing their short stories from almost every conceivable point of view. Nevertheless, the stories selected for study here are worth looking at again for three reasons: first, we can analyze them individually as examples of the fantastic within the theoretical framework of the genre; second, we can consider them together as a unit because they share important structural and stylistic features, as well as common themes; and third, we can determine what they represent specifically in terms of the development of the fantastic genre in Spanish America. Today their importance seems obvious, but it is crucial to remember that they appeared at a time when European theorists like Todorov were declaring with authority that the fantastic was "dead." Pacheco, whose fantastic stories appear a generation after those of Borges and Cortázar, establishes beyond any reasonable doubt that such a claim is false. Together, the five stories discussed here debunk the assertion that the fantastic in Spanish America is merely an imitation of European models, for by foregrounding the literary process that brings the texts into being, they reveal the mastery of those who work in the genre.

The questions of originality, of who writes fantastic literature, and who reads it are addressed in the texts themselves through the use of narrators and characters who also happen to be readers and writers engaged in the production of a literary text. On the one hand, there is a tendency to define the fantastic, like most other types of genre fiction, in fairly narrow terms so that a work can be classified and discussed as representative of the genre. The genre dictates that a number of rules and conventions should be followed in order to maintain its defining boundaries, and a text that exceeds the boundaries too greatly may no longer be considered fantastic. Fans of genre literature usually want to read texts that conform to their expectations about the genre because they enjoy the experience of reading something familiar. At the same time, sophisticated readers and critics tend to expect originality from writers, even when they are working within the confines of a tightly defined category of fiction. These contradictory expectations force the writer-characters in the stories examined here to confront their readers and critics in the text. The stories raise questions such as: Is originality possible? How is originality measured? What value does originality have? Another issue that is addressed directly in the texts is who is the ideal reader of a fantastic story? What qualities does this reader possess that will allow him to experience the full effect of the fantastic? Will the implied reader of the text possess the same qualities as the ideal reader, or will the implied reader assume an ironic distance from those reading practices and introduce a countervoice in the text? Because the fantastic often calls attention in subtle ways to its own literary mechanisms and constructions, it interrogates literary practices that extend beyond the boundaries of a genre. For example, if we are reading a story or novel that we think of only as popular entertainment, do we read it differently than we might a work that has been identified as a serious or important piece of fiction? If we have been told by critics that a particular writer is original and important, do we approach that writer's work the same way we might read a work by an unknown author? How do the attitudes and expectations we have as readers influence the way we interpret and understand a work of literature?

Julia Kristeva coined the term "intertextuality" in the mid 1960s to refer to the shaping of one text's meaning by other texts, but the idea was not new. It was already apparent in the fantastic short stories of Spanish American writers, such as those presented here. Borges, Cortázar, and Pacheco, for example, knew that what readers bring to any given work of fiction determines to some extent their interpretation of it. Semiotic and cultural "codes," as Kristeva and her followers called them, tie readers, writers, and the texts together in ways that play off and against each other. What makes the stories under examination here particularly interesting is that they use intertextuality as a tool to bring the fantastic to life and to question the process through which literature takes on meaning. More than the retelling of a familiar story in new terms, or imitation with a critical difference, intertextuality becomes in the hands of a fantastic writer a way to interrogate the notion of originality and the limits of language. They contest the claim that great literature is directly linked to the uniqueness of writers and their texts, and they urge us to think instead about the process through which individual works pass into the literary canon. The stories presented here are, to borrow a term from Mikhail Bakhtin, "dialogic" texts in that they engage in communication with other works, and the communication runs in both directions. When a given text directly or indirectly references other works of literature, it influences the way we think about them, just as they inform the way we think about it. This process calls into question the means by which we assign value to individual works and how we situate them in relationship to each other.

In Spanish America, the fantastic has often carried with it the stigma of being a variation on penny-press literature, a popular genre that follows established conventions and relies on the emotional response of naive readers for its power. This notion stems from the use the fantastic as a blanket term to describe any kind of supernatural fiction, and from the abundance of inexpensive, mass-marketed anthologies that exploit the public's taste for horror. Even today, some readers associate the genre with conventional ghost stories, tales of demonic possession, or science fiction; they find it acceptable reading for airports but not for serious study. Despite the fact that some of the best writers in Spanish America have worked in the genre, the fantastic continues to have an amorphous and sometimes misunderstood character, especially in terms of its place in the canon and its reception by critics. This situation was even more evident during the first half of the twentieth century, when the realist novel reigned supreme in Spanish America, and the fantastic was often dismissed as marginalized, escapist literature. Writers interested in the genre used such attitudes as building blocks in their stories, to question and dismantle common assumptions about literature and the way we read and interpret texts. The metaliterary qualities of these fantastic texts not only address important critical issues of the times but also point the way toward a more self-reflexive kind of literature in the second half of the twentieth century. In that sense, they are an important bridge to the postmodern period in Spanish American fiction.

Three Stories by Jorge Luis Borges

Many of Borges's short stories deal with the nature of literature, but the mechanisms that inscribe an implied author and implied reader into the text are often veiled and indirect, making it difficult for real readers to find a way out of the labyrinth Borges has constructed for them. For example, in "Pierre Menard, autor del *Quijote*" and "Tlön, Uqbar, Orbis Tertius," the "I" who speaks in the text could easily be confused with the author, himself, who is well known for his nonfiction essays on literature and language and who may be speaking as a researcher rather than a creative writer. The implied reader is someone who shares Borges's interests, who may think that he is reading an autobiographical anecdote about one of Borges's many intellectual pursuits rather than a work of fiction. Naturally, real readers who have experience with Borges's fiction will be skeptical and watch for traps that are being laid in the text, but any extratextual notions we may have about Borges as a writer must be laid aside if we are to understand and appreciate the way the stories function as fantastic texts. This is the "suspension of disbelief" that is often mentioned in relationship to the reading of the fantastic, and it is accomplished in the case of Borges's writing through an implied reader who accepts things at face value until the texts themselves give him reasons to doubt. In the 1930s and 1940s, when the stories first appeared, Borges was already established as an important name in the field of literary studies through his work in the journal *Sur* and other publications. This fact introduces the possibility that in "Tlön . . . " and "Pierre Menard . . . " Borges may be speaking in his own voice and describing his scholarly work rather than something he has invented. At the same time, however, the implied reader is required to be a critical thinker; he must distinguish between what is possible and what is not; and, as the scholarly details offered in the texts become more and more improbable, he must question the validity of what he has been reading. Narrative tension develops between an attitude of acceptance and one of doubt and hesitation, as both are inscribed in the text. Whether the implied reader ultimately chooses to believe or disbelieve, the incongruities in the texts remain and open up to multiple ways of reading and understanding the material contained within. The stories raise questions about the role of critics in shaping the way we read, and they undermine the credibility of the "I" who writes with such complete authority about theories that can never be proven. It is not merely a case of an unreliable narrator, but rather an implied author who seems intent on dismantling the very text he has created before the reader's eyes.

In "El milagro secreto," Borges takes a slightly different approach to the inscription of multiple readings in the text. Unlike "Tlön" and "Pierre Menard," this story does not pretend to be other than what it is, a work of fiction. The use of an omniscient narrator, a foreign setting, and a detailed characterization and plot make it clear from the beginning that we are reading a literary short story rather than an academic essay, but there is still some degree of ambiguity about the way in which we are supposed to look at the text. For example, one reading of "El milagro secreto" encourages us to focus on the suspension of time that occurs in the narrative. Looking at the story from this angle, we become caught up in how the miracle comes about, but we fail to ask why it happens. We become technicians, interested in the workings of the story's language and structure, but we are blinded to other aspects of the creative process. If, however, we focus on the way the story deals with the issue of creativity and literary production, we see why the miracle takes place, but we no longer care very much how it happened. We become intrigued by the concepts contained in the story and do not stop to think about how those concepts have been conveyed to us through language. Each reading produces a different interpretation of what the story is about, but these multiple ways of looking at the text are not necessarily contradictory or incompatible. Each contributes something to the reader's understanding of the story, but neither closes the text to other ways of reading.

Although Borges obviously concerns himself with the issue of readership in these three stories, he is equally if not more interested in the question of authorship. How can we grant a writer ownership of the words he writes, Borges asks, when all writers working within a given language have access to essentially the same body of words? If originality lies in the composition of those words, what is to prevent two writers from hitting upon the same pattern, quite incidentally and independently of one another? What constitutes originality in literature if all works in one way or another borrow elements from other preexisting works? In Borges's "Pierre Menard, autor del *Quijote*," these questions lie at the very heart of the text. Even the title of the story disconcerts us, for we cannot imagine what it means. We have never heard of Pierre Menard and certainly do not recognize him as the author of the Spain's most famous novel. The narrator provides us with names, dates, footnotes, and facts that make the story seem less like a piece of fiction and more like a scholarly article. This technique permits him to write with all apparent seriousness about the literary production of a Frenchman named Pierre Menard, who lived at the end of the nineteenth century. The narrator refers to Menard as the author of a number of poems, articles, monographs, and translations, but in addition, he credits him with a text that had previously been ignored by other critics. Because he claims to have known Menard personally and to have access to the author's manuscripts, he is in a unique position: he can uncover what he terms the "invisible" portion of Menard' s work, that is, a text that is identical to but not a copy of Miguel de Cervantes's *Don Quijote*. According to him, "No quería componer otro *Quijote*—lo cual es fácil—sino *el Quijote.* Inútil agregar que no encaró nunca una transcripción mecáncia del original; no se proponía copiarlo. Su admirable ambición era producir unas páginas que coincidieran—palabra por palabra y línea por línea—con las de Miguel de Cervantes" (49–50).

The narrator does not explain how such a thing is possible or how Menard accomplished his task. He merely states that Menard did produce a "fragmentario *Quijote*," which although textually identical to the *Quijote* written by Cervantes, is "más sutil" (53). He claims, "El texto de Cervantes y el de Menard son verbalmente idénticos, pero el segundo es casi infinitamente más rico. (Más ambiguo, dirán sus detractores; pero la ambigüedad es una riqueza)" (54). To prove his point, the narrator compares fragments from the two texts; we see identical words on the page, but he, in the role of critic, points out differences in style and tone: "También es vívido el contraste de los estilos. El estilo arcaizante de Menard—extranjero al fin—adolece de alguna afectación. No así el precursor, que maneja con desenfado el español corriente de su época" (55).

René de Costa notes that irony is inscribed into the text by "the use of a dramatized narrator whose voice in the text supposedly penned by him is decidedly different and distanced from that of its real author, Borges" (50). But as de Costa points out, Borges's "joke" was so well constructed that it fooled even sophisticated readers of the literary journal *Sur*, where it appeared disguised as an article rather than a short story. Borges later explained, "No one thought of me then as a fiction writer, but rather as an essayist" (qtd. in de Costa 51). Despite the use of invented names based on puns, the "supercilious tone," "the comic-parodic nature" of the article, the "quaint capitalizations and typographical emphases" to indicate a "hysterically effete narrator," many readers took (and continue to take) the story seriously (de Costa 50–51). Borges's "game of transformation" consisted in "making the serious silly and the silly serious," (de Costa 52), but the willingness of many readers to take the story at face value (at least on first reading) allows it to function well as a fantastic narrative, too. It asks us to accept the impossible as if it were real, while simultaneously casting doubt on the validity of the narrator's perceptions. In this way, it emphasizes how the reception of meaning may vary from reader to reader, and how critical judgment is marked by individual idiosyncrasies.

The narrator's insistence that one writer could reproduce the work of another writer without committing an act of plagiarism goes against the grain of everything we consider literature to be. We are indoctrinated from the time we are capable of reading and understanding literary works to believe that each text is the product of one writer's genius, and that much of its value, as literature, resides in its originality. A literary work gains in status precisely by becoming a model that can be imitated (but it is implied, never surpassed) by newer writers. The narrator of "Pierre Menard" asserts that the opposite is true: he would have us believe that two writers could produce the same text without imitation coming into play, and that the two texts, although identical in terms of the words that are used, can be different in terms of the way the reader (or critic) chooses to *perceive* them. The newer work is not necessarily inferior to the earlier one; in fact, he suggests, "Ser, de alguna manera, Cervantes, y llegar al *Quijote* le pareció menos arduo—por consiguiente, menos interesante—que seguir siendo Pierre Menard y llegar al *Quijote*, a través de las experiencias de Pierre Menard" (50). By foregrounding his role as critic in the text, the narrator reaffirms (and, at the same time, parodies) the power that those who write critically about literature exercise over those who write creatively. He demonstrates how it is possible for the critic to elevate or denigrate a given work using criteria that is entirely subjective and arbitrary but appears, within the context of a well-written scholarly article, to be grounded in some absolute, authoritative truth to which only the critic has access. The fantastic element in the story, the idea that one writer could produce a work identical to that of another writer without knowing it, takes on supernatural qualities only because it contradicts what we hold true about the creative-writing process. It defies logic because it changes the way we think about literature and language. The story does not depend on otherworldly elements like vampires, ghosts, or monsters to achieve a fantastic effect; rather, it firmly grounds the fantastic in the human realm. Man no longer is the victim of supernatural forces in the universe; instead, he is the instigator of them.[2]

Another of Borges's assertions, that a writer may have both a visible and an invisible body of works, is repeated in his story, "El milagro secreto," in which a writer produces his masterpiece entirely in his imagination and never commits it to paper. No one, other than the author himself, is even aware that the piece has been written; yet, Borges suggests, this does not prevent it from being the writer's greatest achievement. "El milagro secreto" is more obviously a fantastic story than is "Pierre Menard" since it treats a traditional theme in fantastic literature, the suspension of time. The writer, Jaromir Hladik, is arrested by the Nazis in Prague in 1939 for pro-Semitic scholarship and sentenced to die before a firing squad. His biggest regret is that he will not have time to finish his play, *Los enemigos,* but in a dream a few hours before his death is to occur, God tells him that he has been given a year in which to complete his work. The omniscient narrator of the story confirms that the information in the dream is true when he tells us, "El universo físico se detuvo" (165), and we see Hladik, during what appears to be a full year, constructing his play and committing it to memory: "No trabajó para la posteridad ni aun para Dios, de cuyas preferencias literarias poco sabía. Minuscioso, inmóvil, secreto, urdió en el tiempo su alto laberinto invisible" (167). The miracle is a secret one in the sense that only Hladik is aware of it. It takes place in his imagination, where time literally does stand still and the outside world is frozen in place waiting for him to be reunited with his destiny. The moment that he acknowledges the play as finished, time is readjusted back to the exact moment when a drop of water was about to fall against Hladik's cheek. The drop splashes against his skin, the bullets rip into his chest, and he dies on the morning following his arrest, as if the miracle had never occurred.

The existence of two parallel but distinct time frames, a common theme in fantastic literature, is an important aspect of the story, but it is not its main focus. Instead, Borges looks at the similarities between the concept of a writer producing a work of literature and that of God producing a miracle. In "El milagro secreto," both the miracle and the literary work are invisible and secret. Only the writer and God know what has taken place, but Borges seems to ask if that makes the work any less impressive. Does a miracle occur only when it is publicly recognized as a miracle? Does a literary text have meaning only when it is placed in the hands of a reading public? Hladik's story, when we look at it as one about a writer and his work, makes us question some of our most basic notions about literary value and meaning and suggests, as does "Pierre Menard," that the literary canon should not be limited to those texts that are visible to us as readers. Borges shows us through his fantastic tales that literature is not just a finished product; it is also a creative process. It is sometimes what goes into the process rather than what comes out of it that determines the greatness of a work, but like the miracle experienced by Hladik in "El milagro secreto," the process may escape the notice of all those not directly involved in it. When we look at literature as a commodity, to be weighed, measured, and examined for its worth, we automatically cast into the void all those invisible works that are, for one reason or another, beyond our grasp but which may, nevertheless, represent the writer's most creative moment. Coming from a man who is, himself, firmly established inside the canon and whose visible literary production is overwhelming in its breadth, scope, and brilliance, this is a rather unexpected stance for Borges to take, for by rejecting the notion of literature as a product to be consumed, he in effect dismantles the idea of an established canon and surrenders the position of power he occupies within it. Whether this stance is sincere or feigned scarcely matters, for by opening up the question, he encourages us to think about writing, authorship, and originality in ways that may well go against the grain of our most firmly established beliefs. He interrogates in his stories, as literary critics will do later on in their academic essays, the notion of literature versus textuality. As Barbara Johnson puts it, "While Literature is seen as a series of discrete and highly meaningful Great Works, textuality is the manifestation of an open-ended, heterogeneous, disruptive force of signification that erases and transgresses closure—a force that is operative even within the Great Works themselves" (40). By privileging textuality over literature, practice over product, and interrogation over closure, Borges encourages us to conceptualize artistic achievement in a new (and, some would say, subversive) way.[3]

"Tlön, Uqbar, Orbis Tertius" goes one step further by making us aware of the power that the written word can exert over us as readers and by inciting us to rebel against the authority of the text. While we often assume that we have the power to shape and interpret meaning from the words we find in a text when we take part in the reading process, Borges, speaking as the implied author and the narrator of the piece, asks whether it is possible for a text to shape the meaning of our world. In other words, when we attribute authority to certain kinds of written texts and regard books as the vessels of truth and knowledge, are we not permitting our vision of the world to be shaped by those books? When we set out to study history, science, sociology, linguistics, or any other field of human endeavor, do we not turn to books to tell us what we need to know about these subjects? And, once we have accepted the truth contained in books, how can we ever see it as something that is untrue, imaginary, invented, or constructed by individuals who are, perhaps, not impartial in their views? To illustrate his point, Borges tells us his experience with "Tlön, Uqbar, Orbis Tertius."

A nonfictional tone is established by Borges's reference to his friend, the writer Bioy Casares, who found an entry in an encyclopedia about a place called "Uqbar." Bioy Casares's mention of this place provoked Borges to search for it in his own encyclopedia, an edition that he had assumed to be identical to that of his friend. To Borges's surprise, however, he could not find "Uqbar" listed, and to his chagrin, he discovered that Bioy Casares's encyclopedia was four pages longer than his own, these four pages being of course the article on "Uqbar." With time and scholarly devotion, Borges tracks down information and learns from his research that Uqbar is a land situated somewhere near the juncture of western Asia, eastern Europe, and the Middle East; its geographical ambiguity stems from the reference to Armenia as one of its neighboring regions but without specific reference to which border they share. Tlön is one of two imaginary regions in the literature of Uqbar.[4] Borges discovers later that Orbis Tertius is an imaginary expansion of Tlön, from region to planet, and it is tied to an elaborate hoax created first by a group of scholars, philosophers, and poets in the seventeenth century, who amused themselves by describing an invented world in a series of books that they wrote about it. Later, in the nineteenth century, a North American millionaire continued the project, this time incorporating made-up facts about the nonexistent planet into *A First Encyclopedia of Tlön,* which described in detail the history, language, religion, and philosophy of the imaginary inhabitants. Slowly, books about this place, a planet that had no existence outside of the minds of those who created it, fell into the hands of readers who accepted them at face value. Those who compiled Bioy Casares's 1917 edition of *The Anglo-American Cyclopaedia,* for example, had obviously found information in other books about Uqbar and had incorporated it into their tome, accepting it (and promoting it) as truth.

The process by which Tlön, Uqbar, Orbis Tertius came into being is described in tedious detail by Borges, who emphasizes the thoroughness of his research and the lengths to which he went in order to accumulate the information he is now sharing with us. He goes on to outline his findings about Tlön, summarizing the various habits, customs, and beliefs of the (nonexistent) people of Tlön, listing facts that defy our most commonly held notions about the nature of the universe we inhabit. If Borges had ended the story at this point, we would have been left with a clever fantasy. The addition of a postscript, however, apparently dated seven years after the original story of Tlön was published, pushes the text into the realm of the fantastic and also raises some important questions about the power of the written word to mold our vision of the world.[5] Here, Borges explains that he began to come into contact with real objects that appeared to be from the planet Tlön. These objects, according to Borges, furnish us with proof that Tlön has been engendered from the written word. Tlön is no longer an invention but a reality, and, Borges conjectures, it is only a matter of time before Tlön becomes the *only* reality we know:

> El contacto y el hábito de Tlön han desintegrado este mundo. Encantada por su rigor, la humanidad olvida y torna a olvidar que es un rigor de ajedrecistas, no de ángeles. Ya ha penetrado en las escuelas el (conjetural) "idioma privimito" de Tlön; ya la enseñanza de su historia armoniosa (y llena de espisodios conmovedores) ha obliterado a la que presidió mi niñez; ya en las memorias un pasado ficticio ocupa el sitio de otro, del que nada sabemos con certidumbre—ni siquiera que es falso. Han sido reformadas la numismática, la farmacología y la arqueología. Entiendo que la biología y las matemáticas aguardan también su avatar. . . . Una dispersa dinastía de solitarios ha cambiado la faz del mundo. (34)

Borges concludes, "El mundo será Tlön" (34), thereby suggesting that "el mundo" (or reality, as we know it) will be consumed by a fiction (or Tlön), simply because we have allowed it to happen. By permitting books to have the power to shape our beliefs, our understanding of truth, our conception of reality, we become the victims of writers like those who invented Tlön, who hide behind the authority of the textbooks they produce.

Borges, however, tells us, "Yo no hago caso" (34); he plans to ignore the fact that the world as he knows it will disappear and to spend his days, instead, translating "Urn Burial" by Sir Thomas Browne. As Marina Kaplan has so aptly noted, "Y al hacerlo opone, implícitamente, a las ficciones de la enciclopedia, su concentración en otro texto, otro sueño, el de la fe y el misterio inasequible a la razón que afirmaba Sir Thomas Browne" (331). Browne's meditation on death and man's futile attempts to gain immortality share structural similarities with Borges's story, according to Kaplan; both stories are framed by a specific system of cultural references (that is, Christian faith versus skepticism), and only at the end does the author present "una alternativa, una disyunción" that challenges the dominant paradigm (332). As Kaplan says, "Ambos son la contraparte de los sueños de la razón, cuya impotencia última para trascender el misterio de nuestra temporalidad o para develar el enigma de la realidad ponen de relieve" (332).

James Creech has referred to the encyclopedia as "the genre [which] pretends fully to answer the questions it raises" (187). In this sense, then, it is the epitome of all forms of empowered discourses that close in on themselves and shut the door to further speculation about the knowledge that is being imparted to us. When we confront this kind of text, we generally believe what we are told; even when we question what we read in one book, we turn to another book to find the answers rather than question the concept that *any* book can speak to us with absolute authority. Borges demonstrates very well as he outlines his own scholarly research into Tlön how we come to espouse as truth something we have read, without stopping to consider who wrote those words on the pages we are reading or what his or her motives may have been. It is the same innocent or naive approach to reading that comes under attack in Cortázar's "Continuidad de los parques," for regardless of whether we are reading fiction for pleasure or a textbook for knowledge, we cannot afford to lose sight of how the words were chosen, from what position they were enunciated, or how we are being manipulated as readers unless we are prepared to let others do our thinking for us.

Only by changing some of our attitudes about the written word, Borges seems to suggest, can we resist the authority of the text. On the planet Tlön, he explains:

> Es raro que los libros estén firmados. No existe el concepto del plagio: se ha establecido que todas las obras son de un solo autor, que es intemporal y anónimo. La crítica suele inventar autores: elige dos obras disimiles—el *Tao Te King* y las *101 Noches*, digamos—, las atribuye a un mismo escritor y luego determina con probidad la psicología de ese interesante *homme de lettres* ...
>
> También son distintos los libros. Los de ficción abarcan un solo argumento, con todas las permutaciones imaginables. Los de naturaleza filosófica invariablemente contienen la tesis y la antítesis, el riguroso pro y el contra de una doctrina. Un libro que no encierra su contralibro es considerado incompleto. (27)

Obviously, in a society where books inscribe multiple readings as a matter of course and present both sides of an argument to their readers, where the notion of authorship is openly acknowledged to be the creation of literary critics, where the concept of plagiarism does not exist because all books are regarded as variations on other books, it would be difficult for readers to be manipulated by a writer into accepting a written text as the voice of authority. The playfulness with which the inhabitants of Tlön approach literature does not appear to lessen their production or their enjoyment of books, but it does give literature a different function in society: it is more like a toy or a game than a source of knowledge and truth. No one on Tlön, it seems, could confuse literature with real life. This attitude disempowers the written text and the author by drawing attention to their arbitrary nature, and it undermines the role of the literary critic by showing him to be the master game player that he is. If we were able to see literature in the same light as the inhabitants of Tlön, then ironically, our world could never become Tlön, as Borges predicts, because the texts that brought Tlön into being would never have possessed the power to engender it in the first place.[6]

More than twenty years after the publication of "Pierre Menard," "El milagro secreto," and "Tlön," Roland Barthes sent shock waves through the world of literary criticism by outlining in his essay, "The Death of the Author," many of the same ideas expressed by Borges in his fantastic stories. Notions that once seemed impossible or absurd no longer were considered so strange, for critics like Barthes had discovered that "a text is made of multiple writings, drawn from many cultures and entering into mutual relations of dialogue, parody, contestation, but there is one place where this multiplicity is focused and that place is the reader, not, as was hitherto said, the author" (148). Brown notes, for example, that "Borges's destabilization of his own 'author function' forms part of another fundamental aspect of his work in which he constantly draws into question the way a reader conceives of an author" (511). For this reason, Brown concludes, "we see a Borges much more in line with the developments in twentieth-century thought in which a positivistic faith in science was seen to fail spectacularly" (511). A contemporary reader schooled in deconstruction and postmodernism will find in Borges's short fiction a message that now seems commonplace; but in order to understand how these fantastic stories contributed to and shaped modern thinking about literature, it is important to look at them through the eyes of the implied reader, who is seeing them for the first time. Emir Rodríguez Monegal recalls, for example, that his early reading of Borges influenced his reception of critical theory:

> Educated in Borges's thought from the age of fifteen, I must admit that many of Derrida's novelties struck me as being rather tautological. I could not understand why he took so long in arriving at the same luminous perspectives which Borges had opened up years earlier. Derrida's 'deconstruction' impressed me for its technical precision and the infinite seduction of its textual sleights-of-hand, but it was all too familiar to me: I had experienced in Borges *avant la lettre*. (128)

Borges's choice of the fantastic as a vehicle through which to interrogate literary practices like reading and writing is crucial to the delivery of the message, for the fantastic as a genre must engage the reader in the text if it is to have its intended effect. Through the construction of implied readers and authors who mimic the reading and writing process on the level of plot, the stories illustrate the subtle tensions between these two positions. Who makes meaning, and how? Who controls the text, and how? How do we know what to believe in a text, and how do we make that determination? These three stories by Borges inscribe doubt and hesitation into the texts by undermining the foundations on which so many of our assumptions about literature rest.

"Continuidad de los parques" by Julio Cortázar

Like the Borges's stories examined above, "Continuidad de los parques" relies heavily on the preconceptions about literature that the implied reader brings with him to the text. For example, it mirrors what most of us assume to be the natural process of reading a fictional thriller: first, it acknowledges that the world of the implied reader and the world of the characters are not one in the same, but it suggests that there are similarities between them; second, it invites the implied reader to enter into the literary world of the characters as a silent witness and to become emotionally involved in their intrigue; finally, it allows him to be swept away by the reading experience so that the suspenseful plot and intriguing characters of the fiction appear, at least for a moment, to stand in for reality as he knows it. In the case of "Continuidad de los parques," however, the reading process is more complex, for the main character of the story is both the actual reader of the thriller and also the implied reader encoded into the fantastic story we have set out to read. This character approaches literature not in search of metaphysical messages or as fuel for thought, but rather as a diversion. He is a well-to-do businessman, but he is tired, overburdened with responsibility, and in need of relaxation. He chooses to read a novel of intrigue as an escape from his own life, for, although it is set in a recognizable world with characters who could be real, the vicarious danger and excitement he experiences through reading the novel give him the temporary illusion that he has been transported to another world that is infinitely more interesting than his own. As he is drawn into the novel, he loses the sensation that he is merely reading words and becomes a witness to fictionalized events that take place in the text. The hypnotic prose of the opening paragraph of the story captures very well the sensation we, as real readers, have probably had at one time or another as we surrendered ourselves to the innocent pleasure of naive reading. It is, to a large extent, the recognition of this sensation and our subsequent identification with the fictional reader as he engages in the act of reading that allows the fantastic to come into play in the story. Significantly, it is not the reader who narrates the story, but a third-person omniscient narrator who positions us as voyeurs to the act of reading. Through his seemingly neutral descriptions, he encourages us to surrender to the pleasure of the text just as the fictional reader does.

Because the implied reader's role is entrusted to a character who happens to be reading a fictional work, it is easy to overlook the fact that he is actually guiding us through the reading of two texts at the same time. Real readers can observe him in the act of reading, they watch him caress the velvet of his chair, smoke his cigarettes, and lose himself in the novel he reads. Because they are in essence reading over his shoulder, real readers assume the role of witnesses to his actions, just as he is a witness to the actions of the characters in the thriller. It is at this point that the experience of real readers begins to parallel and reflect that of the character seated in the green-velvet chair. As the divisory lines begin to blur between the fictional reader's world and that of the characters in the novel, a way of reading is inscribed into the short story. Real readers are encouraged to follow the gaze of the fictional reader as his attention shifts away from his own surroundings to the setting of the novel. He becomes so intrigued by the events taking place in the mountain cabin that he is unaware of his own actions; at this point, as the focus of the story moves from man reading in his house to the intrigue taking place in the novel, the fictional reader almost disappears from view as a character. Real readers are no longer watching the man read, but are reading through his eyes about the characters in the novel. Because the fictional reader is so absorbed in what he is reading, he is not immediately aware that a shift has taken place, however. His world and that of the characters are temporarily conflated into a single moment, the moment he is engaged in the reading of the text. As he is driven forward by a desire to know what happens next, he does not stop to think how the words got on the page, what selection process is at work in the creation of the images, or how his readerly gaze is controlled by the force of the narrative. Instead, like many people who read for pleasure, he is caught up in an intriguing plot and the presentation of characters. The mechanisms that divert attention away from the fictional reader and toward the novel are disguised by a continuity in the enunciation practice that allows no new paragraph, no change in narrative voice, in fact, no textual marker of any kind to signal a move from one level of the narrative to another. The narrator quietly glides from the library, where we have been watching the man read, to the mountain cabin, where we witness an illicit rendezvous between lovers, as if these two settings were contiguous. It is precisely the erasure of difference, which had been so carefully established in the opening sentences of the text, that allows the fantastic to come into being at the story's conclusion. Contrary to expectations, the two settings actually *are* contiguous, bringing the fictional reader of the novel into contact with one of the characters about whom he has been reading.

The implied reader of the story (who also happens to be the fictional reader of the novel) has fallen into the trap that has been set for him: he is caught off guard when the two levels of narration merge because he believes that he, as a reader, is somehow more "real" than the characters he is reading about. Through identification with the implied reader, it is possible that real readers have also been lured into that world, forgetting temporarily that everything in the story is a fiction. The implied reader initially positions himself apart from the other characters, providing a model for how to read. He does not identify with the characters in the novel to the extent that he feels he is one of them; instead, he is simply a witness to their actions, privileged to information (through the omniscient narrator) that they perhaps do not know, and in a position to observe them without being observed in return. From this secure spot, he can safely enter the text, knowing that he is able to participate in the fictional world of the characters while they have no access to his. In short, he can enter and exit their world by merely opening or closing the book he holds in his hands, and there is no reason for him to think that they exist outside of the text that contains them. Regardless of how absorbed he becomes in the novel, the solidity of his world does not appear to be threatened by anything that happens on the pages of the book. The book exists to entertain him, nothing more.

As one might expect in a fantastic text, however, the lines between fiction and reality, reader and characters, or literature and life are not clear-cut. The closing sentences of the story reverse the situation that has been set up in the initial part of the tale, as the fictional reader and the characters he has been reading about are suddenly, inexplicably brought together on the same level. Whether the man in the green-velvet chair has been transformed into a character in the novel he was reading, or the characters have found some way to break out their fictional world to invade his world is a moot point. Either way, the seemingly impossible has occurred: the boundaries between fiction and reality are erased within the text, and the inviolability of the fictional reader's position has been exposed as a hoax. By extension, the real readers of Cortázar's story, who have been encouraged to assume the same position as the fictional reader, will find themselves in a less secure stance, for if the divisory lines between fiction and reality can be erased in the text, what absolute security is there that these same lines will hold firm in real life? The fantastic does not aim to change the way we think about the world around us; rather, it asks us to consider (if only for a moment) that our way of thinking may be limited or flawed. While few readers will seriously believe that fictional characters can come to life and invade a space recognized as the real world, if they can be made to question the way they think about fiction and reality, the modern fantastic has achieved its effect. It briefly attacks the stability of our perceptions and beliefs, and it gives us a glimpse into a topsy-turvy world that seems vaguely menacing to us, if only because we have no system of reference to understand it completely.

The reader who approaches "Continuidad de los parques" with the same expectations as the fictional reader of the thriller that makes up part of the text experiences a shock as he learns that so-called escapist fiction does not necessarily provide one with an escape. As Cortázar's fictional reader discovers, mindless surrender to a text can lead to trouble. When the implied reader of the story provides a model for reading that leaves us, as real readers, in an impossible situation, a space suddenly opens up in the text where we are expected to question our notions about literature and the reading process. His mistake, of course, is to identify the characters of the novel as literary creations but to think of himself as an autonomous agent, the one who brings them to life through the act of reading. By asking us to read through his eyes, he brushes aside some of the most elementary facts about literature, that *everything* contained in the story is an invention, *nothing* in the text is real, the laws that govern the extratextual world do not necessarily apply to the world of the character, and any similarity between what we read in a text and what we see around us is an artistic construction, meant to deceive us and make us think that mimetic fiction is capable of capturing reality in words. The appearance of the fantastic forces us to remember that we are dealing with fiction, and that literature always involves a manipulation of the reader by a writer who hides behind his words and shapes them into forms that may or may not have anything to do with the real world. In other words, it reminds us that "literary texts never 'mean what they say' because they are fiction" (Eagleton, *Text,* 155).

A second, more critical reading of the story allows us to see how Cortázar makes his point. Once we know how the story ends, the fantastic effect no longer depends on surprise, but instead becomes deeply rooted in the story's language and structure. Here, the role of the implied reader becomes even more important, since the implied reader will experience the same reaction every time, but real readers will not. Whereas on a first reading of the story, the implied reader may lead real readers astray, on subsequent readings, most real readers will approach the text with ironic distance. This distance encourages an intellectual response rather than an emotional one. The lengthy description of the man seated in his library reading a novel, for example, provides us with important background information that we can use to guess what is going to happen when the character from the novel invades a country house, silently goes up the steps, and enters a library where he finds a man seated in a green-velvet chair reading a novel. First, we notice that the two actions (reading and entering the house) occur at the same time of day: as the man picks up the novel, he observes that "danzaba el aire del atardecer bajo los robles" (312). As the character from the novel leaves his mountain retreat and makes his way downhill, we are told, "empezaba a anochecer" (313). As twilight falls, then, the two levels of narrative come together in time. They also come together in space, as the character of the novel passes through "la alameda" (313) that surrounds a large house, checking to be sure that "el mayordomo" has left for the day (313). Previously, we had seen the fictional reader looking at the "parque de los robles" (312) that surrounds his house. We had also been made aware of the presence of a "mayordomo." The most important verbal clue, however, is the green-velvet chair, placed so that its back is to the door of the study. This chair is described several times on the first page of the story; when it reappears in the last line of the text, it seems clear that the man who is about to be murdered is our fictional reader. Although we assume that it is the same man, it can never be anything more than an assumption since it is not explicitly stated in the text. He is, after all, an anonymous character in both parts of the story. There might possibly be two men seated in velvet chairs, looking out at two different parks of trees, but the way we choose to think about him is up to us as readers.

Cortázar seems to suggest in "Continuidad de los parques" that readers supply the ultimate meaning of a story, if it is to have any. They may hesitate between a natural and supernatural explanation, allowing the story to remain in the realm of the fantastic if they choose to do so, but the act of reading always involves a deliberate, conscious choice. Readers may dismiss the story as fantasy, they may interpret it as a metaphor, they may simply let it exist as an open-ended text. Regardless of how they decide to look at it, however, they must react to it as *literature* and acknowledge it as a *construction*. In this way, the story not only entertains us as an exercise in the fantastic but also teaches us something about the process of reading. It shows us that "we are all the time engaged in constructing hypotheses about the meaning of the text. . . . The text itself is really no more than a series of 'cues' to the reader, invitations to construct a piece of language into meaning" (Eagleton, *Literary Theory*, 76). The fantastic, despite our hunches and inferences about its meaning, remains a stubbornly interrogative narrative mode for, although it challenges us to concretize it and thus explain away those elements that escape our comprehension, it does not inscribe closure in the text. Instead, it reminds us that any meaning we attach to the text is likely to be unraveled by another reading of it. Together with the fictional reader of Cortázar's tale, we learn that the way we choose to interpret what we read often depends on the position we are occupying at that particular moment.[7]

"La fiesta brava" by José Emilio Pacheco

"La fiesta brava," like "Continuidad de los parques," offers us not only multiple ways of reading the text but also presents us with multiple levels of fiction to read. First, we encounter a story entitled "La fiesta brava," supposedly penned by an unknown writer named Andrés Quintana. This tale stands out visually from the others in the collection because it appears to be a typed manuscript that has been inserted into the printed pages of a book. It is also the only story in the collection that is attributed to someone other than Pacheco, the author of book we are reading. Furthermore, it bears the author's name in capital letters immediately after the title of the work, a stylistic feature that does not recur in any of the other stories in the collection. The second part of the narrative returns to the standard format used elsewhere in the book, reconfirming its connection to the anthology we are reading by explaining that Andrés Quintana, the supposed creator of the story we have just read, is actually a fictional character. The new story has no title page of its own but is placed at the end of Quintana's manuscript, as if it were a continuation of the same story. It immediately becomes apparent, however, that structurally and stylistically, they are miles apart. In the second version of "La fiesta brava," an omniscient narrator positions us as witnesses to the act of writing so that we can see how the manuscript we have just read came into being. In this way, we are given access to the creative process and perhaps even more importantly, to the work of critics, who take it upon themselves to determine the literary worth of a newly created text.

The first part of the story, that which passes as the work of Quintana, calls attention to itself as literature by emphasizing the production process that went into its making. Before the narrative begins, for example, we are told that we are going to be reading "un cuento de ANDRES QUINTANA" (79). The writer's name and the use of the word *cuento* clearly establish that we are reading a piece of fiction. The role of the implied reader is not so clearly defined here as it was in "Continuidad de los parques," but there are still clues about how the story should be read. For example, Andrés's story is written in a self-conscious literary style, reminiscent of some of the more experimental writing in Latin America in the 1960s. It is fragmented, it ignores the rules of punctuation, and it employs a second-person narrative voice addressed to the main character of the story, Captain Keller, as if to suggest that he is engaged in dialogue with his subconscious. The implied reader is kept at a distance through these rhetorical devices, a witness to events described in the story, but not emotionally drawn into the world of the protagonist, who is an alienated and psychologically damaged Vietnam veteran on leave in Mexico. Although the story contains some realistic detail, it does not fit into the traditional category of realist fiction, primarily due to the way in which it is written. At the same time, it cannot rightly be called fantastic because there is no attempt to convince the implied reader that he is reading about his own recognizable world. Captain Keller may walk the streets of Mexico City, but his experience there is strange and unfamiliar. The story relies heavily on uncanny elements to create an air of mystery or intrigue, but there is no suggestion of the supernatural at work. Instead, it more closely resembles a nightmare: when Captain Keller is murdered by a group of men who seem to be reenacting some sort of ancient Aztec ritual, the implied reader has no way of knowing what motivated the men to act as they did. We are left with a sense that something odd has happened, but we cannot understand what it means. It is possible to find some symbolic or metaphorical meaning hidden behind the textual images that relate Captain Keller's experience to modern-day Mexico, but because it is clear from the outset that the story is fictional, there is no reason to believe that the experience of the characters have any existence outside of the text that contains them.

In contrast, the second part of the story, which deals with Andrés's struggle to write and publish "La fiesta brava," seems much more grounded in the recognizable world of Mexico City in the early 1970s. Unlike "Continuidad de los parques," which structurally and stylistically disguised the movement from one level of fiction to another, the second part of "La fiesta brava" is clearly meant to be read in a different way from Andrés's story of the same name. A change in narrative voice, a new style, a repositioning of characters and settings, a return to the book's familiar typeset, and the silent acknowledgment that we are now back under Pacheco's implied authorial control all signal that we are moving into another level of narration and that the first part of the text is now closed. An omniscient narrator frames the story we have just read, going back in time to the moment when Andrés was asked to write the piece for the journal; next, we see him struggle with the creative process as he writes; and finally, we witness the painful rejection of the manuscript by the editors of the journal who had invited him to submit it. This section of the narrative has more simple, traditional style that stands in marked contrast to what we found in Andrés's manuscript. It relies on an omniscient narrator who scarcely makes his presence felt; the story is told in chronological order with little or no fragmentation; there is a solid narrative thread that gives tight coherence to the plot; and there is character development and psychological penetration of Andrés, the protagonist, which encourages a degree of sympathy for him. More importantly, there are no visible reminders of an author's presence behind the words we read, which promotes the illusion that the story we are reading is a mimetic representation of our own world. Compared to Captain Keller's extraordinary experience, we seem to be back on recognizable solid ground when we read about Andrés's day-to-day routine, which resembles that of almost any modern city dweller. He strikes us as a more believable and realistic character than Captain Keller, perhaps because he is so ordinary. He is also a familiar figure to readers who recognize him as the modern antihero, the alienated twentieth-century man, the struggling writer, the frustrated artist, the unappreciated and undiscovered talent who has reached the point of despair, surrounded by a hostile city and people who are indifferent to him. The implied reader of the story (who like Andrés is familiar with the world of literature) will at least recognize if not share some of the qualities that make Andrés what he is. He will have an understanding of what it means to be an unknown writer in Mexico in the wake of the Boom, and this extratextual system of reference allows him to feel more deeply Andrés's disappointment and humiliation when his work is rejected by unfeeling critics. Through identification with or sympathy for Andrés, the distance between the character and the implied reader narrows; at the same time, he seems less like a literary character, himself, because he has been cast in the role of creator of fiction. As the author of the text we have just read, he seems more real than Captain Keller because he seems to be an autonomous subject, the maker of meaning, rather than a literary construct. It is at this point, of course, when his identity as a fictional character fades, that the fantastic begins to work its way into the text.

Although it has come about in a different way, the process we have been subjected to as readers is similar in "Continuidad de los parques" and "La fiesta brava," for in both cases the texts encourage us to forget, at least for a time, that we are reading a work of literature. Just like the fictional reader in Cortázar's story who is so caught up in plot and characters that he temporarily forgets that he is reading fiction, the implied reader of "La fiesta brava" has a similar reaction when he reads about Andrés. To accept Andrés, even briefly, as the author of the manuscript that deals with Captain Keller, the implied reader will be asked to believe that Andrés is somehow more real than his literary creation, and that his life extends beyond the pages of the text into the recognizable real world. This effect is achieved through concrete and detailed descriptions that allow the implied reader to imagine Andrés inhabits the same space as he. They walk the same streets, use the same metro stations, and look out their windows at the same city. Although Captain Keller technically inhabits the same city, his experience there is distorted and strange, and as a foreign visitor, he has no real idea of what is happening around him. He seems displaced in time and out of sync with the ordinary world that Andrés inhabits. When, at the end of the story, Andrés thinks he sees Captain Keller in a subway station and believes that the American is about to die, the encounter strikes us as fantastic because it is unclear how the writer of a story could come face to face with a character of his own invention. Andrés's disappearance, which until now has been shrouded in mystery, is inexplicably but directly linked to the dangerous men he had written about in his story. The fantastic component of the story is not the ritualistic murder that takes place in Mexico City's subway tunnels, but rather the collision of two distinct narratives in a single time and place. The seemingly impossible has come to pass—an author and his characters come together in defiance of the story's internal logic—and there is no way to understand it except to unravel our reading of the text and begin again at the start. Like "Continuidad de los parques," "La fiesta brava" works to blur the distinctions between fiction and reality and to interrogate the practice of reading and writing literature, in an effort to make us question the way we read and understand a text.

A second, more informed reading of the story naturally supplies us with clues as to what will eventually happen to Andrés. For example, the newspaper ad that appears on the first page of the narrative explains that he went missing "el martes 5, en el trayecto de la Avenida Juárez a las calles de Tonalá en la Colonia Roma hace las 23:30 horas" (78). Later, Captain Keller is told to take the "último carro del último Metro la noche del martes en la estación Insurgentes, el tren se parará entre Isabel la Católica y Pino Suárez" (84). Anyone who has been in Mexico City will recognize that the two sets of information coincide, placing both Andrés and Captain Keller on the same metro line around 11:30 p.m. on a Tuesday evening. A more obvious clue is given on the next to the last page of the story, when the narrator says that Andrés "descendió en Insurgentes cuando los magnavoces anunciaban que era la última corrida y las puertas de la estación iban a cerrarse" (112). We have already been told that it is a Tuesday evening when Andrés delivers his story to the magazine, thus reinforcing the notion that he and Captain Keller may end up in the same place at the same time. Furthermore, if we consider the fact that the first part of the story is written in the future tense and the second part in the past tense, we could make the grammatical assumption that both verb tenses are pointing toward the same moment in time, a present when the action culminates. A detailed description of Captain Keller in each part of the narrative also provides us with a specific visual image that allows us to link the two. The omniscient narrator confirms that Andrés and Captain Keller are in the same place at the same time when he states, "Andrés gritó palabras que el capitán Keller ya no llegó a escuchar y se perdieron en el túnel" (113). Just as the fantastic erupts in the text, Andrés is assaulted by three working-class men who had been traveling on the metro with him and who had spotted him handling a large bank note. It is impossible to know with certainty that these three men are the same three men Andrés had described in his story, or that Andrés did indeed spot Captain Keller in the subway because Andrés disappears from the text and cannot tell us what happened. The omniscient narrator makes no attempt to clarify or explain the situation, and readers are left with the unsettling feeling that something supernatural may have taken place, although the text offers no real proof. Like the fictional reader in Cortázar's tale, it appears that Andrés is in danger of being murdered by someone who may have emerged out of the pages of a book to wreak havoc on a world that we had briefly imagined to be like our own.

"La fiesta brava" contains a metacritical discussion of Andrés's story, in which an editor scolds the author for creating a scenario that is too far fetched and unreal. The editor's assertion that no one will believe the story lays the groundwork for how the implied reader will react when Andrés and Keller finally meet. He also points out how the story is flawed as a piece of literature, which reminds us again that it is not meant to stand in for reality and that Keller is nothing more than a literary construction:

> No se alcanza a ver al personaje. Te falta precisión. Tienes algunos párrafos muy enredados, el último por ejemplo, gracias a tu capricho de sustituir por comas todos los demás signos de puntuación. Tu anécdota es irreal en el peor sentido, muy *bookish,* ¿no es cierto? Además, esto del "sustrato prehispánico enterrado pero

> vivo" como que ya no. Fuentes hizo cosas muy padres con ello y al hacerlo también agotó el tema. Claro que tú lo ves desde otro ángulo pero de todos modos. . . . Y el asunto se complica por el empleo de la segunda persona de singular. Es un recurso que ya perdió su novedad y acentúa el parecido con Fuentes, *you know.* (108)

While we sympathize with Andrés, we may also feel inclined to agree with the critic, for those of us who have read his story with a critical eye will probably have come to the same conclusions about it. It *is* "bookish" in tone and it *does* go over familiar territory covered by Fuentes, Cortázar, Darío, and others, as the critic points out. Captain Keller lacks psychological depth as a character and his situation does not particularly engage us on an emotional level. For this reason, it is all the more surprising when Andrés spots him in the subway because we had safely tucked him away into the category of fictional character without stopping to consider that Andrés falls into this category, as well. Like the fictional critic of "La fiesta brava," we too have made a simple error. We have temporarily forgotten that "realism is plausible not because it reflects the world, but because it is constructed out of what is (discursively) familiar" (Belsey 47). By equating the unreal with that which is foreign and strange, and the real with that which is familiar, we are overlooking the obvious fact that everything inside a literary text is part of the same fiction. Like "Continuidad de los parques," "La fiesta brava" demonstrates that a critical reading of a fantastic narrative may lessen the emotional impact of the story, but it does not necessarily provide the text with closure. Even when we understand how the story is constructed to achieve the fantastic effect, we do not have a clear-cut explanation of what really happened. The issue at stake, whether a reader or writer (albeit fictional) can come into contact with the characters he is reading or writing about, opens the door to larger questions: Does literature imitate life, or life imitate literature? Does the writer have the power to bring his literary characters to life? Does the reader also have this power? Can critics shape the way we think about what we read? These questions are asked but not answered by the fantastic. Instead, the fantastic makes us think about reading and writing as conscious practices and, in this way, interrogates two of the most fundamental aspects of literature. It undermines the notion sometimes espoused by mimetic fiction, that literature is a natural reflection of the world as we know it, simply by reminding us that inside a literary text, reality is always fictional. At the same time, it calls into question the possibility of originality in literature, for as Andres puts it, "Ya todo se ha escrito. Cada cuento sale de otro cuento, ¿verdad?" (108).

Ultimately, each of the five stories examined here teach us in one way or another to be more aware of ourselves as readers and to examine with greater care the process involved in reading, writing, and the production of meaning. They make it clear that when we designate persons, situations, or places inside a literary text as being real or true, we are responding to them as ideological constructions that correspond to the boundaries our own worldview. The fantastic does not merely suggest we replace one set of ideas with another or that we reject the tenets of classical realism and embrace, instead, a fantastic vision of the world. In fact, it shows us that a multiplicity of meanings can coexist, that contradictions cannot always be neatly resolved, and that a literary text that takes upon itself the job of imparting knowledge is only imparting, at best, a specific *perception* of the world. Unlike many works of classical realism that attempt to fix meaning and present a unified, cohesive, and therefore closed text for our consumption, the fantastic opens our eyes and encourages us to think for ourselves. In this way, it is one of the most subversive forms of narrative, for it shows us "the increasing impossibility of defending 'truth' in any metaphysical way and welcomes the political possibilities for self-determination inherent in a recognition that 'truth' is made by humans as the result of very specific material practices" (Bové 55). Stories such as the ones examined here, which deconstruct and decenter commonly held notions about literature, let us understand how and why literary texts can exert such power over us. At the same time, they make us aware that we do not have to surrender to their power unless we choose to do so.

3 / Reclaiming History: Fantastic Journeys in Time and Space

In Latin America, the notion of realism in literature has often been tied to the examination of social problems stemming from centuries of colonization, racism and class struggle, and the development of realist fiction parallels the growth of nationalism during most of the nineteenth and early twentieth centuries. Jean Franco recognizes that literature in Latin America has been "deeply implicated in the process of national formation and its attendant problems of national and cultural identity" (204). However, she also acknowledges that it is the failure of most of these young nations to provide adequate systems of meaning that undermines referential reading and prompts us to see instead of reality "the continued resonance of certain historical events such as the conquest and the impact of succeeding waves of modernization, visible in the fragmented life forms they have left in their wake" (208). Landmark works from the 1950s and 1960s such as *Pedro Páramo, La muerte de Artemio Cruz, Los pasos perdidos* and *Yo, el supremo* reveal that "individual and collective identity, social and family life were like shells from which life had disappeared" (Franco 205). Franco notes that unlike earlier works that attempted to present real-life events as fact, these novels "offer a space in which different historical developments and different cultures overlap. What they enact is the unfinished and impossible project of the modernizing state" (205).

Historical fiction in particular calls attention to the overlapping boundaries between the real and the invented and draws us into more problematic territory when we begin to question, by extension, the discursive power of traditional history books that claim to represent universally accepted truths. As Veeser points out, "No discourse, imaginative or archival, gives access to unchanging truths nor expresses inalterable human nature," and our perception and understanding of the past is informed by both literary and nonliterary texts that "circulate inseparably" in our culture (xi). Hutcheon agrees and argues that "there are important parallels between the processes of history-writing and fiction-writing and among the most problematic of these are the common assumptions about narrative and about the nature of mimetic representation" (58). She reminds us, "Facts do not speak for themselves in either form of narrative: the tellers speak for them, making these fragments of the past into a discursive whole" (58). Past events, of course, exist empirically, but Hutcheon notes that "in epistemological terms we can only know them today through texts. Past events are given *meaning*, not *existence*, by their representation in history" (82).

While the fantastic has sometimes been dismissed by socially minded readers as escapist literature, in Latin America it is a particularly effective vehicle for exploring issues related to national identity, perhaps because as Franco observes, mimetic fiction has not been wholly successful in meeting that need. Common motifs in fantastic fiction, such as time travel or parallel universes, can be appropriated by Latin American writers to reclaim the past and examine history through another lens. Chronological time breaks down and blurs into a continuum without precise boundaries. Physical space becomes deeply layered, allowing the past to reverberate against the present, creating gaps through which a different course of events might emerge. The fantastic allows characters to go back in time, reinvent themselves, and recover what has been lost. At the same time, it deconstructs the concept of individual identity and suggests that the difference between one man's life and another's is only a matter of chance and circumstance. Through the internal conflict of characters who struggle to be both themselves and someone entirely different, the stories reveal a deep concern with history and national identity but ultimately suggest that the past cannot be contained in words. The past will not stay buried in the pages of a book; it will return to haunt the present so long as these conflicts remain unresolved.

Travel in space and time is a familiar theme in fantastic literature, often linked to science fiction, but in the stories to be examined here, travelers move through time and space without the help of technological marvels and supernatural powers. They slip and slide between two worlds as naturally as if they were walking down a city street. The fantastic becomes a discourse that challenges Western notions of time as chronological and linear and dismantles the notion of history as a series of events that move forward and backward in time. The characters find that the past and present coexist and are intertwined because unresolved issues from the past continue to influence the present. Mexico City is the setting for three of the stories because it is a metaphor for the buried past. The modern city, built on the ruins of Tenochtitlán, allow characters in the twentieth century to share the same physical space as characters from pre-Hispanic times. The other story takes place in two locations, Buenos Aires and El Sur (or the great plains of the Pampas), symbolically representing the divided past of Argentines. It evokes the conflict between civilization and barbarism, a constant theme in Argentine literature, and suggests that to travel from one place to another is the same as traveling in time. The south is the past, and the romanticized view of it that permeates Argentine literature from *Martin Fierro* onward reflects the desire for a more authentic existence that has become increasingly elusive for modern Argentines.

As in many fantastic short stories, the characters here are unremarkable middle-class people going through the motions of a dull and unremarkable life until a fantastic encounter with the past changes them forever. The fantastic allows them to come face to face with the past and to choose how they want to live and die. Our perception of who they are changes during the course of the narratives and makes us acknowledge the power of the past to shape the present. Eternity is condensed into a single moment, the instant before their death or final disappearance. The characters and the historical moment they inhabit are not stable entities, but ones that slip and slide in unpredictable ways. In the end, we realize that the stories we are reading have been narrated from a linguistic void, and that no one can tell us what really happened since no one remains in the text who is in a position to know the truth. The main characters are gone, and only their memories and dreams remain as markers of their existence. In this way, the fantastic opens a dialogue with history and reminds us that any confrontation between the past and present "involves an acknowledgment of limitations as well as power" (Hutcheon 58).

Ana María Morales observes, "Hablar de lo fantástico es, de una u otra manera, hablar de fronteras, de deslindes, de límites entre dominios, entre estéticas, entre modos discursivos, incluso—por engañosa que pueda resultar tal postura—entre maneras de apreciar un fenómeno desde distintas perspectivas" (241). These limits or boundaries are inscribed in the texts on both a thematic and stylistic level, for it is through small slippages in the text that ambiguity, contradiction, and doubt emerge and engage the reader in the search for meaning. In order for the fantastic to have its full effect, the reader must look carefully at small details and think about how specific words are used. In order to see how the fantastic is created through language, we must read for not only what happens in the story but how it happens. To these ends, a close textual analysis of specific stories is best because it allows us to focus on technique as well as theme. By looking at how the fantastic is created in the following stories, we can understand better what the fantastic is.

"La noche boca arriba" by Julio Cortázar

In "La noche boca arriba," the past and present coexist in overlapping layers that defy linear models of time and create instead a continuum where distinct moments blend into each other and lose their precise boundaries. In a similar fashion, the story deconstructs the concept of individual identity and suggests that the difference between one man's life and another's is only a matter of perception. When we use a chronological framework to situate a character in a specific moment in time, Cortázar implies, we are making the assumption that both the subject and the time period he inhabits are stable entities. The fantastic shows us, however, that such constructs can collapse at a moment's notice, and the points of reference we have set up for ourselves in the story may disappear without warning. When this happens, we are forced to look more carefully at the way our perceptions are shaped and manipulated by cultural constructs that we accept as givens and to question the so-called natural laws that govern our understanding of the world around us.

"La noche boca arriba" is a perfectly constructed fantastic story because regardless of the conclusions we reach about it, we cannot erase the feelings of doubt and hesitation that arise in us as we read it. The story begins firmly grounded in a world we recognize as our own and introduces a protagonist who, because of his anonymous and ordinary character, could be anyone we pass on the street in the course of a normal day. In the early pages of the text, there are clear markers to help us distinguish between the "real" world of the character and the world of his dreams. Breaks in the page and verbal cues tell us how to interpret what we are reading; for example, the first shift in the narrative from one plane to the other is signaled by the words, "Como sueño era curioso" (74), which tells us two important pieces of information at the same time. We know we are reading about the man's dream, but we are also warned that it is an unusual dream, "porque estaba lleno de olores y él nunca soñaba olores" (74). How unusual the dream is does not become apparent until the story's end. But as the narrative progresses, the dream occupies more and more space in the text. Each time the man falls asleep, the segments of the story that describe the dream grow longer and more vivid. It becomes increasingly difficult for the man to situate himself in the "real" world each time he awakens from his dream. The sensations and emotions he experiences in the dream carry over into his waking moments, further erasing the difference between the two states. Stylistically, the text begins to blur, as well. There are no more breaks in the page to signal a shift from one world to the other. By the end of the story, the shift does not even merit a new paragraph to mark the transition. It occurs in midsentence, as the man floats between a dreaming and waking state. Ultimately, we see the story wrap around itself like a serpent swallowing its own tail because it ends almost exactly as it began, with a concrete reference to the event that had initially set the plot in motion. However, in one of the numerous shifts back and forth between the dream and the "real" world of the character, an inversion has taken place. What was regarded as a dream is now shown to be real, and what we had recognized as our own world is revealed to be a dream. It is impossible to pinpoint how and when the switch occurred, for the borders that had originally defined the two fields of action have collapsed and reconfigured themselves without our being aware of it.

The plot of the story is deceptively simple. One part of the narrative deals with a man who is injured in a motorcycle accident and taken to a hospital, where he undergoes an operation and suffers from a debilitating fever that induces hallucinations and nightmares. Through his dreams, an alternate story line develops about a man who is taken prisoner by Aztec warriors and carried into a *teocalli*, where he will be sacrificed as part of their ritualized *guerra florida*. Although these two incidents are separated in time by perhaps five hundred years, they are brought together in the story in a number of significant ways. First, the protagonist believes from the outset that he is the man in the dream, and he reacts physically and emotionally to the man's experiences as if they were his own. Second, concrete images appear in both parts of the story that suggest a strong similarity between the two places and the two experiences. They function structurally to situate actions in the same geographic location, so that both men are literally moving about in the same space when an accident occurs that changes their destinies forever. These conditions set up a narrative structure that allows Cortázar to play with our perceptions of time, space, and human identity in order to show us that many of the notions we hold to be true and universal are instead cultural constructs that can shift and converge when we move from one framework to another.

Cortázar uses a third-person omniscient narrator to tell the tale, but the story is focalized through the sensory experiences of the nameless protagonist(s). The fact that neither the motorcycle rider nor the *moteca* warrior has a name allows the narrative to shift smoothly from one plane to the other without calling attention to who is doing the action. Most of the story consists of indirect interior monologue to reflect the thoughts and feelings of the character(s) who share many of the same emotions as they face the possibility of dying. What distinguishes one man from the other in the text is not individual traits that define him as a subject, but rather the world that surrounds him. We are able to identify them as subjects and to tell the difference between them because we associate certain images used to describe the settings with distinct moments in time. For example, we understand that the motorcycle rider is a contemporary man living in the modern world. Visual images such as "[el] hotel," "la calle," "la joyería," "los altos edificios del centro," "los ministerios (el rosa, el blanco), " "la serie de comercios con brillantes vitrinas de la calle Central," "las luces verdes," "una pequeña farmacia de barrio" and "la ambulancia policial" situate him in the twentieth century (72–73). The description of the modern city is somewhat generic but, once the young man begins to dream of "aztecas" and "motecas" and to identify with the *moteca* warrior (74–74), we can easily conjecture that the setting is Mexico City/ Tenochtitlán, where modern structures sit on top of buried Aztec ruins. In this way, we establish the first connection in the text between the present and the past and acknowledge the complex and layered identity of the physical setting. Through the use of images such as "un olor a pantano," "la calzada," "las marismas," "los templaderales de donde no volvía nadie," "la selva," "[el] otro lado del gran lago," and "las ciénagas" (75–76), the text evokes the physical setting of the Aztec capital, built on a swampy island in the middle of a lake. Recognition of this place, together with our knowledge that modern Mexico City sits on the ruins of Tenochtitlán, help us to fill in the gaps left in the opening pages of the story so that we can situate the motorcycle rider in a specific place, even though the narrator has not named it for us.

Another important detail that separates one world from the other in the beginning pages of the story is the way the two characters perceive time. The modern man defines his day by the clock and marks off his activities by the amount of time he has to complete them: "vio que eran las nueve menos diez; llegaría con tiempo sobrado adonde iba" (72). In his world, time is measured in precise minutes ("La ambulancia policial llegó a los cinco minutos"), things occur suddenly and move at a rapid pace ("de golpe," "bruscamente"), and even the severity of his injury is described in terms of the time it will take him to recover ("unas semanas quieto y nada más") (73). The *moteca* warrior, by contrast, lives in a world where time is fluid and conforms to ritual: "La guerra florida había empezado con la luna y llevaba ya tres días y tres noches. . . . Pensó en los muchos prisioneros que ya habrían hecho. Pero la cantidad no contaba, sino el tiempo sagrado. La caza continuaría hasta que los sacerdotes dieran la señal de regreso. Todo tenía su numero y su fin, y él estaba dentro del tiempo sagrado" (77). Although the parts of the story dealing with *la guerra florida* are full of action, there are no references to the passing of time other than the acknowledgment that the hunt is taking place during a period of "tiempo sagrado." Time is divided into night and day, but the notion of minutes and hours makes no sense to the *moteca* warrior since he has no point of reference to determine the length of time he has spent in the swamp hiding from the Aztecs other than the total darkness that surrounds him.

The motorcycle accident that sends the man to the hospital occurs in the morning, and his stay in the recovery ward stretches out across a full day. Not unexpectedly, his perception of time begins to change once he is confined to bed because his daily routine has been interrupted and he no longer cares about the minutes and the hours that are passing. He looks, instead, for visual images that mark the passing of time: "Era de tarde, con el sol ya bajo en los ventanales de la larga sala" (75); "caía la noche," "los ventanales de enfrente viraron a manchas de un azul oscuro" (76). As night approaches, he dreams more vividly and for longer periods of time about the *moteca* warrior and his sense of reality becomes blurred. Night is an important visual image in the story, as the title reminds us, because it functions to bring the two parts of the narrative together. Once the characters occupy the same temporal plane of night, the five hundred years that separate them become irrelevant and night becomes the only marker of time. The sense of being divided in two parts, or of watching oneself as if watching a character in a film, foreshadows the split that will occur in the story as the characters shift places and the two distinct nights become one single moment in time that both men will share.[1]

The loss of memory is another signal in the text that the hospitalized man no longer occupies the same temporal plane that he inhabited in the

have set up between the past and present in our minds are arbitrary and weak and may break down at any time.[2]

"La culpa es de los tlaxcaltecas" by Elena Garro

On the surface, "La culpa es de los tlaxcaltecas" appears very similar to "La noche boca arriba." The action takes place in Mexico City/ Tenochtitlán, and the protagonist leads a double existence as a twentieth-century Mexican woman and as a Native American who lived during the Spanish conquest. Unlike Cortázar's story, however, "La culpa es de los tlaxcaltecas" does not rely on dreams to connect the two story lines. Laura Aldama, the story's protagonist, is aware from the beginning pages of the text that she is leading a double life, and she accepts the seemingly impossible with ease as she moves back and forth in time between past and present experiences. Her encounter with the fantastic begins accidentally during a motor trip, when her car runs out of gas. Stranded, she waits for help on a bridge, where she has a vision of herself in another life:

> La luz era muy blanca y el puente, las lajas y el automóvil empezaron a flotar en ella. Luego la luz se partió en varios pedazos hasta convertirse en miles de puntitos, y empezó a girar hasta que se quedó fija como un retrato. El tiempo había dado la vuelta completa, como cuando ves una tarjeta postal y luego la vuelves para ver lo que hay escrito atrás. Así llegué, en el Lago de Cuitzeo, hasta la otra niña que fui. (11)

Her realization that she has lived before and that she is standing face to face with a man who has been dead for several centuries does not alarm her. What propels her from one existence to the other is fear and guilt over her past actions, not hesitation over the nature of events she is experiencing in the present. The sight of her first husband brings back memories she has repressed; as she says, "No me asombré. Levanté los ojos y lo vi venir. En ese instante, recordé la magnitud de mi traición, tuve miedo y quise huir. Pero el tiempo se cerró alrededor de mí, se volvió único y perecedero y no puede moverme del asiento del automóvil" (11). For the reader, it is difficult to reconcile the image of a modern woman sitting in an automobile while carrying on a conversation with a long-dead Aztec warrior. But for Laura, it is a minor detail and not worth addressing. She is too concerned with the memories she has uncovered to pause to consider the effect her words may be having on her listener. One of the tensions that brings the fantastic into the text, then, comes from the reader's reluctance to accept Laura's words at face value and to give credence to her tale. Because her story seems impossible, if not absurd, our natural inclination is to raise an eyebrow and wonder at the reliability of our narrator. The structure of "La culpa" does not allow us to dismiss Laura's narration so easily, however, because it is offset by a second point of view, that of Laura's servant Nacha, who adds another layer of complexity to the telling of the story.

When Laura returns home one night wearing "el traje blanco quemado y sucio de tierra y de sangre" (9), Nacha does not ask her why her dress is burned and stained with blood. Although Laura has been missing for several weeks, Nacha registers no emotion when her mistress suddenly appears at the kitchen door in the middle of the night, enters, and asks for a cup of coffee. Laura sits at the kitchen table, relating her experiences to Nacha as if they were confidants, and through a series of flashbacks, the story of Laura's disappearance begins to unfold. As Laura talks, Nacha avoids eye contact, speaks little, and keeps her hands busy with small chores. The power balance between the servant and her well-to-do employer makes it difficult for us to know what Nacha really thinks about anything because we understand implicitly that Nacha will not contradict la señora, regardless of how strange Laura's comments may be. For example, when Laura exclaims, "¿Sabes, Nacha? La culpa es de los tlaxcaltecas" (9). Nacha remains silent. When Laura forces a response from her and asks, "¿No estás de acuerdo, Nacha?" the servant replies, "Sí, señora" (10), which is the expected reply. It is difficult to know whether Nacha agrees with Laura or whether she thinks Laura is insane. Her reluctance to deny or confirm any of Laura's comments is at once natural under the circumstances and frustrating to us as readers because Nacha's comments do little to guide us in our interpretation of events.

As Laura tells her story, we occasionally have glimpses from Nacha's point of view that confirm certain details of the story. Nacha listens, reflects, and agrees with remarks made by Laura that coincide with her own way of thinking. But Nacha takes pride in her ability to hold her tongue and not cause problems by spreading gossip, unlike the other maid, Josefina, whose verbal blunders sometimes cause Laura's husband, Pablo, to turn violent. In Laura's home, speaking is a dangerous act, and Laura, in particular, runs the risk of a beating anytime she or one of the servants says something that Pablo does not want to hear. Nacha's reticence seems natural under these circumstances, but it is also a highly effective narrative technique that allows a marginal viewpoint to take hold in the story and create a space where the fantastic can grow.

Laura's mother-in-law Margarita attempts to reframe Laura's experience in terms that will be more understandable and more appealing to Pablo; she tells him, "¡Pobre hijo mío! Tu mujer está loca" (28). This opinion is confirmed by Pablo and the doctor, who treat her like a mental patient and find her behavior incomprehensible. Laura continues to insist that she is in contact with her first husband and that she has long conversations with him. She claims that these encounters take place against the backdrop of a horrific battle, in which the city is destroyed, her parents killed, and her husband wounded. She talks freely to Nacha about her former life, but she learns that she cannot talk to Pablo or Margarita about her experiences because it is dangerous to do so. After her first brief disappearance, they decide to hold her prisoner in the house and allow her to go out only for short visits to the park under close supervision. When she disappears for a second time, Margarita reports to Pablo, "¡Se escapó la loca!" (29), and after a few weeks of extensive investigation that produce no results, they give her up for dead. We have no way of knowing where Laura goes when she disappears, who the mysterious man is, or how she has come to be covered with blood and dirt. Her version of events strikes us as improbable, but Margarita's theory that Laura is crazy does not answer our questions, either. Nacha's neutral role of listener restores narrative control to Laura, who tells her story in the way that makes sense to her, even if it strikes us as fantasy. As the story's inscribed narratee, Nacha functions as a guide for readers since we are hearing the story at the same time she does. Her cautious responses slow down the pace of the narrative, allowing Laura to develop the story in a lyrical and intimate style that weaves a spell around her listeners. Nacha's reluctance to accept or deny Laura's story at face value creates a space for doubt and hesitation, which brings the fantastic into being in the text. This effect becomes even stronger once we realize that Nacha has also disappeared and that the story is being related to us from a linguistic void, from a point of view that we can no longer locate in time or space.

As Laura and Nacha talk in the kitchen, it becomes increasingly clear that both women are waiting for something to happen. After Laura has finished her story, she sits in silence looking out the window at the lights of her neighbors' houses that are fading one by one, until she sees nothing but darkness. Unexpectedly, it is Nacha who breaks the silence, exclaiming, "¡Cuánto coyote! ¡Anda muy alborotada la coyotada!" (32). It is a strange remark, considering that Laura lives in modern-day Mexico City, where coyotes are seldom if ever seen. However, it provides the link in the narrative that Laura has been waiting for, since it confirms what she has said all along, that Mexico City and Tenochtitlán exist as parallel worlds, occupying the same point in space and time through means that are not explained. Nacha verbalizes what has been unspoken between the two women, that they are waiting for Laura's first husband to return for her. She says, "Con tal de que no estorben el paso del señor, o que le equivoquen el camino" (33), purposely using the words she had formerly reserved for Pablo, *el señor*, as a way of erasing him from the narrative and replacing him with another character who, we have been led to believe, is a figment of Laura's imagination. The omniscient narrator clarifies, "Fue Nacha la que lo vio llegar y le abrió la ventana," and it is Nacha who tells Laura, "¡Señora! . . . Ya llegó por usted" (33).

While neither the omniscient narrator nor Nacha explicitly identify the man as Laura's first husband, an Aztec warrior from the sixteenth century, it is clear that the man cannot be Pablo. Nacha has already stated, "El señor Pablo hace ya diez días que se fue a Acapulco" (32). Furthermore, the choice of words used by the omniscient narrator to tell us about Laura's disappearance echo what Laura herself had told us earlier about her first husband: "Después, cuando ya Laura se había ido para siempre con él, Nachita limpió la sangre de la ventana y espantó a los coyotes, que entraron en su siglo que acababa de gastarse en ese instante" (33). The mention of the warrior's blood, the coyotes, the word *siempre,* which implies not just a temporary absence but a permanent return to another place and time, and the reference to *su siglo*, a displacement of time that is rapidly fading even as the narrator speaks, suggest a supernatural reading of the story. But because the information is presented in such a matter-of-fact way, it strikes us as incongruous and strange. Nacha destroys any evidence of Laura's visit to the house, along with the "proof" that the Aztec warrior came to take Laura away, and then she herself disappears from the text. In conclusion, the omniscient narrator tells us, "Nacha se fue hasta sin cobrar su sueldo" (33), a statement that does nothing to resolve the mysteries that have been presented to us in the text. Instead, we are left with only the echo of their words that reverberate in the empty space of the abandoned kitchen.

The concept of time and memory play a very important role in "La culpa es de los tlaxcaltecas," since everything related in the story is remembered and the narrative moves in ever widening concentric circles which reach far into the past. The omniscient narrator situates us first in the present, when Nacha and Laura talk about Laura's adventures, but the past catches us up in a vortex and pulls us deeper inside through flashbacks and recollections. The thoughts of the two women jump back and forth between present, past, and future, rarely distinguishing between the different time periods, and the point of view shifts almost indiscriminately from one woman to the other, as if to stress the similarity of their thoughts. Transitions in the narration are very subtle, and the reader must strain to realize when the event described takes place, since past, present, and future begin to resemble each other. For example, when Laura finds herself reliving a moment from her sixteenth-century existence, she is able to "remember" the future: "No pude decirle al indio que me había casado, porque estoy casada con él. Hay cosas que no se pueden decir, tú lo sabes, Nachita" (12). When speaking of the past, Laura ties it linguistically to the present with the frequent use of apostrophe. She punctuates her narrative with constant remarks such as "¿No estás de acuerdo, Nacha?" "¿Sabes, Nachita?" "¿Te acuerdas, Nachita?" and "¿Verdad, Nacha?" at which point the narrative momentarily shifts away from the past and back to the night of the conversation.

The concept of eternity is a very important one for Laura, and each time she is reunited with her first husband, they evoke a sense of timelessness by repeating certain phrases as though they were part of a ritual. Laura repeats, "Este es el final de hombre" (15, 22, 31), while her husband tells her, "Ya va a llegar el último día" (30), and "El tiempo está acabando" (31). Laura reiterates his words: "Supe que se había acabado el tiempo" (32), "Faltaba poco para que nos fuéramos para siempre en uno solo" (31), and "¿Cuánto faltaría para que el tiempo se acabara y yo pudiera oírlo siempre?" (22). Part of their ritual revolves around the notion of waiting. Each time they meet, Laura's husband asks her, "¿Qué te haces?" to which she replies, "Te estaba esperando." The resumption of her relationship with her first husband marks Laura's passage from a world where time is carefully measured to one where time, as Western man knows it, does not exist. With each consecutive visit to the past, she absents herself for longer intervals from the modern world until, finally, she disappears from it altogether.

Laura's unhappy marriage to Pablo provides at least one alternative reading to the story, since readers can readily grasp why she might want to flee from an abusive husband. Pablo's racist remarks, coupled with his violent behavior and obsessive jealousy make him an unattractive contrast to Laura's first husband who treats her tenderly, accepts her with all her faults, and promises her eternal love. Significantly, it is the blood on Laura's white dress that infuriates Pablo the most. He demands, "¿Puedes explicarme el origen de estas manchas?" (19) He beats her when she refuses to answer, and Margarita begs her to invent a story that will satisfy Pablo in his rage: "Tal vez en el Lago tuviste una insolación, Laura, y te salió sangre por las narices" (20). Pablo's mother apparently believes that her son would find Laura's blood normal and acceptable, providing that it not be associated with anything sexual in nature. What Margarita and Pablo, suspect, however, is that the blood on Laura's dress belongs to a lover, and that the dress is a symbol of the "dirty" act she has engaged in. When Pablo finds blood on the windowsill of his bedroom, he becomes violent because he believes Laura has encouraged the man to visit the house. He refers to the man as "el indio asqueroso" and insults Laura, telling her, "¡Nunca pensé que fueras tan baja!" (27). Neither Margarita nor Pablo express concern over the fact that Laura might be hurt or that the blood could be related to an act of violence directed against her. Instead, they turn the dress into a symbol of shame and use it as proof that Laura is mad when she continues to wear the dress despite their strong admonitions.

Given this historical background of the story, the fall of Tenochtitlán and the massacre of the Aztec people, Laura's bloodstained dress speaks volumes about the Conquest of Mexico. Its original color, white, is stained with the blood of her dying husband. Possibly, this is a way of reminding us that the modern Mexican is a mixture of two races that were once at war and that color is an inadequate measure of a person's worth. For example, when Laura's first husband sees her again, he notes that she is very pale. Taking her hand, he remarks, "Está muy desteñida, parece una mano de ellos" (13). Laura reminds him, "Hace ya tiempo que no me pega el sol" (13), which tells us that although she is removed from her Indian heritage in modern times, it is only a matter of being exposed to it again for it to resurface. The fact that her husband's wounds never heal but continue to mark her can be read as a sign that Mexico has yet to resolve the conflicts of the past and find a sense of racial harmony and a create a history that neither casts blame nor glory on the participants on that event. Laura's constant preoccupation with betrayal, with the Tlaxcalans who fought alongside the Spanish and who contributed to the defeat of the Aztecs, and with her own fear of death and defeat suggests that there are no easy answers, but it poses some important philosophical questions for us to consider. Has Mexico taken the wrong turn and identified with the wrong side of her dual heritage? What would it be like if Mexicans could go back and choose again? The fantastic allows Laura to relive moments from the past, to reinvent herself, and to recover what has been lost. It also shows her that history is hard to contain in words because as she discovers there are times when "todo lo increíble es verdadero" (12).[3]

"Chac Mool" by Carlos Fuentes

"Chac Mool" addresses many of the same concerns as Garro's tale, but rather than advance the notion that reconciliation with the past is possible, Fuentes suggests that the past returns to avenge itself against contemporary Mexicans who have turned their backs on their country's indigenous heritage. Filiberto, the protagonist and sometimes narrator of the story, is a weak and ineffectual man, a dilettante collector of pre-Colombian art who enjoys philosophical debates on the subject of his country's history but who knows relatively little about it. He is a lonely, middle-aged, middle-class man, anonymous in his everyday life, who moves through the world as if sleepwalking. His interests and concerns are petty, his worldview materialistic and bound by rules, and his bureaucratic job brings him no satisfaction or rewards. When he falls victim to the fantastic, it comes as almost a relief to him that he is, at last, lifted from the dreary routine of his ordinary life. Ironically, death returns him to the life he hoped to escape and, rather than close the text, it opens it up to polysemic readings.

Like many fantastic stories, "Chac Mool" begins with the complete absence of fantastic elements, but once Filiberto's character has been clearly drawn and an appropriate setting has been created for him, inexplicable events begin to occur. Filiberto is an avid collector of indigenous Mexican art, and one day he is delighted to find a life-size replica of Chac Mool, the Mayan rain god, in the Lagunilla flea market. What interests him most is not the authenticity of the piece, but rather the modest price the vendor asks for it. He believes it is a modern reproduction, and he humorously records in his diary that the vender had anointed the stomach of the god with tomato catsup "para convencer a los turistas de la autenticidad sangrienta de la escultura" (20). Filiberto installs the statue in the basement of his home, but it seems to bring him bad luck. The plumbing in the house stops working, the pipes break, and the basement repeatedly floods. The idol becomes covered with mildew and mold, which gives him an uncanny human look. Filiberto experiences the first subconscious tremors induced by the incursion of the fantastic into his life when he writes, "Le da un aspecto grotesco, porque toda la masa de la escultura parece padecer de una erisipela verde" (21). His expression of hesitation and doubt grow stronger as he notes daily changes in Chac Mool, and his diary changes tone and style after he acquires the statue. Previously, he had dwelled on anecdotes about his life, and the passages tended to be long, elegantly written, and marked by strong currents of loneliness and nostalgia for the past. After Chac Mool comes into his possession, Filiberto begins to feel uneasy and the diary entries turn into short, choppy sentences that hint at strange happenings but that at the same time attempt to explain them rationally. Filiberto becomes increasingly divided: intellectually he rejects the possibility that a statue could come to life, but emotionally he fears that such a thing might happen. The style of his diary reflects his state of mind as he tries to deal with this internal conflict.

For example, Filiberto first describes Chac Mool as a lifeless statue, a "simple bulto agónico" (20), but as the narrative progresses, he attributes more and more human qualities to the idol until he is finally convinced that Chac Mool is a living creature. In the beginning, he talks about his interest in "ciertas formas del arte indígena mexicano" and tells us that he spends his free time searching for "estatuillas, ídolos, cachorros" (20). He has a possessive attitude toward Chac Mool and the other pieces in his collection. He calls them "trofeos" and speaks of the rain god as "mi Chac Mool" (20), but it is clear that the objects have no special meaning for him and are merely things that he collects. Chac Mool is simply "una pieza preciosa" or "una figura," and Filiberto speaks of him in the same breath as other possessions stored in the basement, as if he had no special value. Once Chac Mool is installed in the house, however, the statue begins to take on human characteristics that Filiberto records in his diary. He notes, for example, that "su mueca parece reprocharme que le niegue la luz" (20). The verb *parecer,* commonly used throughout the first part of the story, is important because it shows that Filiberto is hesitant to commit himself in writing to something that he cannot explain logically. Rather than use a more concrete and definite verb, stating that something *did* happen, he tells us that it *seemed* to have happened, creating a sort of linguistic limbo for the reader. He is confronted with daily indications that the statue is coming to life, yet the stronger the proof, the more inclined he is to deny it. He states, "No quiero escribirlo: hay en el torso algo de la textura de la carne, lo aprieto como goma, siento que algo corre or esa figura recostada" (22).

When Filiberto begins to hear strange noises in the night, he dismisses them as fantasy, but his diary entry reveals nervous strain: "Desperté a la una: había escuchado un quejido terrible. Pensé en ladrones. Pura imaginación" (21). The water motif that always accompanies Chac Mool in Filiberto's diary appears in various forms and provides clues for the reader that something inexplicable is taking place. Filiberto mentions broken water pipes, rain, water he carries from a nearby fountain, and finally the ocean, where he dies. Most of the water images are related to Filiberto's growing doubt and hesitation. For example, he covers the statue with rags to protect it from water damage, but a short time later, he discovers "los trapos están en el suelo" (22). His only comment is "increíble," which shows his reluctance to reach a decision about the nature of the events he is witnessing.

As Todorov points out, the hesitation induced by the emergence of the fantastic is usually of limited duration. Once the doubt is resolved in the narrative, it moves into a neighboring category: if there is a logical explanation for the phenomenon described, it belongs to the uncanny, and if the phenomena is accepted as a natural occurrence, it belongs to the marvelous. In "Chac Mool," Filiberto attempts to explain events with rational arguments, but they fail to resolve his doubts. Eventually he must admit that the seemingly impossible has come to pass. He writes, "No cabe duda: el Chac Mool tiene vello en los brazos" (22). This is the first time Filiberto does not preface his remarks with the verb *parecer*. Significantly, this same night, Filiberto awakens to find a living Chac Mool hovering over him. The scene is reminiscent of one from a gothic horror story. The senses are on edge, sharpened by fear, and doom seems to hover in the air. However, the scene ends not with death, but rather with a sudden rainstorm, which temporarily dissolves the spell of the fantastic:

> El cuarto olía a horror, a incienso y sangre. Con la mirada negra, recorrí la recámara, hasta detenerse en dos orificios de luz parpadeante, en dos flámulas crueles y amarillas.
>
> Casi sin aliento encendí la luz.
>
> Allí estaba Chac Mool, erguido, sonriente, ocre, con su barriga encarnada. Me paralizaban los dos ojillos, casi bizcos, muy pegados a la nariz triangular. Los dientes inferiores, mordiendo el labio superior, inmóviles; sólo el brillo del casquetón cuadrado sobre la cabeza anormalmente voluminosa, delataba vida. Chac Mool avanzó hacia la cama; entonces empezó a llover. (23)

This is a turning point in the story, for we must now reach a conclusion that will account for Filiberto's experience, and once a conclusion is reached, the story leaves the narrowly defined realm of the fantastic. We may choose to believe that Filiberto is mad, that he has imagined the episode, or that it is some kind of fantasy, but the story does not encourage us to think, for more than an instant, that Chac Mool has indeed come to life. Parenthetical statements, made at the beginning and end of this entry in the diary by a second narrator, suggest that we should not trust Filiberto. This other, seemingly objective narrative voice offers a temporary refuge of sanity and allows the narrative tension, which Filiberto's revelation had created, to dissipate. As a result, we grow wary of Filiberto's remarks and the remainder of the story is understood to be a product of Filiberto's imagination.

The narrative moves into the realm of the marvelous when Filiberto overcomes his terror and accepts Chac Mool as a companion. He notes, "Chac Mool puede ser simpático cuando quiere" (24), yet Filiberto comes to resent the rain god's interference in his life. Chac Mool asserts control over Filiberto, forcing him to act as a servant in his own home and holding him prisoner in the basement, while he occupies the master bedroom upstairs. When an opportunity arises to escape the watchful eye of the rain god, Filiberto runs away to Acapulco, where he drowns. His diary ends a few days before his death, and one of the last entries contains a reference to a threat made by Chac Mool to kill him should he try to flee.

If Filiberto were the only narrator of the story, the fantastic would cease to exist when Chac Mool comes to life, since this supernatural event is portrayed without further doubt and hesitation on the part of the main character. At the same time, the reader's uncertainty comes to an end when he is confronted with Filiberto's startling revelation. The tension, which has been steadily building in the narrative, is diffused by the unlikely descriptions of the living rain god and his relationship with the hapless Filiberto. However, a second narrative voice is introduced into the story when a nameless friend travels to Acapulco to collect Filiberto's body and discovers the diary. Through this new narrator, the reader is exposed to a series of logical explanations that counterbalance Filiberto's allegations, and a new feeling of doubt and hesitation arises as the story once again wavers between a natural and supernatural explanation of the events described in the diary. In this way, Todorov's conditions for the fantastic are met a second time in the story, although tension is purposely kept at a minimum now so that the reader will be off guard when the story reaches its true climax.

As the friend reads Filiberto's diary, his reactions mirror the process that Filiberto had undergone when confronted with the fantastic. At first, he tries to analyze the situation logically: "No supe qué explicación darme; pensé que las lluvias excepcionalmente fuertes, de ese verano, lo habían crispado. O que alguna depresión moral debía producir la vida en aquel caserón antiguo, con la mitad de los cuartos bajo llave y empolvados, sin criados ni vida de familia" (24). Because there is no clear explanation, he dismisses the problem : "No quise volver a pensar en su relato" (26). But he becomes obsessed with what he does not understand. This narrator, more so than Filiberto, is characterized by a detached, logical attitude toward life. He raises a number of questions about Filiberto that make the reader hesitant to believe anything written in the diary, but confident in the friend's ability to sort out the truth. Excerpts from Filiberto's diary reveal that he has lost his grip on reality, but the second narrator's comments remain cool and analytical. This narrator assumes the task of putting Filiberto's story in proper perspective. He says, "Pretendí dar coherencia al escrito, relacionarlo con exceso de trabajo, con algún motivo psicológico," but despite his efforts, he fails: "Aun no podía concebir la locura de mi amigo" (26–27).

Unlike Filiberto, who gradually came to accept the inexplicable as part of reality, the second narrator leads the story toward the realm of the uncanny by explaining the fantastic events described in the diary as madness. Indeed, this explanation would be perfectly acceptable to the reader, as well, and the fantastic could be dismissed were it not for the final, unexpected scene of the story, where the second narrator confronts a character who may or may not be Chac Mool. When the friend arrives at Filiberto's house with the corpse, he is greeted at the door by a stranger. Doubtlessly, this stranger closely resembles the description of Chac Mool in the diary, yet the image is vague and ambiguous. The narrator is taken aback by him: "Su aspecto no podía ser más repulsivo; depedía un olor a loción barata; su cara, polveada, quería cubrir las arrugas; tenía la boca embarrada de lápiz labial mal aplicado, y el pelo daba la impresión de estar teñido" (27). This scene differs markedly from the one in which Filiberto discovered Chac Mool leering at him in his bedroom one night. There is less overt horror, but much greater hesitation on the part of the character and the reader. The concluding lines of the story are highly suggestive, but open to various interpretations: "—Perdone . . . no sabía que Filiberto hubiera . . . / —No importa; lo sé todo. Dígales a los hombres que lleven el cadáver al sótano" (27). The fact that Chac Mool once occupied the basement space where Filiberto's body will now be laid to rest suggests that a role reversal has occurred between the twentieth-century man and the ancient rain god. However, we cannot accept that explanation without embracing the fantastic.

In Latin America, where fiction is often judged by its social content rather than its clever form, the fantastic has sometimes been considered escapist literature because it does not always appear to be grounded in real-life issues. For Fuentes and others examined here, however, the fantastic is not a way of escaping reality, but rather of penetrating it and uncovering new dimensions. "Chac Mool" reminds us that the past is not dead, that indigenous Mexico has not been smothered and buried under the mask of European culture, and that it will come back to haunt us until we confront it and learn to deal with it in a more direct and honest way. Chac Mool is portrayed in Filiberto's diary as a character who is bitterly resentful of the present. He was once a god, a respected deity, but in intervening centuries he has been desecrated and forgotten. He condemns the attitude of modern Mexicans like Filiberto who have abandoned their nation's indigenous heritage and are ignorant of their cultural history. Filiberto purchased Chac Mool as a curiosity piece, he has no knowledge of the culture that Chac Mool represents, and he feels no spiritual bond with him. Ironically, as Chac Mool comes to life (according to Filiberto in his diary), he loses the dignity he had as a statue and grows old and ugly. His divine poise gives way to bourgeois tastes. The transformation process is one of corruption and decay, for when Chac Mool abandons his ancient ways and adapts to the twentieth century, his identity is irreparably altered. At the end of the story, he is a culturally hybrid character who, rather than benefiting from the blend of two heritages, adopts and maintains the worst characteristics of both. He is dangerous, despotic, and fickle, a pathetic imitation of something totally alien to his essential being.

"Chac Mool" is not an allegory, but it does have meaning as a metaphor. The rain god's story speaks eloquently about contemporary Mexicans like Filiberto who have turned their backs on their cultural heritage. The transformation that Chac Mool undergoes is not unlike the change millions of Mexicans have experienced since the Conquest. As Laura Aldama discovered in "La culpa es de los tlaxcaltecas," self-deception and self-denial cripple the human psyche and block the emergence of an authentic national and personal identity. Laura reconnects to the past and opts for a different path in life; Filiberto is unable to respond to the challenge and becomes permanently fixed in time and space. His body in the basement is a reminder that moving ahead is not the only way to go through life. Occasionally, one needs to look backward and reexamine what has been lost.[4]

"El Sur" by Jorge Luis Borges

"El Sur" is set in Argentina, but it shares the same deep concern with history and national identity as the other stories examined here. Borges plays with the theme of *civilización y barbarie*, a constant preoccupation in Argentine literature, and pits the empty barren spaces of the pampa against the crowded streets of Buenos Aires as his protagonist, Juan Dahlmann, learns to negotiate the time and space that separates these two mythic places. As Dahlmann makes a journey from the city to the countryside, he begins to suspect "que viajaba al pasado y no sólo al Sur" (211). Although he initially dismisses the thought as a "conjetura fantástica," he eventually comes to believe that he has been transported in time as well as space, and his life, which has inexplicably split in two and taken different paths, comes together again only in death, similar to the way in which the character in Cortázar's "La noche boca arriba" dies. A fantastic reading of the story suggests that Dahlmann has engendered his own double: in one life, he is a lonely librarian dying of blood poisoning in a city hospital; in the other life, he is a man returning to his roots in the south, a romantic hero who is prepared to die to defend his honor in a knife fight. It is difficult, if not impossible, for us to know which death is the real one because Borges creates an open-ended text that suggests that identity is not so much a matter of what *is*, but rather what one *wishes* it to be.

Like Filiberto from "Chac Mool" and Laura from "La culpa," Dahlmann is faced with issues of both personal and national identity. He is an ordinary middle-class man living a life that is predictable and routine. The opening pages of the story are set in 1939, a time when Buenos Aires had been transformed by European immigrants like Dahlmann's own grandfather, an evangelical pastor "de . . . sangre germánica" (205), and the epic struggle of Spanish settlers to wrest the Argentine frontier from its indigenous peoples was relegated to history and confined to books like *Martín Fierro*. Dahlmann, despite his Germanic surname, "se sentía hondamente argentino" (205) because of his maternal family line, the Flores, who had participated in the wars of territorial acquisition. In particular, he admires "su abuelo materno . . . aquel Francisco Flores, del 2 de infantería de línea, que murió en la frontera de Buenos Aires, lanceado por indios de Catriel" (205). As a quiet, timid man working in a library in the city, Dahlmann has time to reflect on "la discordia de sus dos linajes," and he comes to the conclusion that he prefers the Spanish grandfather, "ese antepasado romántico, o de muerte romántica" (205), perhaps because he represents the type of man that Dahlmann is not, a man who possesses and displays strength and determination that comes from "ese criollismo algo voluntario, pero nunca ostentoso" that links him so solidly to the land where he lived and died (206). Dahlmann attaches great importance to the ranch in the south that he has inherited from the Flores family; he has managed to hold on to it "a costa de algunas privaciones," although "las tareas y acaso la indolencia lo retenían en la ciudad," and "verano tras verano se contentaba con la idea abstracta de posesión y con la certidumbre de que su casa estaba esperándolo, en un sitio preciso de la llanura" (206). This brief introduction to Dahlmann's personal past allows the south to function in the text as a symbol of all that is authentically Argentine for him. In order to connect to his more authentic self, he must return not only to the south but to the past, even if it leads him to the "muerte romántica" that awaits him there.

Unlike most other fantastic stories where the fantastic announces itself through uncanny events and inexplicable happenings that inspire doubt and hesitation in the characters and readers alike, in "El sur" there is relatively little tension in the narrative as Dahlmann travels toward death. Instead, his actions seem normal and natural, predestined somehow, and even when faced with certain defeat in the knife fight, "Sintió que si él . . . hubiera podido elegir o soñar su muerte, ésta es la muerte que hubiera elegido o soñado" (216). What allows the text to function so well as a fantastic narrative, then, is not the actions or events that are described in the story, but instead the words the narrator chooses to tell the tale. The contrast between very precise, carefully chosen turns of phrase and imprecise, purposely vague language creates the uneasy sensation that we are reading two stories at once, and that the meaning of what we are reading is falling through the gaps in the text. Whether Dahlmann is dreaming the trip to the south or whether the trip took place is never clarified for us, but we are left with the impression that something fantastic has happened because Dahlmann has been transformed into a character we scarcely recognize. A hole in time seems to have opened up so that he can return to a place that no longer exists and can become the person he always wanted to be. At the same time, the text encourages us to find another story told between the lines, that of Dahlmann's death in the hospital, and to question how both stories can coexist without wiping each other out. The supernatural effect comes from our belief that it is not possible to be in two places at one time, or to live in two time periods simultaneously. Without ever stating so explicitly, the narrator of "El sur" seems to be telling us that we are wrong, that time and space may be more fluid than we know, and that identity can also shift and slide, depending on the way we choose to view it.

The omniscient narrator calls attention to a change in Dahlmann's life by stating simply, "En los últimos días de febrero de 1939, algo le aconteció" (206). The use of a precise date with the indefinite word, *algo*, underscores the strategy that he will take in the telling of the tale. It appears, at first glance, that he is referring to Dahlmann's accident, an unlucky cut on the head caused by a distracted encounter with a doorjamb; however, by the time we reach the story's end, the meaning of *algo* has changed and seems refers to something else, to Dahlmann's encounter with the south and with his other self. On the one hand, the narrator tells us the Dahlmann "estaba a punto de morir de una septicemia," and then almost immediately he adds, "Otro día, el cirujano le dijo que estaba reponiéndose y que, muy pronto, podría ir a convalecer a la estancia" (208). The narrator adds, as an afterthought, "Increíblemente, el día prometido llegó" (208). Again, the narrator uses a phrase that functions as a floating signifier, *el día prometido*, which initially seems to refer to Dahlmann's release from the hospital, but in retrospect, it may also refer to his death in the clinic, since both possibilities have been mentioned by the doctor. The narrator's use of the word *increíblemente* calls attention to both Dahlmann's impatience to leave the clinic and to the improbability of his being able to do so, since only recently he had been "en un arrabal del infierno," tortured by high fever and pain (207). Furthermore, the *estancia* the doctor refers to has already been presented to us in the text as merely "el casco de una estancia," a place that has been abandoned for many years (206). While it seems unlikely that a patient in Dahlmann's state would be sent on a long train journey to an abandoned ranch, Dahlmann receives the news with great enthusiasm and the details of his journey are narrated with precision. However, the description of the journey is swathed in nostalgia and literary references that call attention to its artificiality, "como sueños de la llanura" (211), and make it seem less like an actual place than a mythic recreation of Argentina's past. Dahlmann realizes that "su directo conocimiento de la campaña era harto inferior a su conocimiento nostálgico y literario" (211), and he recognizes the tavern where he stops to have a meal as "un grabado en acero, acaso de una vieja edición de Pablo y Virginia" (212). Everything seems familiar yet strange at the same time: the owner, who inexplicably knows Dahlmann's name although they have never met, bears an uncanny resemblance to "uno de los empleados del sanatorio" (212). An old gaucho "estaba como fuera del tiempo, en una eternidad," and Dahlmann sees him not so much as a real person as "una cifra del Sur (del Sur que era suyo)" (215). These comments suggest that perhaps Dahlmann has not left the clinic but is merely dreaming about the journey; we cannot be sure, however, because the narrator tells us, "y era como si a un tiempo fuera dos hombres: el que avanzaba por el día otoñal y por la geografía de la patria, y el otro, encarcelado en un sanatorio y sujeto a metódicas servidumbres" (210).

The two grandfathers mentioned early in the story remind us that Dahlmann has not made peace with "la discordia de sus dos linajes" (205), and the division in Dahlmann's own life manifests itself through feelings of self-hatred; while lying in the clinic, "Dahlmann minuciosamente se odió; odió su identidad, sus necesidades corporales, su humillación, la barba que le erizaba la cara" (207–8). The realization that he has been near death without having lived the life he always wanted for himself provokes an uncharacteristic emotional outburst in him: "Dahlmann se echó a llorar, condolido de su destino" (208). Significantly, the clinic is located on Ecuador Street, a reference to an imaginary line that divides the world in half. Dahlmann's arrival and (possible) departure from this place divides his life in two. The steps that led him to the clinic are carefully repeated in reverse, as he makes his way to the train station. The narrator explains, "A la realidad le gustan las simetrías y los leves anacronismos," calling our attention to the fact that Dahlmann's life is doubling back on itself (208). At the same time, small verbal clues are given that Dahlmann's experiences are not quite in sync with the world around him. For example, when he stops to pet a familiar cat in a café, he has the impression "que aquel contacto era ilusorio y que estaban como separados por un cristal" (209). He realizes that it is the perception of time that separates him from the cat; as the narrator explains, "El hombre vive en el tiempo, en la sucesión, y el mágico animal, en la actualidad, en la eternidad del instante" (209). Once Dahlmann ceases to think of time as something that runs in a straight line, he, too, begins to live "en la eternidad del instante," and this is what allows him to reconnect not only with the past but with the person he wanted to be.

En "El sur," individual identity is linked to national identity; one is inconceivable without the other, and both involve personal choice. Although Dahlmann frequently has the sensation that he is pushed along in life by blind fate, it seems that his desire and will also play a large role in reshaping his world. As Dahlmann leans forward to pick up the knife, the narrator states, "Era como si el Sur hubiera resuelto que Dahlmann aceptara el duelo" (215). This contrary-to-fact statement is followed by another that suggests that Dahlmann's death is of his own choosing: "Sintió . . . que morir en una pelea a cuchillo, a cielo abierto y acometiendo, hubiera sido una liberación para él, una felicidad y una fiesta, en la primera noche del sanatorio, cuando le clavaron la aguja" (215–16). Linguistically, the use of past subjunctive in these sentences raises a number of important doubts for the reader: Did the duel occur? Did Dahlmann die in the clinic? Which part of the story has been a dream, and which part has been real? Or, have both experiences happened simultaneously? The narrator suggests, indirectly as always, that we follow Dahlmann's example and simply accept things as they occur, without trying to understand "el mecanismo de los hechos" (211). Understanding experiences is not the same as living them, and at times, it is enough to "simplemente vivir" (210), even if it is outside the normal limits of time.[5]

* * *

Although the fantastic does not answer the questions it raises related to national and personal identity in any of the stories examined here, it does help the characters come to terms with troubling aspects of the past that traditional history books have swept aside. It provides a vehicle for exploring hidden conflicts and revealing alternate paths of self-discovery, even if those paths lead away from rational notions of chronological time and fixed geographical space. The fantastic provides a doorway through which other possibilities can be glimpsed and, sometimes, grasped and transformed into another kind of reality. History is not a fixed entity; it is multilayered and polysemic. There is always a speaker who selects, interprets, and represents facts through a text, be it spoken or written, remembered or experienced, invented or real. Past events exist, but what they mean and how we think about them can shift and slide, depending on who is telling the story. In epistemological terms, the fantastic launches an inquiry into how we conceive and talk about the past, how it relates to the present and future, how we understand notions of time and space, and how we construct an identity for ourselves and others who inhabit our world. It does not attempt to close chapters in history, but rather to open them up to dialogue. Far from being a literature of escapism, the fantastic in the hands of these writers becomes a way of drilling into the core of Latin American reality to uncover an untapped vein of truth.

4 / Psychoanalytic Readings of the Fantastic

Fantastic narratives that call attention to the indeterminacy of language, to the impossibility of capturing reality in words, to the relative nature of concepts like "true" and "possible," and that seek to undermine some of our most commonly held notions about literature, the narrative process, the act of reading, and our relationship as readers to a written text open the door to the interrogation of a notion that lies at the very heart of our conception of the world and our place in it, that of "selfhood" and the way in which we come to identify ourselves as subjects. The close connection between fantastic literature and psychoanalysis has been noted by a number of critics who read the themes of the fantastic as expressions of unconscious drives or desires. Todorov goes so far as to claim:

> Psychoanalysis has replaced (and thereby has made useless) the literature of the fantastic. There is no need today to resort to the devil in order to speak of an excessive sexual desire, and none to resort to vampires in order to designate the attraction exerted by corpses: psychoanalysis, and the literature which is directly or indirectly inspired by it, deal with these matters in undisguised terms. The themes of fantastic literature have become, literally, the very themes of the psychological investigations of the last fifty years. (160–61)

At the same time, however, he observes that literary critics have much to gain "from psychoanalytic writings concerning the structures of the human subject" (152), and he suggests that psychoanalysis can offer useful tools for the better understanding of the fantastic in literature. Jackson agrees and posits that "literary fantasies, expressing unconscious drives, are particularly open to psychoanalytic readings, and frequently show in graphic forms a tension between the 'laws of human society' and the resistance of the unconscious mind to those laws" (6–7). While the images that writers choose for the expression of human desire may have changed over the decades, clearly those aspects of the human psyche that bring us into being as individual, gendered subjects cannot be erased altogether from literature. It is possible, therefore, to look at modern literature of the fantastic not as a substitute for psychoanalysis, as may be the case with literature of the eighteenth and nineteenth centuries, but as an illustration of the workings and malfunctions of the unconscious mind, which psychoanalysis has helped to uncover.

The three stories that appear in this chapter, "La casa de azúcar" by Silvina Ocampo, "En memoria de Paulina" by Adolfo Bioy Casares, and "Casa tomada" by Julio Cortázar, offer especially fertile ground for a psychoanalytic reading of the fantastic, since the doubling that occurs in the texts is closely connected to the male narrator's attempts to position and identify himself in relationship to his female Other.[1] Whether in the guise of sister, girlfriend, or wife, the female occupies a central role in all three stories because the narrator's recognition of himself as part of a couple starts the initial shift of signifiers from "I" to "we" as he attempts to integrate the feelings, attitudes, and actions of his female partner into his discourse. His insistence on identification with the female (and his simultaneous wariness about erasing sexual difference through such an identification) creates a fissure through which the fantastic will appear in the text, as his unconscious Desire seeks an adequate system of self-representation.[2] The conflict he experiences between narcissistic and romantic (or sexual) love, which is so intimately tied to the theme of the double in literature, is in many ways an echo of the conflict described by Lacan when he speaks of the Mirror Stage, when the subject attempts to form a notion of self by establishing relationships of difference and similarity to those around him. The Symbolic order decrees that he cannot be both self and Other, yet the recognition of difference shatters the illusion of wholeness and unity that has characterized his existence in the Imaginary register.[3] Continued identification with the female can bring with it the threat of castration, but separation from the female provokes alienation and sets in motion endless Desire. Obviously the subject cannot resolve this dilemma without sacrificing something of himself; it is, nevertheless, a situation that *must* be resolved for, as these stories suggest, the inability or unwillingness to take one's rightful place within the Symbolic order may result in the disintegration of the self. Failure to line up on one side or the other of socially constructed gendered identity carries with it the implicit threat of breakdown for the social network upon which the self relies: language, interpersonal relations, and ideological constructs that give apparent order to the world. By examining the ways in which a human subject can be deconstructed, the fantastic graphically illustrates the construction process through which subjects come into being. At the same time, it foregrounds the fact that subjectivity is a construction, that the concept of self is not one that is granted to the individual at birth, and that at any step along the way the process can go awry.

"La casa de azúcar" and "En memoria de Paulina" are in many ways mirror images of one another: both deal with a romantically linked couple, focus on the decomposition of that relationship, end with the disappearance of the woman from the text, and involve a third party who functions as a double. In both, the male narrator initially positions the female beloved as his double, stressing the ways in which they are alike and reinforcing the notion that they are two halves of a single whole. This romantic notion presents him with a difficulty, however, for it is basically in conflict with the narcissistic love that has drawn him to the female in the first place. She cannot be both female (Other) and male (his double) at the same time. The perceived need to differentiate on the basis of gender leads the male narrator to create a new double for himself, one which will somehow allow him to get closer to the female and perhaps recover the illusion that he and she are as one. It is not a straightforward process, however, for the narrator's recognition of difference between himself and his beloved tears apart his initial self-image as a being connected to the female and forces him to come to terms with his own identity as a male. The shifting image that the narrator has of himself makes it increasingly difficult to know who is the double of whom, and on what basis identification is constructed or undone.

"Casa tomada" features another type of subject disintegration, one that comes about as a result of refusing to deal with sexual difference as a concept. It also features another kind of couple, an unmarried brother and sister who live together in the family home in what the narrator terms a "simple y silencioso matrimonio de hermanos" (413). It is in large part a story made up of silences; more is left unsaid than is ever expressed in words. The exact nature of the relationship between the narrator and his sister is unclear: although it seems there may be some latent feelings of incest involved, the narrator apparently does not act on them on any conscious level. They are repressed by denying sexual difference and by viewing the sister simply as a projection of himself. They live an asexual existence, with the only markers of difference being her knitting (which he regards as a female hobby) and his reading (which he portrays as a male pursuit). They have no contact with outsiders and, thus, no chance to confront their sexuality in the guise of a potential mate. They live in a state of undifferentiation inside the house, as if inside the womb. Perhaps because the relationship between the couple in "Casa tomada" is so amorphous, the double does not manifest itself in human form as in the other two stories, but rather appears as a nameless, invisible "they." "They" drive the narrator and his sister from the house for reasons that are unclear; what happened to the narrator and his sister after leaving the house is never revealed in the text, and the whereabouts of the sister at the time the narrator is telling his tale is a mystery. The only thing that is certain is that the narrator and his sister no longer live in the family home. As he recounts his experience, the narrator appears to be speaking to us from a void where silence has more meaning than words. But it is precisely because there are so many gaps and holes in the text that the story speaks so loudly to us about unconscious Desire.

According to Todorov, the portrayal of uncanny events in a text is not enough to guarantee the presence of the fantastic; the fantastic emerges through a "special perception of uncanny events" (91). When Todorov speaks of this "special perception," he is generally referring to both the perception of the reader and to that of the narrator or of a character in the text. He explains, "the reader's role is so to speak entrusted to a character . . . —in the case of naive reading, the actual reader identifies himself with the character" (33). In all three stories we have set out to examine here, the narrator speaks with the plural "we" in order to talk about his feelings *and* those of the female with whom he is involved. In all three cases, however, the woman is notably absent; whether she went away, as did Cristina in "La casa de azúcar," or whether she is dead like Paulina, or whether she is simply floating around in the background as she may be in "Casa tomada," she is not allowed to speak in the story unless her words are filtered through those of the male narrator. In each story, the narrator stresses that he wants to tell us about the female, not about himself, yet we are positioned in a way so that we tend to identify with him rather than with her. She is presented to us as the subject matter of the story, but she is, in fact, an object recreated by the narrator through language: what we end up with, then, is not a tale about an actual woman, but a story about the narrator's perception of that woman. Obviously, in stories as carefully constructed as these are, the use of a male narrator and the reader's encouraged identification with him are not arbitrary choices on the part of the authors. The male voice carries with it connotations of authority, knowledge, solidity, and sound judgment, especially when it is presented in contrast to the apparent confusion, strangeness, or vapidity of the female characters in the text. The narrator appears "normal," while the female he describes is either insipid or impenetrable. It is his job as narrator to explain the female's behavior, and we trust that he knows of what he speaks, since he has willingly taken on the task. In short, we are prepared to be passive listeners and to absorb the information presented to us by the narrator as "truth," for such is the premise on which mimetic forms of fiction are based. Here, however, we are dealing with the fantastic, and conventional premises do not hold true. In the fantastic, our expectations are played off and against one another until they finally disintegrate and we see that many of our notions about the wholeness and the cohesiveness of the male subject are incorrect, as are many of our preconceptions about the solidity of language.

The first problem facing the male narrator when he sets out to talk about (and speak for) a female is that he must position himself in relationship to her in both linguistic and social terms. To incorporate her into the plural "we" is one way to deal with her in language, but in many respects it is a false positioning. When the narrator says "we," he really means "I," since he is in effect speaking his own mind and assuming that he knows the mind of the female well enough to speak for her too. He attributes thoughts and feelings to her that parallel and reflect his own, but because she never speaks directly to us in the text, we have no way of knowing whether the narrator's perceptions are true. The use of "we" also functions to erase difference since it implies that the male and female are alike, at least in some regards. It emphasizes the closeness of the relationship between the couple and the bond that ties them together. It also permits the female character to function in the story as the male narrator's double, so long as she comfortably fits inside the "we" marker. Conversely, the use of "she" as a being separate from "I" functions to put the woman in the place of the Other, a place to which the male narrator has no access and which he cannot describe with any degree of accuracy. The swing back and forth between the "we," "I," and "she" markers reflects the narrator's search for (and inability to find) a more secure position from which to tell his tale.

The Threat of the Female Double

"La casa de azúcar" begins with the narrator's open admission that he and his wife do not always think alike and that it is difficult for him to understand her point of view because it is so different from his own. His first act as narrator is to distinguish between himself and his wife, presenting himself to the reader as a rational, sane adult, while he portrays Cristina as a childlike, irrational, and eccentric being, who has become a sort of cross that he must bear as part of the burden of matrimony. The reader is compelled to identify with him due to the intimate, confessional tone of his narration; as he describes the bizarre behavior of his wife, the reader is encouraged to empathize with him and view Cristina through his eyes. The conflict begins over what appears to be a trivial matter; due to its very pettiness, it does not signal immediately that there is a deeper crisis underlying it, and because it introduces an element of levity into the tale, it misleads us into thinking that there is no need to scrutinize with great care what we are being told. The narrator adopts an attitude that reveals a mixture of exasperation and patient good humor, as he explains that Cristina has invented a number of highly personalized forms of superstition that make life unnecessarily complicated for them both. The fact that he moves from the third-person "she" to the plural "we" seems normal under the circumstances, since they are a married couple. At the same time, however, it reveals how he sees his identity tied to hers: "No podía comprar frutillas en el mes de diciembre, ni oír determinadas músicas, ni adornar la casa con peces rojos, que tanto le gustaban. Había ciertas calles que no podíamos cruzar, ciertas personas, ciertos cinematógrafos que no podíamos frecuentar" (32). Before their marriage, he confesses, "estas supersticiones me parecieron encantadoras," but with time his attitude changes: "Después empezaron a fastidiarme y a preocuparme seriamente" (33). It is precisely because her superstitions are personal and because they exclude him that he finds them objectionable. He calls them "manías absurdas" (32), and he attempts to convince her that, if she must be superstitious, she should share the superstitions that he and others have:

> Le hice notar que tenía un espejo roto en su cuarto y que por más que yo le insistiera en la conveniencia de tirar los espejos rotos al agua, en una noche de luna, para quitarse la mala suerte, lo guardaba; que jamás temió que la luz de la casa bruscamente se apagara, y a pesar de que fuera un anuncio seguro de muerte, encendía con

> tranquilidad cualquier número de velas; que siempre dejaba sobre la cama el sombrero, error en que nadie incurría. (32)

The narrator uses Cristina's superstitions to distinguish between her and him (her superstitions are absurd, his superstitions are normal). At the same time, he attempts to eliminate the difference between them by insisting that she give up her superstitions and take on his.

The superstition that most directly influences their lives is Cristina's belief that she cannot live in a house or apartment that has been inhabited by others before her: "Según sus creencias, el destino de los ocupantes anteriores influiría sobre su vida" (33). Although the narrator pretends that his primary objection to this notion is the cost of a new house or apartment, he reveals his real thoughts in a parenthetical statement made to the reader: "(en ningún momento mencionaba la [vida] mía, como si el peligro le amenazara sólo a ella y nuestras vidas no estuvieran unidas por el amor)" (33). Because Cristina's superstitions do not include him, the narrator rejects them. He feels that he does not have to take them seriously or even challenge them openly, since to do so might constitute an acknowledgment of their importance. Instead, he ignores them as he would ignore the ideas of a child: he rents a small house that appears to be new, but in fact is not: "Pensé que esa casa era recién construida, pero me enteré de que en mil novecientos treinta la había ocupado una familia, y que después, para alquilarla, el propietario le había hecho algunos arreglos" (33). The first thing he notices about the house is its extraordinary whiteness "que brillaba con extraordinaria luminosidad," almost as if it were a house made of sugar. This appearance of newness, cleanliness, sweetness, and purity allows him to deceive Cristina, and he finds it easy to convince her that "era el lugar ideal: la casa de nuestros sueños" (33).

No sooner does the newly married couple move into the house, however, than the narrator begins to worry that Cristina will discover his deception. He systematically begins to cut his wife off from the outside world so that nothing can destroy the "tranquility" and "happiness" of their lives "en aquella casa de azúcar" (34). He disconnects the phone and locks the mailbox because he is afraid a wrong number or a letter addressed to the previous occupants will make Cristina suspicious; he discourages her from talking to the neighbors; he prohibits her from receiving visitors or from walking alone in the streets; then, once he has set up these restrictions, he is obliged to follow her and spy on her to make sure she is doing nothing against his orders. Ironically, he does these things in order to preserve what he calls "nuestra felicidad" (34), for as he explains to the reader, "Eramos felices, tan felices que a veces me daba miedo" (33). The narrator is aware that his happiness is based on a lie, but it is not only fear that his lie will be discovered that causes him anxiety. It is also a feeling of repressed guilt, which stems from his refusal to acknowledge difference between himself and Cristina and the simultaneous recognition that difference *does* exist.

Cristina's role as Other acts to remind him that their marital bliss is an illusion, for although the narrator insists that their happiness is mutual, Cristina's behavior demonstrates that she does not possess the feelings he ascribes to her. In order to sustain the fiction that they are happy and that they are united, the narrator must turn a blind eye to Cristina's Otherness and see her instead as a projection of his own ego. The narrator notes a change in Cristina's personality, remarking "de alegre se convirtió en triste, de comunicativa en reservada, de tranquila en nerviosa" (35), but he interprets her behavior as a reflection of his own "inquietud." He is slightly worried that she no longer takes an interest in the "wifely" activities that once filled her days: she no longer prepares his favorite desserts or serves him cookies with his tea or decorates the house "con volantes de nylon" (35). But he does not stop to consider the meaning of her behavior. He continues to insist, "Nos queríamos con locura" (35), although it is apparent to the reader by this time that neither Cristina nor her husband is entirely satisfied in the relationship and that the narrator may not know what Cristina's real feelings are.

The idea that Cristina may be undergoing a supernatural metamorphosis or transferal of personality does not occur to the narrator until the fiction that her behavior parallels and reflects his own begins to crumble. He is bewildered when at one point he notes, "En aquellos días, tan tristes para mí, a Cristina se le dio por cantar. Su voz era agradable, pero me exasperaba, porque formaba parte de ese mundo secreto, que la alejaba de mí. ¡Por qué, si nunca había cantado, ahora cantaba noche y día mientras se vestía o se bañaba o cocinaba o cerraba las persianas!" (40). Her lightheartedness in the face of his sadness strikes him as incomprehensible behavior because it is no longer a mirror of his own. The "impossibility" of the situation leads him to suspect that something supernatural might be taking place. It is not surprising, given these circumstances, that he adopts Cristina's superstition about the house and makes it his own. It conveniently provides him with an explanation for her Otherness: if he believes that Cristina has taken on the personality of the former occupant, Violeta, then her "strange" behavior can be seen as the result of a fantastic occurrence rather than a natural one.

While Cristina's husband struggles with the difficulty of inserting the female into the space occupied by self, the narrator of "En memoria de Paulina" finds it problematic to distinguish the female as Other. Both male characters are figuratively stuck in the Mirror Stage of subjectivity, since they are torn between the need to view the female as an extension of their own being and the need to position the female in opposition to them so that they can take up their positions along socially constructed gender lines. Nevertheless, they approach the conflict from different directions. The narrator of "La casa de azúcar" already speaks from inside the Symbolic order, and as Cristina's husband, he must openly acknowledge sexual difference. At the same time, however, he feels alienated by the female's Otherness and experiences unconscious Desire to return to the realm of the Imaginary, where difference does not exist. The narrator of "Paulina," by contrast, speaks as if he were poised at the edge of the Imaginary, but prevented by a number of obstacles from stepping into the Symbolic order, where his maleness would be clearly defined. His continued identification with the female and his repression of libidinal drives have made it impossible to become Paulina's *novio*. So long as he insists there is no difference between them, they will be tied together in a presexual phase, like mother and child. He cannot possess her sexually without evoking powerful feelings of incest, nor can he compete for her love against a male rival without feeling that he is unleashing the father's threat of castration.

Cristina's husband only suggests indirectly his desire to mold the female into an image of himself, but the narrator of "Paulina" is more overt in his need to be seen as a part of his beloved. He begins the story by telling us how similar he and Paulina were to one another and by stressing that his happiness was dependent on the knowledge that he and Paulina were so much alike. The first memory he offers us of her is of the day when they discovered their affinity for the same things:

> En uno de mis primeros recuerdos, Paulina y yo estamos ocultos en una oscura glorieta de laureles, en un jardín con dos leones de piedra. Paulina me dijo: Me gusta el azul, me gustan las uvas, me gusta el hielo, me gustan las rosas, me gustan los caballos blancos. Yo comprendí que mi felicidad había empezado, porque en esa preferencias podía identificarme con Paulina. Nos parecimos tan milagrosamente que en un libro sobre la final reunión de las almas en el alma del mundo, mi amiga escribió en el margen: *Las nuestras ya se reunieron.* "Nuestras," en aquel tiempo, significaba la de ella y la mía. (11)

The unsuspecting reader may pass over the many clues contained in the above passage because, at least on the surface of things, the narrator merely seems to be telling us a rather conventional and clichéd love story. It is commonplace in this kind of story for the narrator to stress how he and his beloved are mirror images of one another. As Keppler has observed, "Being in love involves a sense of affinity, the lovers ARE each other" (11). Coates has noted the same tendency, pointing out that "in love, the other is one's double. It has been suggested that when selecting a partner, we tend unconsciously to choose persons whose features echo our own" (1). The rather flowery language and the seemingly unconnected images used by the narrator to describe his memory of the event can be attributed to the fact that he is a would-be writer and a sensitive, erudite young man prone to literary forms of expression. There seems to be no reason to question his perception of things, since Paulina herself (in written form) backs up his impression that they are two halves of a single whole.

Lost in his memories of Paulina, the narrator devotes several pages of the story to an elaboration of the similarities between them. She is his salvation, his ideal ego, and the person he could become if only he could attain her state of "resplandeciente perfección" (12). As he tells us, "En lo que me parezca a Paulina estoy a salvo. Veía (y aún hoy veo) la identificación con Paulina como la mejor posibilidad de mi ser, como el refugio en donde me libraría de mis defectos naturales" (11). He refers to himself as "un apresurado y remoto borrador de Paulina" (22), thus emphasizing his belief that his own sense of self depends on that of his beloved. He is so wrapped up in this notion that he cannot conceive of himself without her; his use of "I" and "she" in the early pages of the text only functions to underline the fact that together they form a "we" that is unified and cohesive. They think (so the narrator claims) with a single mind and they speak with a single voice.

Unlike Cristina's husband in "La casa de azúcar," who is painfully aware of his wife as Other and who seeks a way to remodel her into self, the narrator of "Paulina" suffers from his inability to perceive difference between himself and his beloved. For example, so long as he believes that he and Paulina are mirror images of one another, he cannot behave as a sexualized being. If he were to recognize his maleness, it would stand in opposition to Paulina's femaleness and they would no longer be identical. The narrator seems to be aware of the problem, for he occasionally comments on the ambivalent nature of their relationship. He and Paulina are young adults, engaged to be married; yet, as he observes, "Hablar de nuestro casamiento no nos inducía a tratarnos como novios" (11). He calls their relationship "una puderosa amistad de niños," a situation he attributes to his own hesitancy to play the role of lover: "No me atrevía a encarnar el papel de enamorado y a decirle, con tono solemne: Te quiero" (11). He sees their future marriage as "algo natural y cierto," but he projects the carnal aspect of that relationship to a remote future, to "un ordenado porvenir," when they will have "tiempo suficiente para trabajar, para viajar y para querernos" (11). He tells us that he and Paulina often imagined their married life together "con tanta vividez que nos persuadíamos de que ya vivíamos juntos" (11), but it is clear that their relationship is not a sexual one. The narrator enjoys watching Paulina as she "plays" housewife, but he is uncertain about the part he should play in the drama. When he must characterize her relationship to him in words, he generally calls her "mi amiga." Only when a male rival enters the picture does he begin to call her "mi novia." The sight of Paulina talking to a male who may be sexually attracted to her provokes the narrator to exclaim, "¡Cómo anhelé decirle que la quería! Tomé la firme resolución de abandonar esa misma noche mi pueril y absurda vergüenza de hablarle de amor. Si ahora pudiera (suspiré) comunicarle mi pensamiento" (14). The recognition of Paulina as Other has at last come to the surface, and this allows us to re-read the early passages of the text in a different light.

Returning to the narrator's initial memory of Paulina in the garden, we can now see signs of an internal conflict that were not apparent at first glance. For example, the two (identical) stone lions suggest the idea that Paulina and the narrator are replicas of one another. Lions are wild, ferocious beasts under normal circumstances, but the fact that these are made of stone indicates that their natural instincts have been checked and that they are trapped in a static existence. This image captures the potential carnality of the relationship between the narrator and Paulina, but it also emphasizes that the relationship is standing still. Laurel has similar connotations of immobility and frustrated love in that it is associated with the myth of Daphne and Apollo. Just at the moment when Apollo attempted to possess the woman, she was transformed into a laurel tree, thus escaping the consequences of the god's lust. The garden is a motif commonly associated with carnal temptation and the end of innocence (as in the case of Adam and Eve in the Garden of Eden). The conflict between innocence and carnality is highlighted in the case of Paulina and the narrator in their shared appreciation of "el azul, . . . las uvas, . . . el hielo, . . . las rosas [y] los caballos blancos." These images suggest incipient desire that is being violently repressed: grapes are associated with worldly pleasure, with fertility, wine, and life; roses are linked to romantic love and sometimes to passion; horses connote sexual desire (especially male desire) and potency. But ice is cold, frozen, and static (similar to the stone lions); white and blue are colors associated with purity, virginity, the infinite, and the unreachable. Together, these images suggest that the narrator's sexual desire and carnal instincts exist side by side with his desire to maintain a pure and innocent relationship with Paulina. These feelings are not brought to the surface, however, until a rival for Paulina's love appears on the scene. The romantic triangle that emerges between the narrator, Paulina, and Montero is a reflection of the original Oedipal drama, which brings the male subject into being and makes him aware of the mother as Other. Montero is a man with a clear image of himself as male; under his gaze, Paulina becomes transformed into female; as a result, the narrator, in order to take his place as male and to compete for the female's love, must cease to identify with her. He can no longer view her as part of himself if he is able to see her through the father's eyes as an object of Desire. Since incest is forbidden, Desire is repressed and becomes unconscious; but in one form or another it will always be directed at that which he perceives as Other.

The narrators of "Paulina" and "La casa de azúcar" try to set up a situation in which the female acts as their double. By seeing the women as reflections of themselves, they feel less severely the lack that is at the root of unconscious Desire. By denying difference, especially sexual difference, they are able to maintain the illusion of wholeness and completeness that is associated with the Imaginary order. As the male begins to suspect that there *is* a difference between himself and the female, he feels the pressure of the Symbolic order on him, forcing him to take up his rightful place as a male. This means recognizing the female as Other, which in turn brings Desire into being. As the narrators attempt to deal with unconscious Desire, they are symbolically torn between the wish to return to the Imaginary realm (where the female presents no problem because no perceived difference exists) and the need to function in the Symbolic order (where male and female relationships can develop along the lines that society has drawn). It is at this point, as the males vacillate between the two alternatives, that a new double appears in their lives. In the case of Cristina's husband, he believes that his wife has developed a relationship with the previous occupant of the house, a mysterious woman named Violeta. Although he tries to make a convincing case that Violeta and Cristina are doubles, even asserting that Cristina has undergone a supernatural transformation and has become Violeta, we could also say just as easily that Violeta is a projection of the narrator's repressed Desire and that she functions in the story as *his* alter-ego. It is obvious, as the story progresses, that it is the narrator, not Cristina, who is obsessed with the possible existence of Violeta. Violeta can only speak through the filter of the narrator's voice, and she says only what he wants to hear. By claiming that Cristina has become Violeta, the narrator effectively silences his wife while upholding his own discursive power. If he cannot penetrate Cristina's Otherness, he will banish her from the text and substitute her voice with one of his own creation.

The narrator of "Paulina" is more passive by nature than Cristina's husband, and he is also more tortured by his own sexuality. In order to take up his role as Paulina's lover, he must first lay claims to gendered identity and acknowledge repressed sexual desire for her. Unfortunately, as he is quick to point out, he cannot act of his own accord. His shyness, his hesitancy, and his indecisiveness make it difficult for him to move forward in the subjectivity process. He needs the presence of a father figure to spur him to act. Upon Montero's arrival on the scene, the narrator undergoes a definite transformation; he ceases to identify with Paulina and begins to identify on an unconscious level with his rival. The very opposition between himself and Montero is what binds them together as doubles, for Montero is everything that he is not. Melanie Klein sees the double as a product of identification projection: one individual attributes to another those aspects of his personality that he does not want to acknowledge as his own; nevertheless, on an unconscious level, he continues to recognize those characteristics that he has projected onto the other, and for this reason, he identifies with him. The hatred the individual sometimes feels toward his double reflects the ambiguous nature of his own feeling of self-worth, according to Otto Rank, who sees hatred toward the double as a defense mechanism that has its roots in narcissism (the brother or the father is a rival for the mother's love). The narrator both despises and admires Montero because he is the object of Paulina's attention. At the same time, he waivers between self-pity and anger because Montero possesses attributes he cannot find in himself.

When Paulina confesses to the narrator that she loves Montero, the narrator's exclaims, "Todo era absurdo. No había una persona más incompatible con Paulina (y conmigo) que Montero. ¿O me equivocaba? Si Paulina quería a ese hombre, tal vez nunca se había parecido a mí" (16). Nevertheless, it is not difficult for him to work out the unconscious equation that Paulina would desire him too if he were more like Montero. Unlike Cristina's husband, who works toward erasing difference in the story, Paulina's beau feels an intense need to construct difference along gender lines. He must discover the bonds that tie him to Montero (whose maleness can reflect his own), and he must cast Paulina in the role of Other (so that her femaleness can stand in opposition to him).

Paulina initiates the break from the narrator when she announces that she is in love with Montero. Soon afterward, the narrator sails for Europe, leaving Paulina and Montero to their fate. When he returns to Buenos Aires some time later, Paulina pays him a visit, and for a moment, their relationship returns to familiar territory; he tells us, "Nos miramos en los ojos y, como dos ríos confluentes, nuestras almas se unieron" (19). But this is a turning point in the story and the pleasure of the moment is shattered by the introduction of a sexual element into the reunion. The narrator notes an aggressive sexuality on Paulina's part, which both delights him and repulses him. Caught in an Oedipal struggle, the narrator recognizes that it is his deepest desire to possess her, but it is a desire that must be repressed because he has conditioned himself to think of her as M/Other. Failure to heed the incest taboo would evoke the father's wrath, which could result in a symbolic castration or the loss of his self-image as male. The mention of Montero's name during the course of the conversation between Paulina and the narrator shatters forever any possibility of the narrator falling back into an Imaginary state of undifferentiation. Knowing that Paulina has abandoned him for his rival positions both males on one side of the gender line and the female clearly on the other. The female must be put in her place; if she cannot be an extension of his notion of self, then she must be characterized as Other. This necessity pushes the story into the realm of the fantastic, as the narrator soon discovers that Paulina has been dead for two years and that she could not possibly have visited him in the flesh. He concludes that Paulina's ghost must have come to say good-bye.

Far from being a shock, this revelation comes almost as a relief, for it allows the narrator to deconstruct the original version of Paulina's visit and return to his earlier fantasy of her. The narrator transforms the story into a fantastic tale as a way to return to a state of innocence; he declares, "Lo cierto es que Paulina me visitó anoche. Murió sabiendo que el matrimonio con Montero había sido una equivocación - una equivocación atroz - y que nosotros éramos la verdad. Volvió desde la muerte, para completar su destino, nuestro destino" (24). This version of events encourages the narrator to see Paulina as an extension of himself, as he has always been inclined to do. Their "destiny," or the "reunión de las almas" to which the narrator makes reference several times, restores him to a state of Imaginary wholeness and erases sexual difference as well as sexual desire.

But this version of events, however satisfactory, does not put an end to the narrator's worries about Montero as a rival for Paulina's love. Montero continues to symbolize the power of the Phallus and the call to take one's place along socially prescribed lines within the Symbolic Order. He must acknowledge difference, especially between self and other, and between male and female identity, if he is to function as an adult. The story of Paulina must be dismantled and reconstructed again, in order to reassert his identity as separate from the M/Other. As a living woman or as a ghost, Paulina's ability to pull him back into the pre-Oedipal stage is dangerous. The narrator tells us, "Como una fulminación, me alcanzó la verdad" (24); the "truth," he decides, is that the Paulina who visited his apartment was nothing more than a projection of Montero's imagination. For reasons that he never makes clear and certainly never questions, the narrator decides that Montero is capable of projecting images from his mind onto physical space. According to this theory, the narrator had no actual contact with Paulina; instead, he insists, "Yo abracé un monstruoso fantasma de los celos de mi rival" (24). Montero, not Paulina, now functions as the narrator's double in the sense that together they act as one to position Paulina as the forever elusive and unattainable Other. No "final reunion of souls" can take place between the narrator and Paulina so long as Montero exists; conversely, Montero can never fully possess Paulina so long as the narrator exists. By positioning each other as Paulina's lover, they become mirror images of one another; each one perceives that the other possesses what he lacks, and an endless chain of Desire is set in motion. Once this situation is firmly established, Paulina has no further place in their lives (or in the text), except in the role of the absent Other. It is appropriate, therefore, that the narrator acknowledge in the title of his story that he is not attempting to tell us about the actual woman, Paulina, but instead to capture the traces of her that exist in his memory.

The Amorphous Other

Unlike the previous stories, "Casa tomada" does not deal with romantic love. Perhaps for this reason, many of the external conflicts that were immediately apparent in the stories by Ocampo and Bioy Casares are notably absent from Cortázar's tale. The brother and sister couple in "Casa tomada" leads a simple life that appears to be, at least on the surface, entirely free of tension. In fact, it is the very ease with which they go through life that first captures our attention in the story. They have no economic worries, no social demands placed on them, and no existential anguish to plague them. They appear to have everything they want or need in order to feel complete. Nevertheless, the narrator offers us numerous clues throughout the text that everything is not as simple and straightforward as he would have us believe. Like the male narrators of "Paulina" and "La casa de azúcar," he too is a victim of his unconscious Desire, and it is his encounter with Otherness that leads him into the realm of the fantastic.

While all three narrators are instrumental in directing our gaze as readers to those details they wish to emphasize and away from those elements they would prefer to hide, the narrator of "Casa tomada" is both more controlled and more controlling in the way he approaches his task. He attempts to deny us access to his state of mind and to his feelings by focusing our gaze elsewhere; he insists, "es de la casa que me interesa hablar, de la casa y de Irene, porque yo no tengo importancia" (414). Nevertheless, it is clear from the outset that his identity is so closely tied to Irene and to the house that he cannot speak about them without including himself in the discussion. On an unconscious level, he has already set up the equation in his mind that Irene = the house = himself. He cannot separate one entity from the other, even on the most superficial level, for to do so would be to undermine his sense of self. This symbiotic relationship is established with the opening paragraphs of the text:

> Nos gustaba la casa porque aparte de espaciosa y antigua (hoy que las casas antiguas sucumben a la más ventajosa liquidación de sus materiales) guardaba los recuerdos de nuestros bisabuelos, el abuelo paterno, nuestros padres y toda la infancia. Nos habituamos Irene y yo a persistir solos en ella, lo que era una locura pues en esa casa podían vivir ocho personas sin estorbarse. Hacíamos la limpieza por la mañana, levantándonos a las siete, y a eso de las once yo le dejaba a Irene las últimas habitaciones por repasar y me iba a la cocina. Almorzábamos a mediodía, siempre puntuales; y no quedaba nada por hacer fuera de unos pocos platos sucios. Nos resultaba grato almorzar pensando en la casa profunda y silenciosa y cómo nos bastábamos para mantenerla limpia. (413)

The emphasis on shared pleasures ("nos gustaba," "nos resultaba grato"), shared activities ("hacíamos la limpieza," "almorzábamos"), shared family ties and a shared past ("nuestros bisabuelos, el abuelo paterno, nuestros padres y toda la infancia") immediately establishes that the narrator considers Irene and himself to be a couple and that he perceives them to be mirror images of one another. As was the case in the other stories, the male narrator speaks for the female, allowing her no direct access to language. She is incorporated into the plural "we," but the "we" is always articulated from the male position. She is an extension of him, and she takes up her place in the story as the narrator's alter ego. In this sense, she functions linguistically and psychically as the narrator's double. So long as the narrator is able to contain her within the image of self and the house shelters him from the demands of the Symbolic order, he can hover almost indefinitely inside the realm of the Imaginary, where difference (and Desire) are nonexistent concepts. This situation metaphorically illustrates the pre-Oedipal state, where the individual's Imaginary identification with the mother has not yet been shattered by the Law of the Father, which demands that Desire be displaced elsewhere.[4] Because it is an unsustainable state, it inevitably carries with it the threat of loss; it is this anxiety that "Casa tomada" portrays through the use of the fantastic.

While there is nothing unusual about unmarried siblings living together under the same roof, the narrator of "Casa tomada" is aware that his relationship with Irene goes to an extreme in terms of its exclusivity. If we are to believe what the narrator tells us, he and his sister have virtually no contact with anyone but each other; as a result, they have no notion of their own sexuality, no outlet for libidinal drives (if any were to exist), and no means by which to procreate. The "matrimonio de hermanos" they have entered into can engender nothing, since it is a contradiction in terms. It can only bring about what the narrator terms a "necessary" ending to their bloodline. It also threatens to put an end to the established patriarchal order that has characterized the family for generations, since unlike his father and grandfather, the narrator has rejected the role of father for himself. The narrator's choice of the word "marriage" to describe their relationship can be seen as an innocent metaphor, but given the care with which the narrator normally chooses his words, it may function like a Freudian slip of the tongue to reveal the narrator's true feelings. It suggests that perhaps on an unconscious level the narrator is aware of the notion of sexual difference but has resisted the predrawn gender roles that come with it. Since the recognition of sexual difference would position the female as Other and unleash Desire, he represses the thought immediately and attempts to cancel it out by describing the relationship as a "matrimonio de hermanos." The word "hermanos" is both plural and masculine, which erases gendered difference and repositions her as an extension of the male narrator. To further emphasize the point, the narrator calls the extinction of his branch of the family a "necessary closure." It is necessary only in the sense that it arises from the narrator's need to avoid an incestuous relationship with his sister, or a marriage in the true sense of the word. The absence of children is both punishment (for rejecting the demands of the Law of the Father) and proof of innocence (that they have not violated the incest taboo). Knowing that their chosen lifestyle will bring about the end of their family line could provoke strong feelings of guilt in the narrator and in his sister, if they were to recognize that it was a conscious choice. For this reason, in order to draw blame away from themselves and cast it elsewhere, the narrator confides:

> A veces llegamos a creer que era ella [la casa] la que no nos dejó casarnos. Irene rechazó a muchos pretendientes sin mayor motivo, a mí se me murió María Esther antes que llegáramos a comprometernos. Entramos en los cuarenta años con la inexpresada idea de que el nuestro, simple y silencioso matrimonio de hermanos, era necesaria clausura de la genealogía asentada por los bisabuelos en nuestra casa. (413)

The notion that something is perhaps missing in his relationship with Irene opens up a space for Desire in the text, but since Desire has no outlet, it must be repressed and projected elsewhere. The narrator first attempts to do this by insisting that it is the house's fault that he and Irene have not taken up the roles society has ascribed to them (husband/wife, mother/father). If they have ended up with a "matrimonio de hermanos" rather than a real marriage, he asserts, they are not responsible for the situation. It is not his wish, but the wish of the house, that they remain in a perpetual state of undifferentiation in which the female functions as an extension of him and the illusion of a perfect union is maintained. Repression of Desire does not, of course, effectively erase Desire because once it has come into being, there is no way to escape its influence. It must always be directed toward the Other, or that which brought the subject into being in the first place. The narrator cannot acknowledge Irene as Other without converting her into an object of Desire (thus, breaking the incest taboo).

The only solution to the problem lies in the projection of Otherness somewhere else, onto an amorphous and invisible "they" who take over the house and drive the narrator and his sister out into the world. In this way, the narrator's internal conflict can be played out entirely through projection, between "it" (the house) and "they" (who take over the house). As a result, the narrator can see himself and his sister as the victims of forces beyond their control and they need take no responsibility for their actions. According to this interpretation, the narrator and Irene do not abandon the house because they choose to leave it. Instead, they are simply bending to a will that is greater than their own. Just as earlier in the story the house "made" them stay, something else now "makes" them go. Desire is never voiced or even acknowledged as belonging to them; rather, it is projected always onto something or someone else.

Under the tightly controlled gaze of the narrator, the focus of the story is never permitted to stray beyond its perceived "natural" conclusion, when Irene and the narrator leave the house for the last time. We have no way of knowing what happened to them afterward, what became of the house, who or what took over the house, or what Irene thinks about the situation. The narrator appears to be telling his story from a complete void, which might lead us to conclude that the "we" speaking voice has traded places with the "they" who invaded the house. "They" came out of nothingness and took over a concrete space; "we" began in a concrete space and have retreated into a vacuum. Since "they" of the text lie outside linguistic representation and have no concrete identity as subjects, the narrator's "I" (alone or incorporated into the plural "we") in turn undergoes a process of disintegration when the two entities are transposed. Our inability as readers to locate the source from which the narrative voice speaks is disconcerting, for it opens up a space outside the text that allows unconscious Desire to speak through the discourse of the fantastic.

The Self Undone

In the three stories examined here, the narrator loses something or someone who had given him a sense of identity as a subject. As the threat of loss becomes apparent to him, he undergoes a psychic crisis that forces him to reposition himself within the Symbolic (or Patriarchal) order. This process resembles the Mirror Stage when the subject develops an awareness of himself as something distinct from the Other. Recognition of Otherness gives birth to Desire, which is driven underground into the unconscious but which continues to exert its influence on the subject by presenting itself as a lack that must be—but can never be—filled. It is in this way, as Lacan and others have pointed out, that Desire resembles language. Language functions through the substitution of linguistic signs for real objects, but although the sign replaces the object in speech, we are aware that the word is *not* the object it represents. There is always a gap between the signifier and signified, through which absolute meaning escapes us. This problem is especially acute for the narrator of a fantastic tale because the words he uses do not and cannot correspond to the objects they supposedly designate, given the fact that these objects (things, ideas, phenomenon) have no reality outside of the text that contains them. Nowhere is this more obvious than in "Casa tomada," where the supernatural element escapes the linguistic sign altogether. Spanish verb structures allow the subject pronoun to be omitted when it is clear from context who is doing the action. When the narrator tells Irene, "Han tomado la parte del fondo" (416), he speaks *as if* it were understood who (or what) has taken over the house, but it is never put into words. On the second occurrence, the narrator retreats even further from linguistic representation by saying, "Es casi repetir lo mismo salvo las consecuencias" (419). Since he told us virtually nothing on the earlier occasion, for him to "casi repetir lo mismo" is to tell us nothing again. Finally, once the action has been completed, the participle "tomado" is transformed into an adjective; at the end of the story, we are presented with a fait accompli, "la casa tomada," without ever being allowed to see who carried out the action or why. Because he does not tell us what we need to know in order to interpret his reactions and behavior, the story strikes us as incomprehensible and strange. We are led to believe that something supernatural might have taken place, but we are given no clues as to what that thing might be.

In "Paulina," the narrator constructs, deconstructs, and reconstructs the story of Paulina's visit a number of times in the text, thereby setting into motion a spiraling pattern that does not allow us as readers to settle into one definite interpretation of events described. Although the narrator presents us with "la verdad," it is obvious that there are multiple truths at work in the text. He assures us several times that what he is telling us is "lo cierto," or "la verdad," but each version of events cancels out and substitutes for the other. The open-endedness of the story and the lack of fixed meaning allows the story to remain indefinitely in the realm of the fantastic, for although the reader may choose one "truth" over another, there is no guarantee that it is the only or the absolute truth. The narrator's fluctuating vision of "what really happened" emphasizes that all forms of interpretation are arbitrary and subjective and that meaning can never be fixed from a position of absolute authority.

This message is reconfirmed in "La casa de azúcar" where the narrator begins his story with an authoritarian stance, but he is forced to conclude, "Ya no sé quién fué víctima de quién, en esa casa de azúcar" (43). His frequent exclamations of "no sé por qué" and "Jamás comprenderé por qué," which initially seemed nothing more than mild expressions of bewilderment, must now be read quite literally. He does not understand the situation he has chosen to narrate nor does he have the slightest comprehension of his wife's character, which was supposedly the subject of his discourse. The disintegration of his authority as narrator accompanies the disintegration of his notion of self, as well as his realization that language is an incomplete and imperfect system of representation. Numerous times in the text, his ineptness as narrator becomes apparent when he attempts to reproduce verbal exchanges that took place between himself and Cristina, or Cristina and others. His sense that Cristina always means to express more than her words can convey leaves him feeling alienated from her and creates in him a profound sense of lack. He, in turn, cannot find words for that which is lacking and he retreats into silence: "Volvimos a casa. Enloquecido de celos (¿celos de que? De todo), durante el trayecto apenas le hablé" (38). Eventually, it is his inability to find linguistic representation for unconscious Desire that leads to the creation of Violeta, for Violeta personifies the Otherness that separates him from Cristina. How Cristina was transformed into Violeta escapes him, just as meaning always escaped him whenever he attempted to interpret Cristina's words or to express his thoughts to her. The supernatural element of the story slips through the gap left open in language, and we are left with the results of the action—Cristina transformed into Violeta—without knowing how the action takes place. As the narrator attempts to position himself in language to tell the story of Cristina, he is not able to say with certainty "quién fué víctima de quién" because his own notion of self has been decentered. He is not the narrator he thought he was, nor is he apparently the man he assumed himself to be. His only identity in the text, apart from being the narrator, is that of Cristina's husband; therefore, as he deconstructs her being, he inevitably dismantles his own.

It is probably not coincidental, given the complex relationship between the formation of the human subject and the subject's insertion into language as a representational system, that we meet all three narrators at a point in their lives when their notion of self has begun to come apart at the seams. A psychological process that is normally confined to early childhood extends figuratively here into adulthood, as male narrators attempt to come to terms with female Otherness. The telling of the story becomes therapeutic, for if they are able to use words to tie their experiences to real objects, the experience will somehow become more meaningful to them. They are inevitably frustrated in their efforts, however, because the fantastic-like unconscious Desire cannot be contained in language. Words can never stand in for that which outruns our conscious grasp. By foregrounding the gaps that occur in language, the fantastic calls attention to the insufficiencies in the system we must use to represent ourselves whenever we use words in an attempt to capture and convey our experiences to others. In this way, the fantastic acts to revive one of our most basic fears as human subjects, that there is no solid core to the "I" we use to represent ourselves in language, and as a result, the place from which we speak can never be anything more than an arbitrarily assumed position.

5 / The Fantastic and the Conventions of Gothic Romance

Critics have tended to view gothic romances and the literature of the fantastic as closely related genres, sometimes erasing boundaries altogether in their treatment of eighteenth- and nineteeth-century European texts. Seen as a product of romantic sensibilities, this type of fiction reveals "a preoccupation with themes, events, incidents, or characters normally described as impossible, implausible, incredible, uncanny, fanciful, imaginary, delusory, or mad, and with experiences that are excluded from so-called realistic literature" (Jackson, *Miss Darrington,* xvi). Gothic romances such as Radcliffe's *The Mysteries of Udolpho* (1794) and Lewis's *The Monk* (1796) are often cited as examples of the fantastic, yet even in these early works it is clear that the gothic has a nature of its own. As George Haggerty asserts, "It is no mere coincidence that the cult of Gothic fiction reached its apex at the very moment when gender and sexuality were beginning to be codified for modern culture" (1). He believes that "transgressive social-sexual relations are the most basic common denominator of Gothic. … Terror is almost always sexual terror: fear and flight, as well as incarceration and escape, are almost always coloured by the exoticism of transgressive sexual aggression" (1). It is this emphasis on the sexual that opens up gothic romance for exploration in terms of how it treats gender and the body.[1]

Psychoanalytic, feminist, and gender theorists have been particularly attracted to the ways in which female writers and readers respond to the conventions of gothic romance. In *Literary Women* in 1977, Ellen Moers coined the term "Female Gothic" as a way to validate and rescue from oblivion gothic texts written by women since the eighteenth century. During the next decade, a great deal of critical attention was given to the way in which gothic fiction depicts male and female characters, the way gothic plots respond to the pressures of patriarchal culture, and the manner in which modern readers react to a genre that appears to be (at least on the surface) antifeminist in nature. Tania Modleski sums up the Ur-plot of othic romances this way:

> The atmosphere is dark and stormy, and the ethereal young girl comes to a mysterious house, perhaps as a bride, perhaps in another capacity, and either starts to mistrust her husband or else finds herself in love with a mysterious man who appears to be some kind of criminal. . . . She tries to convince herself that her suspicions are unfounded, that, since she loves him, he must be trustworthy and that she will have failed as a woman if she does not implicity believe in him. (59)

But, Modleski reminds us, gothic novels also "testify to women's extreme discontent with the social and psychological processes which transform them into victims" (84). The conventions of gothic romance demand tension in the narrative, which can never be completely erased, even when the novel reaches an apparently happy ending. Because the gothic portrays any attempt to act out feminine desire as a transgressive act, the heroine is extremely confined in terms of her behavior and emotions; she cannot claim a space in the text as a desiring subject without risking the label of "unnatural" woman. Michelle Massé explains:

> Culturally prohibited from speaking of passion, unable to move toward the object of desire, the heroine remains the passive center of the novel and of the female adolescent's erotic dream. The phantasmagoric horrors that bombard her are the natural companions of repression, the price she must pay for her transgression—desire—even when it is only obliquely acknowledged and represented. By being a perennially passive victim, she remains a "good girl," never entirely aware of her own sexual longings. (10)

The two novellas chosen for analysis in this chapter, *La última niebla* (1935) by María Luisa Bombal and *Aura* (1962) by Carlos Fuentes, problematize the issues pointed out by Massé and Modleski by making them central to their narratives. In a self-conscious fashion, Bombal and Fuentes borrow heavily from the conventions of gothic romance in order to subvert them and mold them into the modern fantastic. The fantastic becomes a means of creating and nurturing an impossible love—a theme that lies at the heart of gothic romance—but in the fantastic the texts double back on themselves to interrogate the credibility of the narrator and his or her claim to agency and desire. Specifically, they examine the female body as the locus of sexual desire and longing, and they position male characters in the text as the objects of that longing.[2] The female's right to feel, express, or act on sexual desire is called into question, especially as she ages and her body no longer corresponds to culturally constructed ideas of beauty. At the same time, the texts ask us to consider what role we as readers play in the construction of meaning, since our ability to say what happens to the characters depends so heavily on conjecture. Language is not transparent, it can break down, and meaning can escape us, lying always just slightly beyond our grasp. What assumptions do we, as readers, bring to the texts about romantic and sexual love, about desiring and desirable women, about gendered roles, and about the body? How and why are the narrators consumed by love? And, if we perceive that they have wandered into madness or the realm of the unreal, what encourages us to distrust the "truth" value of their words? These are questions that the novellas address in direct and indirect ways. In addition, they provide meaningful contrasts to each other for an investigation into the ways that female and male writers engage with gothic conventions, and the way that we, as readers, respond to notions of gender in the texts we read. If *La última niebla* illustrates the power of the "Female Gothic" in Latin America, then *Aura* is a response to that power. Fuentes's novella clearly demonstrates that in our postmodern age, women are not the only victims of gothic romance. Whenever socially constructed ideas about gendered identity begin to crumble, the fantastic inserts itself into the text like a wedge, dismantling many of our assumptions about what is possible and real.

La última niebla has generated a considerable body of critical work over the years. Regarded as the beginning of the New Novel in Chile, Bombal' s work has gained a place in the canon and has become a standard text used in the study of the evolution of Spanish American narrative toward a more subjective and introspective kind of writing. Feminists have also been drawn to Bombal's work, in part because it is rare to find a woman author of her generation included in the canon, and in part because Bombal's writing conveys a particularly feminine kind of experience to the reader, which points to the development of a new vein of women's literature that would flourish in the later part of the century. The emphasis on female characters, the intimate portrayal of the workings of the female psyche, and the attempt to find an appropriate language for feminine discourse sets Bombal's work apart from that of her male contemporaries and provides critics with a wide range of issues to be studied. However, relatively little attention has been given to Bombal's work as an example of the fantastic, although it contains many of the stylistic and thematic features associated with that kind of literature. In part, this may be due to the fact that *La última niebla* shares some characteristics with gothic and conventional romance fiction, and its lyrical and philosophical overtones have encouraged readers to think of the narrator's experiences as imaginary rather than supernatural. The oversight, however, also says a great deal about how our perceptions are informed by assumptions about feminine discourse, interpretive power, and authority in a text. The questions raised by Bombal's text open the doors to a detailed investigation of reading practices that the fantastic has consistently urged us to consider over the course of the past century.

Aura is a useful point of departure for a reexamination of Bombal's work because it reiterates a number of important questions about how gender relates to perception, both on the diegetic level of the character and narrator as well as the extradiegetic level of the reader. For example, Fuentes's text also shares many elements with gothic and romance fiction; yet, his work has seldom been read as an example of either. Readers and critics have generally agreed that the experiences of Fuentes's male narrator, Felipe Montero, are supernatural in nature, and although there is a great deal of doubt about the way these experiences occurred and what they mean, Felipe's reliability as a narrator and his sanity are rarely, if ever, questioned. By contrast, in Bombal's text our doubt revolves not around the nature of the events described, but instead around the credibility of the narrator. Both novellas are narrated in a lyrical, intimate style, as if the narrator were speaking or writing for his or her own benefit rather than ours. Both texts deal with passionate encounters between the narrator and a strange lover who may or may not be real. Both narrators are isolated, dreamy individuals who are frustrated and disappointed with life. Both see love as a means of fulfillment. In both works, it is the female who initiates the sexual encounter and whose passion is underscored in the text. The atmosphere in both novellas plays an important role, creating a mysterious backdrop for the action. Finally, both narrators suffer crushing disappointment when their lovers vanish, and both are left to wonder if their lover was real or merely a figment of someone's imagination.

A careful examination of how the fantastic is treated in both novellas reveals that the authors use many of the same strategies and techniques, and while both texts privilege subjective impressions over objective fact, the way in which we react to those impressions is quite different. For example, memory and dreams play an important role in both narratives and provide clues to help us interpret what we read. For both narrators, the perception of what is real is closely tied to what is remembered: Aura is real so long as Felipe can hold on to the memory of her, just as the lover in Bombal's text is real to the narrator so long as her memories are undisturbed. Loss is connected not only to physical separation but to the inability to recall physical sensations and experiences in concrete detail after the moment has passed. Dreams introduce oneiric and lyrical qualities into the prose that permit the blending of categories like real, imagined, dreamed, and supernatural. Through the use of symbolism, the narrators' dreams reveal subconscious desires, fears, and longings that play themselves out in the texts. The supernatural for both narrators is an antidote to the real world that, by comparison, is flat, dull, and unrewarding. The degree to which they give themselves over to their "impossible love" reflects, to a large extent, their willingness to let down the barriers that separate categories like the possible from the impossible, the dreamed from concrete fact. Binary oppositions like old/ young, desiring/ desired, repulsion/ attraction, and other markers of difference break down in the narratives and leave us unsure about where the dividing lines lie. For this reason, both texts resist closure and fit comfortably into a discussion of the fantastic, despite any attempt to reach a conclusion about the nature of what we have just read.

The Male as Victim

Like any well-crafted fantastic text, *Aura* can be read in a number of different ways and leaves much to the reader's imagination. Whether Felipe Montero's encounter with the mysterious Aura is real is a question that remains open to interpretation. A supernatural reading of the novella leads us to believe that Aura is exactly what her name implies, an impression or sensation rather than a tangible form, a subtle emanation from another's body rather than a being in her own right. It also suggests that the ancient Consuelo Llorente, Felipe's employer, has managed to reincarnate herself through witchcraft and has used the beautiful young Aura as bait to attract Felipe to her house. In line with this reading, Felipe appears to be the reincarnation or double of Consuelo's long-dead husband, the General, and Consuelo has fabricated a complex snare to bring him back into her arms. Felipe's initial ignorance of Consuelo's plot makes him the perfect narrator for a fantastic story because as events unfold, he must grapple with a way to make sense of them. His hesitation and doubt are passed on to the reader, making it difficult for us to reach an immediate conclusion about what is happening in the text. Felipe is typical of many other narrators of fantastic fiction in that he is bored by the normalcy of his life. He is dissatisfied with the niche he has carved out for himself in the world, he is solitary, understimulated, and overly imaginative, and he secretly longs for an escape from "la larga fila detenida de camiones y autos [que] gruñe, pita, suelta el humo insano de su prisa" (14). He defines himself as a failure, as "Felipe Montero, antiguo becario en la Sorbona, historiador cargado de datos inútiles, acostumbrado a exhumar papeles amarillentos, profesor auxiliar en escuelas particulares, novecientos pesos mensuales" (11). Consuelo's money, her appeal to his vanity, and above all, Aura's irresistible beauty convince him that he belongs in Consuelo's house rather than in the world outside. The strange, eerie, almost menacing quality of the house simultaneously repels and attracts him, feelings that are echoed when he meets Consuelo and Aura for the first time. The binary opposition of repulsion/ attraction underscores one of the novella's major themes, that of the double. It also suggests the idea that opposites are not always as distinct from one another as we suppose, and the difference between them is sometimes only a matter of perception.[3]

Initially, Felipe expresses uncertainty about the choice he has made to live in Consuelo's house, but he has two powerful motivations: one is Aura, a young woman who entrances him with her beauty, and the other is the appeal of the work Consuelo has offered him. Overcoming his anxiety about the strangeness of the old woman and her household, Felipe reminds himself of the good salary and the few demands that the job will place on him. He is both romantic and practical; his two sides reveal themselves clearly as he debates the merit of staying or leaving, and for every disturbing thing that happens in the house to unsettle him, he confects a rational explanation and a reason to remain there. Most of the narrative consists of an internal monologue about the meaning and significance of what he sees, thinks, and feels while he is in the house with the women. However, as Felipe falls deeper under the spell of Consuelo and Aura, he finds it increasingly difficult to explain away their strange behavior. Ultimately, he appears to embrace Consuelo's beliefs that Aura is her double, a younger version of herself, and that he is Consuelo's dead husband, but it is not clear how fully he believes this or how he accounts for it.

When he sees a photograph of the General, for example, Felipe exclaims, "Es él, es . . . eres tú" (58). The recognition of his own image in the photograph may literally signify that he believes he is the General, or it may be merely a dramatic reaction to the discovery that he looks very much like the dead man. As he looks at the photo, he states, "siempre te encuentras, borrado, perdido, olvidado, pero tú, tú, tú" (58). This is the closest Felipe comes to stating openly that he believes something supernatural has occurred, but it is important to note that he is speaking only of his *perception* of the photo, not of an actual supernatural event. Crucial to the fantastic effect of the novella, Felipe's reluctance to take a firm stand about the seemingly impossible details he narrates leaves the reader without a sense of closure. For example, Felipe does not state categorically that Aura is a specter but instead records what Consuelo tells him: "Ella ya se agotó. Nunca he podido mantenerla a mi lado más de tres días" (61). Felipe does not respond when Consuelo asks him to become her accomplice. She promises, "Volverá, Felipe, la traeremos juntos. Deja que recupere fuerzas y la haré regresar" (62). But, significantly, the novella ends before we know Felipe's reaction. This truncated ending successfully diverts attention away from the supernatural aspect of the narrative and points it in another direction. What shocks Felipe and perhaps most readers into silence is the discovery that Consuelo has taken Aura's place in bed and Felipe has been making love to the old woman instead of her young niece. The substitution of one woman for the other suggests that they are one in the same person, but it does not offer us absolute proof. Felipe is faced with the necessity of deciding what caused him to mistake Consuelo for Aura, and a supernatural explanation is one way to erase the natural conclusions he might otherwise reach, that he is literally and figuratively blind to the difference between the women that he has so painstakingly constructed throughout the narrative.

Felipe's interior monologue has several important functions in the text. First, the use of the second-person familiar, *tú*, creates a floating signifier with multiple meanings. Felipe appears to be talking to himself, but he may also be talking to his double (the General) or he may be having an intimate dialogue with an outside observer (the reader). Any of these narratees could identify with the use of *tú* as a form of address and, therefore, live Felipe's experiences at the same time he does. To further create doubt and hesitation, Felipe uses the present and future tenses when he speaks to give immediacy and indeterminacy to his discourse, as if the story he is telling were about to unfold and the outcome still uncertain. In addition to facilitating the reader's exposure to the fantastic, the interior monologue allows us to share Felipe's desire for Aura. This element is important because it prepares us for feelings of horror and revulsion when Consuelo takes Aura's place in Felipe's arms; Aura's soft skin, firm body, and smooth flesh are replaced by Consuelo's "rostro desgajado, compuesto de capas de cebolla, pálido, seco y arrugado como una ciruela cocida" and "labios sin carne que has estado besando, . . . encías sin dientes que se abren ante ti" (61–62). The use of *tú* in these passages situates the reader firmly in Felipe's place and encourages us to feel what he feels: the monster in the tale is not the phantasmagorical Aura but Consuelo, the living woman. The lesson to be learned from this encounter is that the supernatural is not as frightening as old age, and desire, when misdirected, is the most dangerous trap of all.

There are signs that Aura is not of this world from Felipe's initial encounter with her, but he is reluctant to attach any negative meaning to these clues because he is so attracted to the young woman. For example, Felipe first perceives her not through sight but through sound, through the sensation of "esa respiración agitada a tu lado" (19). Her otherworldliness is suggested by the fact that she appears silently, unexpectedly, and is visually elusive; Felipe sees nothing but a fragmented body part, a hand that suddenly extends itself between him and Consuelo in the dark room, as if it were emerging from a void. Her silent entrance strikes him as unreal, and he notes that "su aparición fue imprevista, sin ningún ruido—ni siquiera los ruidos que no se escuchan pero que son reales porque se recuerdan inmediatamente" (19). His choice of words is important for it establishes the relationship between memory and existence in the novella: that which is remembered becomes real. This idea plays itself out in the narrative on two levels, as Consuelo explores methods to turn memories of her dead husband into reality and Felipe seeks a means to hold on to Aura, who may only be the phantom of Consuelo's youth.

Felipe's active imagination, coupled with an attraction to the mysterious and unknown, become apparent as soon as he arrives at Consuelo's house. For example, he notices that the doorknocker looks like "la cabeza de un feto canino," a simple fact that sparks a dramatic reaction in him: "Imaginas que el perro te sonríe y sueltas su contacto helado" (13). This chilling sensation encourages him to enter the house rather than retreat from it. The front door opens with the slightest pressure from his fingers, beckoning him inside as if it had been left open for him. Felipe obviously feels anxiety about the strangeness of the situation, but he also has a strong desire to escape from the world outside, and when he looks over his shoulder at the street, he feels that he is seeing it for the last time. Although he tries, he cannot retain "una sola imagen de ese mundo exterior indiferenciado" (14). This passage across the threshold is symbolic as well as physical, for it marks Felipe's transition from one world to another. Consuelo's house is in ruins, the patio dark and sparsely populated with mysterious herbs and shade-loving plants, every door inside the house is a swinging door without a lock, and the furniture is an eclectic mix of dusty, outmoded furniture from the nineteenth century. Nevertheless, it is a world where Felipe feels curiously at home.

Consuelo uses language at times to manipulate and confuse Felipe, knowing that her words will awaken curiosity on his part and, at the same time, subdue him. For example, her references to "mi compañera" and "mi compañía" in their initial interview are purposely obscure, making it difficult for Felipe to know if she is talking about her pet rabbit or her niece, Aura. When the rabbit exits the room, Aura enters, as if they were different incarnations of the same being. Through language, Consuelo creates an air of mystery around the young woman before Felipe has met her. Perhaps for this reason, Felipe's first impression of Aura is extraordinary. Her eyes, like Consuelo's, exert an almost hypnotic power over him, and under her gaze, Felipe surrenders completely to the old woman's will. Aura's eyes seem to be offering him "un paisaje que sólo tú puedes adivinar y desear" (20). This impression echoes Felipe's earlier belief that Consuelo's ad was aimed directly at him, that their meeting was predestined, and that he is meant to play a significant role in both women's lives. It is a balm to Felipe's wounded ego and shows a desire on his part to see himself and his life in more positive terms. The underpaid part-time teacher is instantly transformed into a respected scholar and becomes the suitor of a beautiful woman. Inside Consuelo's house, Felipe can live out his fantasies and have the life he feels he deserves.

The darkness of Consuelo's house does more than create a mysterious atmosphere in the novella. It literally and figuratively blinds Felipe so that any exposure to light (or reason) stuns him momentarily and makes him hesitate and doubt his own perceptions. For example, in order to see Aura's eyes clearly, he must move away from the light into the darkness, "para que la luz de las veladoras no te ciegue" (20). These words suggest that Felipe sees best not from a position of clarity and illumination, but from the dark corners of his mind. From this vantage point, he sees what he wants to see: Aura is a powerful seductress and her eyes have a strong, almost magical power over him. Uncomfortable with this thought, however, he quickly denies the power he has attributed to her by telling himself, "no es cierto . . . son unos hermosos ojos verdes idénticos a todos los hermosos ojos verdes que has conocido o podrás conocer" (20). Unsure whether to surrender to Aura or resist her, Felipe allows his thoughts to flow back and forth, matching their rhythm to the ebb and flow he finds in her eyes. This indecision, or the ability to see things from two points of view almost simultaneously, characterize Felipe's narrative throughout the text. For each theory he constructs, a contrary thought immediately appears to wash it away.

Felipe's room is the only one in the house that is well lit, and it is significant that the time he spends there is empty time, a time when he sleeps or daydreams or idly passes the hours until his next encounter with Aura or Consuelo. The electric light that exists in the hallway outside his room reveals nothing but "ese largo pasillo desnudo," an empty space (23). It is below, in the darkened rooms the women inhabit, where Felipe's new life unfolds. He accepts darkness as a natural condition for the time he lives with them, and he tells himself that it is useless to rely on light "porque ya sabes que esta casa siempre se encuentra a oscuras. Te obligarás a conocerla y reconocerla por el tacto. Avanzas con cautela, como un ciego, con los brazos extendidos, rozando la pared" (23). The reliance on senses other than sight guides Felipe in his search for Aura, and it prepares us for the realization that he may not find her through usual means.

Unlike traditional heroes of romance fiction, Felipe falls easily into the role of victim, especially when he presents himself as the object of the female gaze. A magnetic, powerful gaze is a common attribute of the male in gothic fiction, and it renders the female protagonist powerless against him. Here, a reversal in gendered roles creates a transgressive situation that threatens to emasculate Felipe as Consuelo's penetrating eyes reduce him to a state of defenselessness. As she lays out her conditions, he can only mutter "No sé" and "Quizás" (19), as if his will were being drained from him. Her gaze disturbs him because it is strong, relentless, and inscrutable. The description of Consuelo's eyes is important because it establishes a clear connection between the old woman and her young niece, Aura. When Felipe first meets Aura, he is strongly attracted to her eyes. Her eyes are fluid and hold him in a hypnotic trance, but because Aura is young and beautiful, Felipe considers her gaze seductive. She stares at him in the same way as Consuelo, but the effect on Felipe is completely different. Her eyes are "ojos de mar que fluyen, se hacen espuma, vuelven a la calma verde, vuelven a inflamarse como una ola" (20). The sexual imagery suggested by words like "espuma," "inflamarse," and "ola" stand in strong contrast to the words used to describe Consuelo's eyes such as "seca," "amarillenta," and "caída." Whereas both women are portrayed in the text as strange, almost otherworldly creatures, Felipe perceives them as extreme opposites because of the feelings they evoke in him. Consuelo is the monster, Aura the damsel in distress, and he is, he believes, the hero of the tale. It is ironic that he casts himself in this role when it is he, not Aura, who has become Consuelo's real prisoner.

The atmosphere of Consuelo's house and the old woman herself are evocative of gothic romances, and Felipe is unsettled by them. More perturbing still is the suggestion of transgressive sexual desire linked not only to the young and beautiful Aura but also to the ancient Consuelo. Consuelo's passionate marriage to General Llorente took place during Mexico's most romantic period, the reign of Maximilian and Carlotta. Carlotta's obsession with her husband, her madness, and her inability to accept his death echo strongly in Consuelo's character and reverberate throughout the text. For example, in one of the novella's most disturbing scenes, Felipe spies on Consuelo as she dances an imaginary waltz with her husband's old military tunic: "Ves a la señora Consuelo de pie, erguida, transformada con esa túnica entre los brazos: ese túnica azul con botones de oro, charreteras rojas, brillantes insignias de águila coronada, esa túnica que la anciana mordisquea ferozmente, besa con ternura, se coloca sobre los hombros para girar en un paso de danza tambaleante" (40). This image of Consuelo clearly mirrors well-known stories of the Empress Carlotta who, as a very old woman, wrote passionate love letters to her husband, Maximilian, a man who had died sixty years before. It is unsettling because in addition to signaling that Consuelo is perhaps mad, it also shows that she still feels intense sexual desire. He comes to the conclusion "que por eso vive Aura en esta casa: para perpetuar la ilusión de juventud y belleza de la pobre anciana enloquecida" (42). Consuelo as madwoman is consistent with the treatment of aging women in gothic romances. As Jackson points out, "Displaced from their society and history, dislocated from their bodies, minds and marriages, [these characters] move into another realm, in between things, to a kind of no-man's land. Feeling that they do not belong socially, they come to occupy the ultimate non-social, asocial position—that of specter, madwoman or ghost" (*Miss Darrington,* xx). Consuelo's self-imposed exile in the decaying house is symptomatic of the way elderly women are made invisible in a youth-obsessed culture and helps Felipe to understand her obsession with her "niece," Aura.

In the role of romantic hero, Felipe imagines that he can free Aura from the madwoman's control. However, he is not adept at the role of savior, and he procrastinates beyond all reason, telling her, "No, quizás todavía no. Estoy contratado para un trabajo. Cuando termine el trabajo, entonces sí" (54). He slips back into the role of victim as soon as he realizes that the women are manipulating him and using him as a sexual object. For example, when Aura and Felipe make love in Aura's room, she takes control, assumes the dominant position, and tells him "Tú no hagas nada. Déjame hacerlo todo a mí" (47). After the act, Felipe realizes that Consuelo has been present in the room, too, that she has been watching everything, and that Aura's performance was for the old woman's benefit: "Las dos te sonríen, te agradecen" (50). The realization that Consuelo still feels desire unsettles Felipe as much as the fact that she has been watching him make love to Aura.

The idea that Consuelo's sexual desire might be directed toward him occurs to Felipe in dreams and shows that he has already begun to confuse Aura's identity with that of her elderly aunt. For example, in the first dream, Aura's hand takes on the characteristics of Consuelo's hand; it becomes "esa mano descarnada que avanza hacia ti con la campana en la mano, gritando que te alejes, que se alejen todos," and her face becomes "el rostro de ojos vaciados [que] se acerca al tuyo" (37). The attribution of characteristics that Felipe associates with Consuelo (*mano descarnada, ojos vaciados*) to Aura turns her into something to be feared. The manifestation of desire in the woman, indicated by the outstretched hand and the face held close to him, creates a sensation of panic and an urge to flee. When he awakens from the nightmare and finds that Aura has crept into his bed, the sexual encounter that takes place between them is like the echo of his dream, with Consuelo and Aura playing the same role. He cannot see her face, but he assumes the woman in his bed is Aura because he touches "la piel más suave y ansiosa," he smells "el perfume de las plantas del patio," and he identifies the key that he saw Aura place on a ribbon around her neck (38). Felipe's assumption that it is Aura in his bed is logical, but again, it is based on perceptions rather than certain knowledge. Later, when he finds himself in bed with Consuelo, he kisses and touches her "sin pensar, sin distinguir" (61), and it is only when the moonlight invades the room and he sees Consuelo's face that he realizes what he has done. The dream has prepared him subconsciously for this outcome, but he has chosen to ignore the warning.

Felipe's second dream repeats the same kind of imagery and reveals even more clearly what he fears: Consuelo is the powerful, sexualized woman, the one who approaches him as a predator might, and Aura is an empty shell, easily broken, and in danger of disappearing altogether as "sus piernas desnudas, caen rotas y vuelan hacia el abismo" (44). Consuelo's open mouth is like the female sex organ; it is bloody and toothless, and to Felipe, it is menacing. He screams at her to go away. In retaliation, Consuelo destroys Aura with a diabolical grin, as her mouth superimposes itself on Aura's mouth and Aura slips away. This dream, like the earlier one, plays with Felipe's fascination with and terror of Consuelo as a sexual being. In large part, the dreams also lay the groundwork for the novella's conclusion, encouraging many readers to think, as Felipe perhaps does, that Consuelo and Aura are, literally, one in the same being. In addition, the dreams invert the message contained in the epigraph, where Jules Michelet writes, "El hombre caza y lucha. La mujer intriga y sueña; es la madre de la fantasía." In the case of *Aura*, Consuelo is the true hunter and fighter. She has fought for a hundred years to preserve her youth, keep her passion alive, and hold on to the man she loves. Felipe is her prey, and Aura is her weapon. Although Consuelo is portrayed in the text initially as the one who dreams and intrigues, it becomes apparent as the story line unfolds that Felipe is more of a dreamer than she is. His fantasies of Aura, his illusions about himself as a romantic hero, and his half-hearted intrigues to manipulate Consuelo and rescue Aura come to nothing. They are only dreams, whereas Consuelo reveals herself to be the one character in the text capable of taking concrete action. This inversion of traditional roles undermines many of the conventions associated with gothic romance and effectively dismantles the power of the male hero to seduce and subdue the female object of his desire.

The Madwoman's Desire

The scene in which the narrator of *La última niebla* finds her ideal lover is similar to Felipe's first encounter with Aura in a number of important ways. As might be expected in a story with gothic overtones, the meeting takes place in a dark, deserted space, "entre la oscuridad y la niebla" (18). The only light comes from a streetlamp in the mist, a light so strange that it makes her own shadow unfamiliar to her. The "silueta confusa" that she does not immediately recognize as her own reveals that her identity has been altered and positions her as an outside observer to her actions, as if a person other than herself were carrying them out. She notes that the stranger appears through the midst, not as an incarnate body but as a shadow, "otra sombra junto a la mía" (18). Like Aura, he approaches in silence and his appearance is unexpected. Like Aura, he does not speak, but instead establishes communication with the narrator though his penetrating gaze. Like Aura, he is so close to the narrator that her vision is distorted and she sees only a fragment of his body. She notes that his face has "un aspecto casi sobrenatural," which she relates to his unusual eyes, "unos ojos muy claros en un rostro moreno" (18) with "pupilas luminosas" (19). His body emanates "un vago pero envolvente calor," which pulls the narrator to him like a magnet (18). Uncharacteristically, she initiates sexual contact with him by throwing her arms around his neck, and when he silently guides her through the dark abandoned streets, she does not resist. This behavior, so atypical of the narrator, is not totally unexpected, since many clues have been planted early in the novella that hint at frustrated desire and lack of satisfaction in her marriage. However, it is difficult for the reader to pinpoint which element in the story is the more shocking and disturbing: the supernatural aspect of the narrator's lover, a nameless man who appears to have materialized from thin air, or the sudden outburst of passion and desire that transforms the narrator into a person we can scarcely recognize as the meek, undemanding woman who appeared in the early pages of the narrative.

In both novellas, unrestrained feminine desire is portrayed as something vaguely threatening and dangerous; however, there is a difference in terms of who might be harmed by it. Felipe has moments of fear and anxiety about his own safety, believing that he may be the victim of a madwoman or a witch. By contrast, the narrator of *La última niebla* expresses no concern about the physical danger she is placing herself in when she agrees to have sex with a stranger, despite her awareness of him as an "almost supernatural" being. At no time does she express fear of him, since her desire for him outweighs all other feelings. Her inability to contain and channel her desire in socially acceptable ways is dangerous to no one but her, since it causes others in the text (and many readers) to question her sanity. One important difference between the two texts is that the narrator of *La última niebla* believes that she is the agent of her own desire, that she is equally desiring and desirous, and she feels comfortable with that role, whereas Felipe is reluctant to give up agency to Aura or Consuelo and surrender desire to a female. He perceives his desire for Aura as normal and natural, but female desire is mysterious, strange, and sometimes horrifying. Consequently, although the two narrators have almost identical experiences with their lovers, they tell their stories in very different ways because of the way they position themselves in relationship to desire and agency.

Another element that the two novellas have in common is the importance of setting. Just as Consuelo's house is a throwback to an earlier era, a historical relic that is falling into ruin, so too is the house where the narrator of *La última niebla* and her lover have their sexual encounter. The "jardín abandonado" is the first sign that the house represents a different world and a different reality for the narrator. The house she shares with her husband is characterized by formal, manicured gardens that require the upkeep of numerous servants, and they stand in strong contrast to the natural world of woods, ponds, and fields that surround them. By contrast, the abandoned garden of her lover's house enchants her. The chains that lock the garden gate are rusty and difficult to open, signaling once again that the house is isolated from the world the narrator usually inhabits and that the passage from one space to another is symbolic as well as physical for her. Inside the house, "la oscuridad es completa," as was the case inside Consuelo's house (19). The narrator cannot see where she is going, and like Felipe, she feels her way through deserted halls and up dark stairs, following her lover who guides her through a space he seems to know well. In the dim light, she makes out "una habitación cuyas cretonas descoloridas le comunican no sé qué encanto anticuado, no sé qué intimidad melancólica" (19). The breakdown of language ("no sé qué"/ "no sé por qué") and the inability to articulate what she sees and feels are further signs that the old rules no longer apply and the narrator cannot depend on past experiences to guide her in the interpretation of what she senses now.

Sensations described as heat, movement, smells, and sounds dominate the narrator's description of the physical act that she participates in with her lover. Here, the multiplicity of senses that are evoked downplay the importance of visual images and call attention to other ways of perceiving experience. This technique undermines any attempt by the reader to occupy the role of voyeur and, instead, encourages us to imagine the sensations through her body rather than see them with our eyes. Hours later when she leaves him, it is her ability to recall physical sensations in detail that makes the experience undeniably real to her. She notes, "Un perfume muy suave me acompaña: el perfume de mi enigmático amigo. Toda yo he quedado impregnada de su aroma. Y es como si él anduviera aún a mi lado o me tuviera aún apretada en su abrazo o hubiera deshecho su vida en mi sangre, para siempre" (21). The use of contrary-to-fact statements here is telling: although they acknowledge, on the one hand, that the sensations she describes are not real, they emphasize the notion that memories can be so vivid that they seem real, as if they were happening in the present moment. The importance of memory and its relationship to the perception of reality is a theme that unfolds in *La última niebla,* just as it does in *Aura*. Yet, the question of whose memories are real and whose memories are invented is a complex one that cannot be easily answered. It is precisely through this gap in the text that the fantastic emerges.

Because of the ambiguous and open way in which Bombal has structured her novella, and because of the poetic, imprecise use of language in the text, many key scenes in the work resist a straightforward, literal reading. *La última niebla* employs many of the strategies associated with the best kind of fantastic literature, carefully laying the groundwork for doubt and hesitation not only on the part of the fictional character but on the part of the reader as well. Structurally and stylistically, the novella allows, even encourages, a certain degree of openness by refusing to take a firm stance on the issue that occupies the central part of the narrative, which is the nature of the relationship that exists between the narrator and her lover. He may be a ghost, he may be real, or perhaps she dreamed him; we simply cannot be sure. The novella's resistance to closure has positioned it somewhat at odds with masculinist reading practices that encourage us, as readers and critics, to impose meaning as a method of control over a work that constantly threatens to escape our grasp. *La última niebla* does not focus on the task of separating the real from the imagined or the supernatural; instead, it permits us to see that the real is an arbitrary category whose meaning can shift and slide, depending on who is telling the story and how much power or authority that person is assumed to have.

In a sense, the novella offers a key to the strategy of its reading early in the text. The second narrative sequence involves the narrator's encounter with a dead girl, apparently at a funeral, where she stands and contemplates "la muchacha que yace en ese ataúd blanco" (11). It follows the opening scene of the novella that is, despite the strange relationship between the narrator and her new husband, Daniel, a fairly realistic description of the their arrival at their country estate on the eve of their wedding. In this initial segment, the narrator discovers (or is reminded) that Daniel is still passionately in love with his first wife, who has been dead for less than a year. She remains curiously aloof from her husband's inner turmoil and grief on their wedding night, turning instead to a pastime that will give the novella its basic narrative structure, the writing of a diary or record of her innermost thoughts and emotions. Here, the theme of escape through dreams is established for the first time, as she records her response to Daniel: "Lo dejo pasar al cuarto contiguo sin esbozar un gesto hacia él, sin balbucir una palabra de consuelo. Me desvisto, me acuesto y sin saber cómo, me deslizo instantáneamente en el sueño" (11). The narrative sequence ends with a brief reference to the following morning, when she awakens to find that she is alone in the bed. Further, the sequence is physically separated from the following entry by a break in the page and three asterisks.

Because of the lack of chronology in the diary, and because the narrator writes in a disjointed style, not bothering to introduce or explain new topics, it is difficult to pinpoint when the funeral episode takes place, or to be sure that it does, in fact, refer to an actual event and not merely a dream or mental image that passes through the narrator's head. Critics have interpreted the scene in vastly different ways, often citing it as an example of the influence of surrealism on Bombal's writing style. Some assert that the dead girl is the narrator, herself, metaphorically killed by the stifling atmosphere of the house, which she compares to "una tumba" (12). Others speculate that the dead girl is Daniel's first wife. Since the narrator and Daniel are cousins, it is possible that she attended the funeral and images of it have remained in her mind; it is equally possible that she is simply imagining the funeral as a reaction to Daniel's obsession with his first wife. Some critics read the scene quite literally, as the funeral of an unidentified dead girl, which the narrator attends for unspecified reasons. There is also ample evidence that the scene may be remnants from a dream, given the oneiric quality of the language and the narrator's cryptic remark that follows her description of the funeral scene: "Desde hace mucho, flota en mí una turbia inquietud. Cierta noche, mientras dormía, vislumbré algo, algo que era tal vez su causa. Una vez despierta, traté en vano de recordarlo. Noche a noche he tratado, también en vano, de volver a encontrar el mismo sueño" (12). An equally convincing case could be made, however, for reading the funeral scene as a foreshadowing of the suicide attempt made by Regina, the wife of Daniel's cousin, at the end of the novella and for the narrator's own brush with death as she leaves the hospital where Regina lies dying. The fact that the same scene can be read in several different ways, all legitimate and all to some degree true, shows to what extent we, as readers, are called upon to impose meaning on the text as we attempt to fill in the gaps with our own interpretations of events. At the same time, however, it teaches us that our readings are nothing more than interpretations based on conjecture, and as such, they can be endlessly deconstructed and reconstructed as our perception shifts and changes. As Jackson tells us, fantastic narratives "frequently point to the serious limitations and inadequacy of language to capture something ineffable, beyond the human and therefore beyond words. Instead, they have resource to a language of allegory and symbolism—suggestive, parabolic, dreamlike, surreal, hinting at supernatural events, sketching them in, for when they are made too literal ... they can become dangerously clumsy and incredible" (*Miss Darrington,* xxii).

Linguistically, the funeral scene is important because it introduces the poetic language that will characterize so much *of La última niebla,* and it calls our attention to the function of the fog or mist, which is to become the central leitmotif of the novella. In this narrative sequence, we experience the same sensation described by the narrator as she attempts to remember her dream and fails: we are left with "una turbia inquietud," a feeling that there is something just beyond our grasp, which we are unable to comprehend. It is, in a sense, the realization that language involves a process of sending and receiving messages and that breakdowns in the system can occur; when this happens, it emphasizes the failure of language to communicate a fixed signification and throws doubt not only on our own ability to perceive meaning in a text but on the narrator's ability to convey meaning to us. For example, although the narrator describes her actions, her feelings, and the setting in which events took place, we are left with the impression that her words do not "make sense" because they do little to clarify the points that are most obscure to us. She does not tell us who the dead girl is, what she was doing at the girl's funeral, when the event took place, or what makes her suddenly shout "¡Yo existo, yo existo . . . y soy bella y feliz! Sí, ¡feliz! la felicidad no es más que tener un cuerpo joven y esbelto y ágil" (12). The equation of happiness with a youthful body is a theme that the narrator will take up later in the text, but at the time she utters these words, they seem out of place. They draw attention away from the mystery (who is the dead girl?) and refocus our attention on the narrator's sense of self. Language becomes, for her, a weapon she can use against what she perceives as "silencio, un gran silencio, un silencio de años, de siglos, un silencio aterrador que empieza a crecer en el cuarto y dentro de mi cabeza"(12). In her diary, she gives language free rein, using words and images that vividly conjure up the strength of her emotions but do little to convey the precise meaning of the scene to us. Unlike traditional narratives, where communication between the narrator and reader appears relatively free of obstacles, *La última niebla* leaves us with the uncomfortable feeling that we are reading a text that is not directed at us. We approach the text not from a straightforward, direct path, but by peering over the shoulder of a woman who is essentially writing for herself and who uses language in a private, therapeutic way. As we discover in this scene, we cannot rely on language alone as a key to understanding the novella, for there often appears to be a layer of meaning behind the narrator's words, which we can glimpse but never fully perceive.

Careful readings have been done of the scene in which the narrator claims to have met her lover for the first time, and of subsequent parts of the narrative where she believes she sees him again. Equal attention has been paid to the scene in which Daniel informs her that she imagined the entire episode, and of her shattering encounter with "reality" when she returns to the place where she thinks her experience occurred and finds it substantially changed. It is remarkable that despite the degree of sympathy critics may feel for the narrator's plight, they have tended to accept Daniel's word as law and to interpret the changed condition of the house to mean that the event described by the narrator never took place. When we compare *La última niebla* with *Aura*, it is significant that Felipe's sanity has not been seriously questioned by critics, but the narrator of Bombal's text has almost uniformly been regarded as a hysterical female, an overly imaginative narrator, or a madwoman. While much doubt surrounds Aura as a character and the question of her existence is never completely resolved in the novella, most readers accept Felipe's words at face value. Aura, if she is supernatural or unreal, is a product of Consuelo's imagination, not Felipe's. Felipe is perhaps deluded in the sense that he seeks an impossible love, but he is generally seen as an innocent victim of the women. By contrast, the narrator of *La última niebla* is seen as the perpetrator of her own delusions, and it is the actual existence of her lover rather than the nature of his existence that is called into question. *Aura* lends itself easily to supernatural readings because we are not sure that Aura is a living woman, but Felipe's perceptions of Aura and his narration of what he sees while in the house carry a certain degree of authority, like Daniel's words. Ironically, we also doubt the mysterious man in *La última niebla* is real, but rather than lead us in the direction of the supernatural, our doubt tends to circle around the narrator's reliability. Bombal's work clearly illustrates that "speaking of things that man has declared nonexistent has always made women vulnerable to charges of exaggeration, neurosis, madness . . . because their way of seeing is not restricted to the central, normal, rational one" (Jackson, *Miss Darrington,* xxii).

Supernatural readings of Bombal's work are not common because critics have tended to accept Daniel's explanation over any other, thereby closing the text to further hesitation and doubt. By most standards, his story is reasonable and possible, whereas the narrator's story appears farfetched and improbable. What determines our perception of possible and probable, however, is a socially constructed norm that privileges the masculine and effectively silences the feminine, thereby denying the female narrator authority over her own text. For example, critical readings have tended to promote Daniel's point of view, accepting the following scenario as the one most likely to have happened: on the night in question, the narrator had too much to drink; she fell asleep and did not wake up all night; she did not go out, meet a man, and make love to him; the house she claims to have visited does not exist in reality; and her belief that the experience was real is proof of her delusional or neurotic personality. The textual details on which this interpretation rests are relatively scant; nevertheless, they provide us with enough information that we could easily construct an alternate reading of the text from the point of view of the narrator, if we were inclined to do so. For example, Daniel also had a considerable amount to drink on the night in question; he fell asleep and, by his own admission, does not remember waking during the night; the narrator went out, met a man, and made love to him; many years later, she cannot find the house where the encounter took place, having visited it only once; or, possibly she does find it but does not recognize it because it has changed significantly over time; her distress at the end of the novella is sadness at the loss of her lover, but not necessarily an admission that he was never real.

A number of details in the text work toward creating doubt and hesitancy about the narrator's experiences, but although the issue remains unresolved on the textual level, critics have tended to read the scene as unreal because the behavior exhibited by the narrator is so unusual and so unlikely for a woman of her class living at that time. For example, the first encounter, as it is described by the narrator, takes place at night in a deserted plaza and, later, in a vacant house. The lover does not speak, nor does she, since they communicate on a purely physical level through embraces, kisses, and gestures. The narrator states that she understands what he wants without his speaking. She follows him to a house that is completely empty, except for a bed in one of the rooms, and she is led through the vacant space in an almost dreamlike state. Before they make love, she has the impression that her lover is watching her, appreciating her beauty. Their sexual encounter is described in poetic terms, emphasizing the physical and the sensual aspects of their coupling, but what is perhaps most remarkable about the scene is that it is narrated without reference to dialogue. Once the man falls asleep, the narrator gets up, dresses, and leaves; she returns home to her husband, who is asleep, and slips into bed without waking him. The similarities between this encounter and Felipe's experience with Aura are striking: both lovers are ghostly apparitions, both are distinctly eerie, and both behave in improbable ways. Both encounters take place during the night, when the narrators had been sleeping or dreaming; both narrators awake fully believing that the episode did, in fact, occur. Why, then, have the texts been read in such very different ways?

The narrator's closing words, "todo se ha desvanecido en la niebla," have generally been taken to mean that she realizes she has been mistaken about her lover: he is not real, her encounter with him was an illusion, and she has wasted her life dreaming about a figment of her imagination. The words themselves, however, do not carry this meaning. As established much earlier in the novella, the narrator is prone to poetic turns of phrase, and she uses language in a highly personal, often ambiguous way. When describing her feelings about her experience, she chooses the verb *desvanecer,* which simply means to suppress or erase an idea or an image from one's mind. It may be that she is referring to nothing more than the impossibility of retrieving the past, or of keeping alive an old memory. Although the narrator appears rather despondent at the end of the novella, there are numerous causes for her unhappiness that are suggested by the text: she is growing older, she feels unloved, her relationship with Daniel is not particularly stimulating or satisfying, she is ill with a fever, she is concerned about Regina's attempted suicide, and she is disturbed by the way in which Regina's lover has apparently abandoned her. All of these elements, added to the narrator's feelings of loss caused by her inability to reestablish contact with her old lover, are sufficient to explain the note of despair on which the novella ends.

Although the narrator does not stop to consider other interpretations of what may have happened, readers can easily do so if inclined. For example, when the narrator attempts to find her lover's house a second time, several years after their initial encounter, she is suffering from a fever and is distraught over Regina's attempted suicide. She is not very familiar with the city, since most of her life has been spent in the country, and she visited the house only once before, at night, in the fog. Her attention was diverted from her surroundings by the intensity of her desire for the mysterious man. Given these factors, it is quite possible that she does not accurately remember the location of the house, and that she visits the wrong place when she seeks it out a second time. Another explanation could be that the lover took her to the house, which was at the time uninhabited (perhaps following the death of the owner?), and in the ensuing years, the man's widow has returned, resumed occupancy of the house, and changed the furnishings to match her taste. Or, perhaps the narrator's lover was the woman's husband at the time; she may have been away when the tryst took place. The woman claims that her husband was blind; he could have been blind at the time of his meeting with the narrator (thus explaining the "casi sobrenatural" aspect of his eyes), or he could have gone blind after meeting her. Because she saw him only in the dark, was with him only a short time, and because she was slightly drunk and excited by the sexual nature of the encounter, it is possible that she could have made love to a blind man without being aware of his condition. Although she believed at the time that he was watching her and admiring her nakedness, it may have been merely a wish on her part that he see and appreciate the slimness and beauty of her body. Whether he was married at the time of their encounter is impossible to know, since no words were spoken between them. Finally, Daniel's theory that the man was a ghost may literally be true, if she visited the house after the death of the man and had an encounter with his spirit in corporal form. While none of these readings are privileged over others, they are textually just as valid as the theory that the narrator imagined her lover. The lack of traditional narrative devices such as a clearly framed chronology make it difficult to know how many years have passed since the narrator's first encounter with her lover. We know only that she had celebrated her tenth wedding anniversary some time before this scene, and shortly after it she notes how old Daniel has become, thereby suggesting an additional passage of time. Considering the looseness of the novella's time frame, it is quite possible that the narrator's lover has been dead for many years, or that at some point he could have moved or otherwise vanished in the mist, as she tells us.

These alternate ways of reading the novella are no more valid than any others that have been put forth by critics, but they do call attention to the open-ended character of the text and show that any conclusions can be dismantled by approaching the novella from a different point of view. So why have critics and readers almost unanimously agreed for more than fifty years that the narrator's voice carries less authority than her husband's in the determination of values like true and real? To dismiss her as nothing more than an example of the unreliable narrator we find in so much contemporary fiction is to ignore the importance of gender-related issues in the novella and in the body of criticism that has grown up around it. The narrator is acutely aware of herself as a woman and speaks to us with a woman's voice, using language in a highly personal way that corresponds to her innermost feelings, with little regard for our reception of it. Through a complex series of interconnecting relationships with other female characters in the text, she speaks not only for herself but also for her sex, despite the degree of isolation in which the individual women live. Her experience becomes, in this light, not so much an individual one but a shared one, for it functions on a symbolic and metaphorical level as a confrontation with feminine desire, and it provides us with a theoretical framework in which we can examine the notion of female agency.

Throughout the novella, the narrator finds herself positioned between two other female characters who have a strong impact on the way she thinks about herself. She can never live up to Daniel's first wife, his dead child-bride, who is "una mujer perfecta" (13); her only other model for womanly behavior is Regina, the unfaithful wife of Daniel's cousin, who exudes raw sexuality. Although the narrator initially feels a certain amount of jealousy and distrust toward Regina, she is also fascinated by the way the woman interacts with her lover. The funeral scene acts as a bridge between two important moments in the narrative: it occurs immediately after Daniel reveals he is still in love with his dead wife, and immediately before the narrator meets Regina and her lover for the first time. The narrator's initial encounter with Regina seals the impression that she will forever have of the other woman: "En la penumbra dos sombras se apartan bruscamente una de otra, con tan poca destreza, que la cabellera medio desatada de Regina queda prendida a los botones de la chaqueta de un desconocido" (13). Finding Regina in the arms of her lover provokes an identity crisis in the narrator, as she becomes increasingly aware of her own sexuality and the lack of passion in her marriage to Daniel. It is not long after this meeting with Regina that the narrator finds her own lover and begins to enjoy the same kind of relationship that Regina has. The narrator's feeling for her lover also echoes the passion that existed between Daniel and his first wife, "aquella muchacha huraña y flaca a quien adoraba"(9). By placing herself strategically between Regina and Daniel's dead wife, a deep interconnection is established between the three women that will be played out in the remainder of the novella.

While we tend to think of *La última niebla* as a love story, and certainly many parts of the novella deal with the narrator's longing for love and fulfillment through a sexual relationship with a man, it is significant that male characters in the work occupy a shadowy role. The narrator's lover, whose very existence is called into question by the ambiguity with which he is treated in the text, occupies her mind not so much as a flesh and blood character, but as an idea, as the representation of desire, and therefore as something that is by its very nature unattainable. Daniel, her husband of many years, elicits little response from her; even when their relationship develops into a physically satisfying one for her, she remains emotionally aloof and indifferent to his presence. At the end of the novella, when he pulls her from the path of an oncoming car, her only response is one of slight surprise, which underlines the little importance she attaches to him as a man: "Aturdida, levanto la cabeza. Entreveo la cara roja y marchita de un extraño. Luego me aparto violentamente, porque reconozco a mi marido. Hace años que lo miraba sin verlo" (42). The narrator's cool, unemotional response to Daniel contrasts strongly to the emotions she feels when she learns of Regina's suicide attempt and offers an important clue regarding her state of mind. As she has done throughout the novella, the narrator finds a reflection of herself in another female character, and by comparing own loss to Regina's, she understands her position better. She realizes that are no models of happiness for her to aspire to: Daniel's first wife, the girl of his dreams, died after only a few months of marriage, and Regina, the unfaithful wife, has been driven to suicide by her lover's abandonment. The notion of romantic love, so enviable in the novella's early pages, has turned out to be an illusion, and it is perhaps the loss of this dream that the narrator mourns more than anything else.

Bombal, like Fuentes, problematizes the notion of feminine desire and suggests that once it is unleashed, it becomes a dangerous and destablizing force. Clearly, one way to neutralize the threat is to strip the female body of its ability to attract, seduce, and exert any form of power over the male. In the case of *La última niebla* and *Aura*, this shift is achieved through the image of the aging or aged woman who still feels desire but who is no longer desirable to her male lover. Felipe's horror at finding himself in bed with Consuelo is an extreme example, but Bombal's narrator also condemns herself to a future without love, believing that her once youthful body has now become "carnes mustias y pegadas a un estrecho esqueleto, un vientre sumido entre las caderas" (42). She is "una mujer casi vieja, qué cosa repugnante e inútil," and she laments that "un destino implacable . . . me ha ido acorralando lentamente, insensiblemente, a una vejez sin fervores, sin recuerdos . . . sin pasado" (42–43). Her slow descent into nothingness reminds us of Consuelo's long life as a widow, completely shut away from the world, unloved and unwanted.

No longer able to attract and hold a lover, she slips into what she calls an "inmovilidad definitiva," a permanent mist that shrouds her and makes her invisible (43).

* * *

As Kathleen Woodyard has observed, "For women, the cultural dichotomy of youth and old age has long been underwritten by the biological dividing line between the reproductive and postreproductive years, with the symbolic date of older age for women understood as coinciding with menopause around the age of 50" (168). It is, perhaps, no coincidence then that the aging narrator of *La última niebla* sees her future as a blank slate. Anne Fauto-Sterling's study of postmenopausal women shows that in Western culture, women's usefulness is tied to their reproductive capacity, and that menopause means the "death of femininity"; the postmenopausal body is believed to be more prone to disease, and the aging female is seen as "emotionally unstable, depressed, hysterical, irritable, even insane" (170). As late as 1945, doctors and psychologists continued to tell women that "at menopause woman has ended her existence as a bearer of future life and has reached her natural end—her partial death—as a servant of the species" (Deutsch 458). If, as Nancy Chodorow claims, sexual love "is a fulcrum of gender identity, of sexual fantasy and desire, of cultural story, of unconscious and conscious feelings and fears about intimacy, dependency, nurturance, destructiveness, power and powerlessness, body-construction, and even of self-construction" (71), then the absence of the possibility of sexual love for an aging woman would signify the inevitable erasure of selfhood. The aged female body, no longer able to engender or act on sexual desire, becomes a symbol of the abject, that which culture abhors and excludes as a way to sustain itself.

The aging narrator of *La última niebla* and the hundred-year-old Consuelo stand in strong contrast to their youthful selves, emphasizing the difference that age makes in our perception of them as desirable and desiring women. Because of their aging bodies, they are denied an outlet for that desire, and the fantastic emerges in the narratives as a result. The fantastic becomes a way of creating and nurturing an impossible love, a sexual union in which the female's ability to possess the male is at least as strong as the male's ability to possess her. The lover in the text, whether real, imaginary, or supernatural, allows us as readers to explore some of our preconceived notions about women, their sexuality, and their bodies. The qualities that make Aura so attractive to Felipe are the same qualities shown by the narrator of Bombal's text when she interacts with her lover: she is the agent of her own desire, a powerful female who steps outside conventional behavior to act out her sexual fantasies. This inversion of roles is dangerous, however, since it positions the male lover as the desired object rather than the desiring subject. It becomes even more threatening when the female is no longer young and beautiful because it calls into question the relationship between desire and the aging female body. In the case of Consuelo, desire takes on nightmare proportions, and in *La última niebla*, it is systematically erased from the text. Both narratives call attention to gender-related issues and make us question our perceptions of unrestrained feminine desire as a threatening and potentially dangerous force. By linking the desiring female to the emergence of the fantastic, they effectively problematize the restrictions that have been imposed on female agency in gothic romances and interrogate the relationship between the fantastic and the female body.

6 / Women Writers of the Fantastic

Whenever an author sits down to write a piece of narrative fiction, one of the first issues he or she must face is the question of who will tell the story and from what perspective. More than a mere technical detail, the choice of narrative voice and the vision that gives rise to that voice implies an ideological stance on the part of the writer, for as Michel Foucault has taught us, no aspect of the enunciation process can be regarded as an innocent and neutral practice. When an author settles on a given way of seeing and speaking, he or she automatically privileges one set of ideas or one group of people over another. Whether the text seeks to uphold the status quo or subvert it, whether it works within the bounds of an empowered discourse or explores the creative possibilities of marginalized and/or unrecognized discourses, it will ultimately say something to us in favor of or against the "normal" way of seeing and voicing human experience. The notion that there is some kind of universal truth, some absolute knowledge, or some inherently correct way of perceiving the world has come under a good deal of attack in recent decades, both from Foucauldians and feminists who have each in their own way attempted to show how Western society has been dominated by hierarchical modes that privilege a masculine elite. With increasing frequency, women writers have experimented with narrative strategies through which they might appropriate the male gaze and the male voice, transform them into something more authentically feminine in character, and employ them as tools in the creation of a female body of literature. One way in which women have attempted to accomplish this goal is to use the subversive capacity of the fantastic to undermine patriarchal authority and disempower male discourse. Through the fantastic, alternate ways of seeing, thinking, feeling, and speaking are presented for consideration and are often subtly upheld as viable models for emulation. While these texts seldom address radical feminist concerns in a straightforward manner, they nevertheless can be considered feminist works, for they provide, at least temporarily, the marginalized and muted members of patriarchal society a voice with which to speak. In this manner, they call attention to the limitations imposed by the rationalizing discourses that have characterized so many of the "Great Works" produced by male writers and they open our field of vision to encompass that which has previously been unspoken, unwritten, and unseen.

Obviously, the fantastic is not a literary mode that is limited to or dominated by women writers; nevertheless, as Jackson has observed, women are especially attracted to the fantastic as a way of subverting patriarchal society and the norms of a male-dominated symbolic order. According to Jackson:

> The dominant literary forms in Western culture from the eighteenth century onwards have been realistic and mimetic. . . . There has been no room in such fiction, nor in such a worldview, for anything not immediately knowable, for anything invisible, unseen, inexplicable. These areas have been prohibited from mainstream literature just as they have been tabooed by culture at large; a rationalistic, materialistic, scientific, and secular culture has restricted its definition of the "real" to what is familiar and under rational control. This culture is also a patriarchal one, and many of its values and definitions are male-determined. . . . To challenge this history of writing by producing texts that are outside the frame of reason, that are anti-reason, unreasonable, unrealistic, is to simultaneously challenge the "reality" that frame contains and upholds—the "real" as defined by a materialistic, masculine, patriarchal culture. (*Miss Darrington,* xvii)

In this sense the fantastic, like feminism, can be regarded in Foucault's terms as a "reverse discourse" for both systems challenge the normalizing powers of society's "regime of truth," or the mechanisms through which truth and knowledge are produced and disseminated. Jackson believes that women writers use the fantastic "to provide serious explorations and dramatizations of issues at the heart of human existence.

They raise profound questions about the nature of identity, about the limitations surrounding earthly experience, the restrictions of body, mind, space and time, the distinction between life and death" (*Miss Darrington,* xvii). The expression of these concerns is by no means limited to fantastic texts written by women. Nevertheless, what sets women's writing apart from similar texts produced by men is an insistence on viewing the events narrated from a distinctly feminine point of view and on speaking (or writing) in a way that addresses women's frustration with a system that has for so long worked to exclude them.

The stories to be examined here, "Su demonio privado" by Elvira Orphee, "El robo de Tiztla" by Elena Garro, and "El cuaderno," "El goce y la penitencia," and "El vestido de terciopelo" by Silvina Ocampo, employ a number of narrative strategies that lead us to question the authority normally attributed to first-person male narrators and the omniscient narrative voice that speaks from the perspective of a male. At the same time, they show us that for a woman "to speak—or to try to speak—is to experience difficulties in finding an appropriate speaking-position in an andocentric mode of discourse which designates men as the enunciators and relegates women to the position of the enounced" (Ruthven 60). By undermining the telling-power of the male speaker and authorizing that of the female, these women writers create a space for the feminine fantastic, where ambiguity in the text reflects the ambiguous position of women in patriarchal society and the ambiguous nature of language itself. The question of who speaks and who sees is an essential one for these writers because, as Todorov and others have observed, it is the *perception* of events rather than the events themselves that brings the fantastic into being. John Berger posits, "The way we see things is affected by what we know or what we believe. . . . We see only what we look at. To look is an act of choice" (8). If our gaze as readers is directed and manipulated by a gaze inside the text that focuses our eyes on certain images and away from others, we can scarcely call our perceptions our own; yet, as the stories we have set out to examine here show us, we seldom pause to reflect on the fact that we are looking through someone else's eyes rather than through our own once we are caught up in the thread of a narrative. Only by making us aware of how the process works to exclude marginalized discourses from mainstream literature can women writers of the fantastic call attention to the eye behind the "I" who speaks and the power it exercises over us in shaping our worldview.

Addressing the Limits of Language

"Su demonio privado" by Orphee and "El goce y la penetencia" by Ocampo provide interesting contrasts to one another in the sense that both stories are narrated from the first-person point of view, yet the experience of narrating is entirely different for each of the speakers. The male narrator of "Su demonio privado" reveals himself to be incapable of penetrating what he perceives to be the essential Otherness of the female; his inability to see her clearly, to capture her image visually or verbally, or to make sense of his relationship with her results in a narrative that is fragmented, incoherent, and full of puzzling gaps. It is through these gaps, of course, that the fantastic emerges, but whether it is a consequence of supernatural forces, a manifestation of madness, or a misreading/ mistelling of information presented in the text is a question left open to the reader's imagination, since the narrator's confusion about the story he has set out to tell does not permit us to grasp it in any concrete way. "El goce y la penitencia," by contrast, is a relatively straightforward narrative. It is told in the first person by the story's female protagonist, who experiences the fantastic and relates it to the reader with ease. Tension is created in the text not by her own doubt and uncertainty about the nature of what she relates but by her refusal to look for explanations or to offer logical conjectures to us as readers. The supernatural does not pose the same threat to her that it does to the narrator of "Su demonio privado" because in her mind it is linked to positive elements (sexual gratification, spiritual communion, motherhood, an escape from a tedious marriage) rather than to negative forces (sexual jealousy, fear, aggression, violence, death), as is the case with Orphee's tortured male speaker. Perhaps for this reason, Ocampo's protagonist sees no need to understand the fantastic or to explain it but is content, instead, merely to acknowledge its presence in her life. As readers, we may choose to believe her story or not. We may look for explanations and arrive at our own logical conclusion that negates the fantastic in the tale, but the narrator does not lead us to these actions. The model she provides for us is one of quiet acceptance, flexibility, and openness to things that have no rational basis but that nevertheless touch our hearts and minds. By suggesting that there is more than one way to view reality and by granting power (albeit temporarily) to a marginalized discourse, Ocampo calls attention to the ways in which we as readers have been conditioned to respond to male-dominated discursive practices as if they were "normal" and "natural" rather than see them as the ideological constructs they are. "Su demonio privado" carries a similar message but conveys it in a different way. In Orphee's tale, it is through the breakdown of language and the fragmentation of the speaking subject that the authority of the male voice is decentered. It is the male narrator's inability to find an absolute truth and voice it, his inflexibility when confronted with anything that lies outside rational understanding, and his stubborn adherence to a discursive system that is inadequate for his needs as narrator that ultimately lead him to madness. His refusal to bend when confronted with the impossible demands of "normalcy" points to the rigidity of the system and to its imperfections, thereby undermining the notion that any discursive system can encompass all facets of human experience and speak for all people.

The title of "Su demonio privado" gives a clue as to the narrative strategy that will be used throughout the story because it is intriguing and it encourages us to read on in hopes that its meaning will become clear. Yet even as we read it, we realize that words are being used and combined in a purposely ambiguous way that may represent an obstacle to us as readers. The possessive pronoun *su* could refer to any number of people and the odd mixture of the adjective *privado* with the noun *demonio* suggests that we are not dealing with ordinary devils or demons but, perhaps, with something symbolic or metaphorical that plagues some individual in the story that we are about to read. It is not immediately clear as we turn to the text who the narrator is, from what perspective the story is going to be told, through whose eyes it will be focalized, or who the main characters of the story will be. The first paragraph would lead us to believe that we have a third-person omniscient narrator who will focus on the master painter. However, the narrator's unexpected confession that he does not know what the painter is thinking and can only conjecture about it effectively undoes our initial impression of the narrative voice that is being used in the story and presents us with an alternative theory that the narrator may be one of the characters in the story who is witnessing the events he describes. This impression is confirmed immediately when the *yo* reveals itself in the second paragraph, but we still do not have a clear notion of who the narrator is or what his relationship is to the characters he describes. He appears to be directing himself to a listener or a reader outside the text, but he does little to clarify the story he has set out to tell. Characters are introduced only obliquely and without any indication of their role in the development of the narrative. Fragments of their conversation are wedged in between the narrator's commentary about portrait painting, his observations about the scene he is witnessing, and strange non sequiturs that reveal his thoughts about life and art. Although his words are ordinary enough, they are combined in unexpected ways that produce ambiguous, jumbled meaning. For example, he explains that he is not able to paint the young female model who has appeared in the master's studio because she too closely resembles the painting of San Giovanni Battista by Leonardo DaVinci, "aunque esta vez fuera mujer y tuviera cabellos lisos en lugar de abultados" (61). What this young woman has in common with a male saint is never addressed in any direct way; instead, the narrator closes the subject to further speculation by emphatically stating, "Habilidad y reincidencia podrán dar combinaciones premiadas, pero el premio a la recaída en la misma sonrisa se viene prolongando demasiado" (61). While these kinds of enigmatic statements do little to advance the plot or develop characterization, they effectively show us that we are dealing with a story that foregrounds its own enunciation practice. The difficulty we have in grasping the meaning of the narrator's words, in identifying the object of his gaze, or in piecing together the narrative fragments he appears to offer at random suggests that at least one valid reading of the story's title would permit us to see "su demonio privado" as the narrator's painful struggle to tell his story in a way that makes sense both to himself and to us as readers. Rather than smooth over the troublesome process of molding language into meaning, Orphee's narrator calls our attention to the gaps that exist between what is perceived and what is said, between what is thought and what is put into words, between what we are told and what we understand those words to mean. By telling a story whose meaning seems to lie continually just beyond our grasp, the narrator of "Su demonio privado" makes us aware of how dependent we are on the voice and the vision that guides us through any text and how strongly we rely on that voice and vision to help us make sense of what we read.

The narrator's opening remarks about his inability to paint an image of the young female model foreshadow the difficulty he will have when he attempts to create a verbal portrait of her in the text; as he confesses early in the tale, "¡De ella supe siempre tan poco!" (63). His lack of knowledge, however, does not prevent him from telling the story from his own point of view. He describes the way in which they met, fell in love, married, and produced a child, stressing his own thoughts and feelings but systematically excluding the female from any role in the text other than that of the passive object of his gaze. Despite the almost clichéd elements of his story, the tale does not unfold in any predictable way because the narrator is constantly distracted from the thread of his narrative by random thoughts about the female's impenetrable Otherness and about the difficulty of understanding her words or actions. He is particularly troubled about his wife's past because it excludes him; he tells us, "Quería meter sus recuerdos en mi vida" (67). But the impossibility to doing so brings him face to face with the fantastic or the strange forces that shape the woman's life to fit the image he has created of it in his imagination. Since he cannot participate in the woman's past or appropriate her memories and make them his own, the fantastic enables the narrator to control the woman's future but only in a way that erases chronological boundaries and collapses her life into a single, still frame. Shortly after their marriage, she begins to receive mysterious photographs of herself in poses that she cannot recognize, with people she does not know, and in places she claims never to have been. The narrator, unable to accept her at her word, assumes that she is lying and interprets the photos as proof that his wife had a child before her marriage to him and that she is hiding the unsavory details of her past life. Gradually, however, the narrator begins to suspect that the photos do not reflect the past at all, but rather show what is going to happen in the future. He also becomes convinced that his wife's destiny is somehow being controlled by an enigmatic figure referred to in the text as el Desconocido. According to the narrator's theory, el Desconocido represents everything that his wife wants and desires; therefore, he regards el Desconocido as his greatest rival. Ultimately, it is jealousy of el Desconocido's control over the female that drives the narrator to destroy her. When he sees a photo of his wife's dead body laid in preparation for her funeral, he believes that el Desconocido plans to kill her. In order to "save" her from el Desconocido's grasp, he concludes that he must be the one to kill her (in a way that does not correspond to the image in the photo, so that the prediction cannot come true). He believes that his wife's pride makes her incapable of resisting el Desconocido's power over her; as he puts it, "Quería ser tan desconocida como el Desconocido que había rastreado antes ferozmente" (86). Therefore, he concludes:

> No me quedaba, por amor, otro remedio que hacerme cómplice de su orgullo. Le llevé la comida yo, llena de un somnífero, forcé la puerta más tarde, la vestí, me la llevé cayéndose y levantándose hasta el automóvil, corrí distancias, lancé la máquina contra un árbol y salté afuera. Se incendió sin que yo tuviera que hacer esa horrible cosa que temía: quemarla. Oh no, él no la tendría con las manos piadosamente cruzadas. (86)

Apparently, the narrator feels that the murder of his wife was justified because the most important goal in his life is not to understand the woman or to build a better relationship with her but to act in such a way "para burlar al Desconocido, para que supiera que eso él no lo había previsto" (87). Throughout the story, the narrator explains his hostility toward his wife, his jealousy, and finally his murder of her as the effect of the fantastic rather than of his own doing; yet, the unreliability of his voice as narrator makes us suspect that we may be dealing with a madman rather than with a victim of the supernatural. A psychological reading of the story does not reduce the fantastic effect since there is no way for us to penetrate the many layers of ambiguity that have been woven into the text through the breakdown of language and the absence of traditional narrative structures. How can we attach clear meaning to anything the narrator relates when we are never entirely sure what he is trying to tell us? To dismiss the supernatural as the ravings of a madman is to impose an extradiegetic solution to an intradiegetic problem. But the text itself offers no clue as to how we are to interpret the meaning of what we read. To accept the narrator at his word is almost out of the question since we can make no sense of what he tells us, but to impose our own reading on the story is equally problematic because the text does not provide us with the information we need to draw meaningful conclusions. By positioning us in this kind of narrative void, Orphee encourages us to interrogate the entire process of narration, to see the restrictions that are automatically imposed by the writer's choice of one narrative voice over another, to question the ability of any narrator to tell an absolute and unshakeable truth, and to consider the ways in which language sometimes functions as a barrier to communication rather than as a bridge to it.

"El goce y la penitencia" tells a story that is very similar to the one contained in "Su demonio privado," but it is told from a female point of view and in the words of the story's female protagonist. Here, a young woman visits a painter's studio to have a portrait made of her son. Over time, the woman and the painter become attracted to one another, first as friends and then as lovers; they take advantage of the portrait sessions to consummate their relationship while the woman's son is locked away in the attic, happily playing games on his own. The painter, however, like the narrator of "Su demonio privado," does not seem to be able to capture his subject's image on canvas; he finally produces a painting of a child, but it is a child who in no way resembles the woman's son. As it turns out, this painting like the photos in "Su demonio privado" reflects something that has not happened yet: it is a portrait of the child the woman is going to have in the future, and it shows what he will look like when he is five years old. Not surprisingly, the father of the new child is the painter of the strange portrait. As he was committing the child's image to canvas, it seems he was simultaneously impregnating the woman with his son-to-be. These "facts" are related by the female in the most open and direct way possible. At no point does she hesitate over the nature of the events she describes, nor does she stop to wonder at the apparent impossibility of what she tells us. She expresses a certain amount of amusement at the joke that has been played on her rather boring husband, and she delights in the new child's resemblance to the portrait that was painted of him, but she does not seem to be concerned with the supernatural implications of her tale or feel it necessary to explain to us how the impossible took place. She treats it, instead, as if it were all a coincidence, one that is entertaining and pleasing but not necessarily important enough to merit speculation or comment. She dismisses it by simply stating, "Nunca sabré si ese retrato que tanto miré formó la imagen de aquel hijo futuro en mi familia o si Armindo pintó esa imagen a semejanza de su hijo, en mí" (215).

Neither explanation is possible in rational terms, yet both are acceptable to her. She does not insist on establishing hierarchies of truth in her story; for her, there are multiple truths, multiple ways of looking at things, and multiple ways of understanding. Her willingness to admit that there are certain things that she "will never know" opens a space in the text for that which lies outside of language, for that which cannot be spoken, seen, or understood but that nevertheless forms a part of her life experience. Unlike the male narrator of "Su demonio privado," she does not allow herself to be bogged down by the desire to understand or to possess knowledge about things that are, in essence, unknowable. She tells us what she can, skips over what she cannot tell us, and openly admits the shortcomings of language when it fails her: "A veces quisiera reproducir esos diálogos que eran el fruto de mi aburrimiento; no puedo" (212). While the narrator of "Su demonio" must undergo a rather lengthy and torturous process of mental gymnastics to arrive, finally, at the conclusion that he is dealing with the fantastic, the narrator of "El goce" appears to accept this possibility at once, without hesitation or doubt. Both narrators ultimately embrace the fantastic as reality, but once the narrator of "Su demonio" becomes convinced that he is the victim of fantastic forces, he attempts to dominate those forces by giving them a name (el Desconocido), by humanizing them (el Desconocido = a rival for the wife's desire), and by creating a parallel system of topsy-turvy reason that will allow the fantastic to function as a substitute for and a mirror image of the world of the narrator. The rules of the Desconocido's world may be different, but the narrator still understands the game: if only he can penetrate his rival's thoughts and second guess his motivations, then he has a chance of winning the contest. He learns to think like el Desconocido and to see the world through el Desconocido's eyes, just as a soldier in battle learns to think like his enemy in order to survive. The narrator of "Su demonio" sees the fantastic as a threat or a challenge that must be dealt with in a decisive, forceful way. In his view, it cannot be allowed to exist in peace, side by side with the real world, for patriarchal society has conditioned him to believe that two opposing systems cannot simultaneously occupy the same space. The weaker one must be relegated to a position of less importance, while the dominant one rises to the top. The narrator of "El goce," however, appears to be free of such conditioning. In her story, the fantastic does not stand in for the real world, but instead forms a part of it. She does not approach the fantastic with an antagonistic attitude, nor does she attempt to justify its existence. For her, it simply *is*.

Tension is created by somewhat different means in the two stories, then, due to the differing attitudes professed by the two narrators. In "Su demonio," tension is built into the text through the ambiguous use of language, the resulting breakdown of the narrative process, the gaps in communication between the narrator and the reader, and by the reader's mistrust of the narrator's reliability due to the ineffective way in which the latter tells his tale. The narrator insists that hierarchies of truth be established and that one vision of reality be upheld at the expense of another. His inability to arrive at an absolute truth that is meaningful both to him and to us underlines the flaws in the system through which truth is created and communicated. Eventually, it deconstructs his power as narrator. In "El goce," the narrator does not attempt to close the narrative to a wide spectrum of interpretations by offering explanations of how the impossible came to pass; instead, she redefines the meaning of the impossible and suggests that there are multiple layers of truth behind any story. It is the lack of tension on the intradiegetic level that produces tension extradiegetically, for we have been conditioned to expect in fantastic narratives some degree of doubt or hesitation built into the actual telling of the tale. When we are confronted with a narrator who appears to have a solid grasp of reality as we know it and when she relates her experiences in language that is simple and direct, we expect the story she tells us to conform to the basic notions of what we consider possible and real. When she calmly tells us a story that lies outside of these established boundaries, we are at a loss as to how to proceed: we cannot accept the story at face value without changing some of our notions about the laws that govern the universe, yet on what basis can we dismiss the narrator's words as untruths? She does not appear to be mad, as the narrator of "Su demonio" might be. If she is lying to us or playing with us, there is no clear indication in the text that she is consciously doing so. In fact, there is no reason for us to think that she is even aware that what she tells us transgresses the limits imposed by traditional mimetic fiction. The fantastic comes into being through our reluctance as readers to believe her, not through doubt and hesitation on her part. The unknowable, unseeable, or unspeakable does not disturb her; instead, it disturbs us to find a narrator so unwilling to acknowledge the doubts and reservations that we may feel. She neither helps nor hinders us in the interpretation of the text, but instead leaves us to reach our own conclusions about the story she tells. If we insist on engaging in a power struggle to establish hierarchies of truth, we must engage in the struggle alone, for she appears immune to these pressures. She is content to let the fantastic exist side by side with the real, without establishing relationships of opposition and antagonism. Our reluctance to do the same underlines the power that hierarchical thinking exerts on us and the limitations that it imposes on those who speak through marginalized discursive systems.

Speaking from the Margins

Ocampo's "El vestido de terciopelo" is a more direct attack on patriarchal order in the sense that it makes us aware of how our vision is controlled by the coercive gaze of a narrator and it suggests that the act of seeing, like the act of telling, is never entirely free of bias. Here, the first-person narrator acts as a witness to events portrayed in the text rather than as the story's protagonist. It is through her eyes that the speaking "I" of the tale is focalized, and by stubbornly directing our gaze toward elements in the narrative that do not seem central to the telling of the tale, she frustrates our desire to see, to know, and to understand what lies at the heart of the story. Like the narrator of "El goce," the narrator of "El vestido de terciopelo" is at ease with the art of narration. To her, the story she tells makes perfect sense. It is complete and coherent, and it carries the message she has set out to convey. The problem for us as readers is that she does not tell us the story we expect to hear. How did the fantastic come about? What possible explanation can there be for the supernatural phenomenon she describes? Perhaps more importantly, why does she not respond to the supernatural with fear, hesitation, or uncertainty? As narrator, her actions go against the grain of what we normally find in fantastic fiction, and it is through this inconsistency that the story achieves its full effect. It reminds us that the fantastic exists only when someone *perceives* that it exists; through the use of a narrator whose vision does not necessarily match our own, "El vestido de terciopelo" leads us to question how our perceptions are shaped, reinforced, or subverted by the "I" who controls our gaze as the story unfolds before us.

The narrative voice used in "El vestido de terciopelo" is that an eight-year-old girl, one that normally lacks authority in mainstream adult fiction. In Ocampo's story, however, it is somewhat more difficult to dismiss her child speaker because it is apparent that the girl has already joined the ranks of the urban working class and she has seen enough of life to erase some of her childish innocence. She is the assistant to a seamstress named Casilda, whom she accompanies to the home of wealthy clients. Contact with the rich has made her aware of her own poverty; with a jaundiced eye for one so young, she notes the luxurious surroundings in which her clients live and she compares it to her own neighborhood where the streets are marred by "perros rabiosos y quema de basuras" (144). Despite the narrator's youth, she is keenly aware of irony, especially when it involves class differences. The constant exclamation of "¡Qué risa!" that she directs toward us throughout the story invites us to look through her eyes at "la señora" and her wealth and to see how they appear to a young girl who is excluded from that kind of life. For example, when the señora asks her, "Cuándo seas grande . . . te gustará llevar un vestido de terciopelo, ¿no es cierto?" the narrator replies "Sí," but she thinks, "sentí que el terciopelo de ese vestido me estrangulaba el cuello con manos enguantadas. ¡Qué risa!" (146). Apparently, it does not occur to the señora that a poor child will never be able to afford to wear the kind of clothes she makes for her clients. For the child, however, the weight of that reality is suffocating, as is the need to respond blandly to the señora, to keep silent and let her true feelings go unvoiced. By contrasting the child's thoughts and observations with the insipid commentary of the señora throughout the story, the child emerges as the one who has a better understanding of real life.

Most of the story is a description of the fitting of a black velvet dress that the señora has ordered for a European vacation, and the narrator insistently focuses on the work the seamstress has put into the dress, as well as on the dress's fine details. She is particularly impressed by a sequined dragon embroidered on the bodice, and she is intrigued by the way it seems to have a life of its own. Numerous times throughout the brief story, the narrator observes that the señora has trouble getting the dress on past her head. This observation is usually followed by the exclamation of "¡Qué risa!" that so frequently punctuates her narrative. The woman's problems with the dress grow progressively more serious, however, until at the story's conclusion the child remarks, "La señora cayó al suelo y el dragón se retorció. Casilda se inclinó sobre su cuerpo hasta que el dragón quedó inmóvil" (147). Neither Casilda nor the child responds to this event in ways that we would expect. The child pays no attention to the woman on the floor, but instead calmly strokes the velvet dress, "que parecía un animal" (147). Casilda, somewhat more practical, remarks, "Ha muerto. ¡Me costó tanto hacer este vestido! ¡Me costó tanto, tanto!" (147). Both Casilda and the child appear to believe that the woman was strangled by the velvet dress, but this thought only evokes the usual "¡Qué risa!" from the narrator. It is possible, of course, that the woman died of natural causes, but remarks throughout the story about the velvet clinging to the woman's neck, her difficulty in breathing whenever she puts the dress on, and the child's offhand reference to the velvet of the dress as a "género sobrenatural" seem to confirm that the woman was killed by the dress (146).

What is most disturbing about "El vestido de terciopelo" is the narrator's refusal to show or tell us "what happened" in the story. What she gives us is a story about dressmaking, with the supernatural entering only in the most indirect and coincidental way. It seems strange to those of us who are used to reading fantastic tales that a narrator would not take advantage of the mysterious elements in the story to build tension and create doubt or hesitation in us. The narrator of "El vestido," like the narrator of "El goce," does not appear to distinguish between the ordinary and the extraordinary; she mentions things that strike us as impossible in the same breath as she describes the most common daily occurrence. While we yearn to know more about this strange dress that may have the ability to kill people, she tells us about the way Casilda pins up the hem of the skirt or smoothes out a wrinkle under the arm. Her final dismissal of the woman's death with "¡Qué risa!" strikes us as inadequate; nevertheless, she apparently has no more to say on the subject for she ends her story without further comment. Like the narrator of "El goce," she leaves us to make of the story what we will. It does not appear to concern her that we may find her version of events lacking in detail or insufficient in terms of rational explanation. She has shown us (and told us) what she considers to be important, and she implies that if we are not satisfied with her story, it is our problem rather than hers.

Underlying the lighthearted tone of Ocampo's stories, there is a serious message about power and the role it plays in the creation of a work of fiction. Whether we realize it or not, our vision and our perceptions are being guided and shaped by a narrator. At times, the narrator hides behind an assumed objectivity and appears to be neutral. But as these stories show us, what a narrator chooses to see, to voice, and to reveal to us is never the result of a natural practice. What a narrator defines as possible, normal, or real influences the way he or she tells the tale. If the concepts expressed and described mirror the thinking of mainstream society and if they are conveyed in a way that does not call undue attention to the enunciation process, the end result of the narrative will generally be considered "realistic" or "true." If, by contrast, they describe an alternative vision of the world and reflect a different way of perceiving or speaking, or if they are communicated in a way that reveals the shortcomings of language or a breakdown in the narrative process, we tend to react to these works as unrealistic or untrue. What we seldom stop to consider, however, is that our perceptions in fiction are never entirely our own. They have been shaped for us to a large extent by the culture in which we live, where rational, patriarchal discourse is upheld as the normal or natural one, and marginal discursive systems are silenced, ignored, or treated with skepticism. A narrator may speak from within the mainstream or from the margins, and while we may respond differently depending on the position from which the story is told, we must remember as we read that no fiction can be more true than another, since both are literary creations, and as such, they reflect an ideological bias.

Wallace Martin has observed that a narrative written in the first person "may prove unreliable because it issues from a speaking or writing self addressing someone" (142). He goes on to say, however, "We cannot question the reliability of third-person narrators, who posit beyond doubt or credulity the characters and situations they create" (142). Women writers of the fantastic would challenge this statement, since the authority, reliability, and discursive power normally attributed to third-person narrators are reflections of patriarchal authority, which generally does not extend to female speakers. As Kathleen Jones puts it, authority demands "some sort of surrender of private judgment—at least in the weak sense of submitting to the judgment of another without making conduct dependent on one's assessment of the merits of the command" (123). Jones believes that "the very definition of authority as a set of practices designed to institutionalize social hierarchies lies at the root of the separation of women qua women from the process of 'authorizing'" (120). Perhaps for this reason, we tend to associate, at least on an unconscious level, the authority of the omniscient narrator with a male rather than a female voice. Seldom do we stop to think about the gender of a third-person narrator as we read, but as feminist critics have shown us, language is never gender free. Therefore, a narrator whose job it is to shape language into meaning for us cannot speak from a sexually neutral position. Behind the omniscient voice, there is still an "I" through whose eyes the story is being focalized. Narrators may absent themselves from the story's frame, of course, but the vision and choice of words that brings the narrative into being still reflects a given way of looking at the world and of transforming images into language. Ruthven asserts, "What are inscribed in our society as cultural practices are reaffirmed as literary conventions, and give the illusion of justifying their existence by imitating life. But 'life' itself, of course, is never pre-given and unconstructed, but always and already culturally coded" (77). Garro and Ocampo play with the fact that as readers we tend to make assumptions about the omniscient narrator's relationship to mainstream, patriarchal culture and rationalizing discursive systems, and they show us how our assumptions can sometimes be wrong. If we are to continue to trust in the reliability of third-person narrators, they suggest, then we must redefine the basis on which we grant authority to narrative voices in a text so that it extends to those whose point of view may differ from our own. By testing our faith in what an omniscient narrator knows and can tell us and by questioning the source of the authority with which a narrator speaks, Garro and Ocampo point out that reliability is never inherent in a speaking voice but is, instead, attributed to that voice by us as culturally conditioned readers.

In Garro's "El duende," "La semana de colores," and "El robo de Tiztla," we are led to believe that we are dealing with a traditional narrative voice that will ultimately untangle the supernatural elements in the story and restore logic and reason to a world that has been turned upside down. In contrast to the characters in these stories who as young girls appear to be gullible and naive, the omniscient narrator strikes us as mature and worldly. We are led to believe that this narrator, unlike the characters, can distinguish reality from fantasy. The girls may believe in fairies, ghosts, people who speak with the tongue of an animal, and other extraordinary beings, but the narrator suggests we are not to take them seriously. We who have left our childhood behind can see (like the narrator) that the children are misreading information and arriving at the wrong conclusions; we laugh along with the narrator at their childish assertions and beliefs. An air of complicity is thus created in the tale between the narrator and an adult reader that encourages us to distance ourselves from the characters and view them as incapable of perceiving or understanding truth. It is as if we were sharing a joke with the one telling the story at the expense of those about whom the story is being told. We are made to feel superior to the child characters, simply on the basis of our maturity and their lack of it. The narrator speaks with authority and in a voice that inspires trust and confidence. Naturally, we expect it to provide the answers to the questions it raises in the text and that these answers will uphold our traditionally held beliefs about what is possible and real.

There is, however, a degree of duplicity at work in each of these tales because all the while the narrator is establishing complicity with us and encouraging us to feel superior to the characters, we are being slowly drawn into their world. The narrator's omniscience allows for the penetration of the children's thoughts and feelings. But this penetration, in effect, causes the focalization to shift, gradually and subtly, so that we are not immediately aware that a change in perspective has taken place. It is only when the story ends that we realize we are no longer looking at the events described in the text through the eyes of an adult narrator but through the eyes of a narrator who sees the world as a child does. Contrary to our expectations, it is not the mainstream view of reality put forth by patriarchal society that triumphs, but rather the worldview of the marginalized and disempowered. By supporting the children's point of view rather than our own and by asserting that the children's perception of events is the correct one, the narrator forces us to reevaluate the qualities we had attributed initially to the voice guiding us through the tale. It seems necessary, after all, to question the reliability of a third-person narrator, for the narrators we confront in Garro's stories are *not* beyond doubt or credulity. We doubt what we are told because it does not conform to our preestablished notions about the nature of the universe that we inhabit and because an empowered discourse has been appropriated by those who normally lack power. In other words, the tale is told in a way that seems inappropriate to us, and it is therefore troublesome, regardless of how we choose to deal with it. If we dismiss this narrator as one who is unreliable, then we can no longer assume that third-person narrators always "posit beyond doubt or credulity the characters and situations they create" (Martin 142). This posture threatens to deconstruct the authority of the omniscient narrator in general and the foundation on which a large body of our literature rests. If, by contrast, we respect the narrator's authority and accept without question the truth of the story we are told, we will have to embrace a worldview that we have been conditioned to believe is not valid in our culture. This stance threatens to decenter patriarchal authority in another way because it opens the doors to marginalized discourses and grants power to those whom the system has sought to exclude.

Of the three Garro texts mentioned here, "El robo de Tiztla" is the most duplicitous in construction since it misleads us on several different levels. Not only are we led to have certain false notions about the adult and child characters in the text and the nature of reality as it is portrayed in the tale, but we are also deceived about the identity of the narrator as well. The main body of the text appears to be narrated by a third-person omniscient speaker, similar to the one who narrates the other stories. This narrator, however, strikes us as slightly more objective than the one who guides us through the other tales because no particular effort is made to emphasize the children's point of view over that of the adults. Language is more concrete and less poetic and from the opening remark, "Tiztla es una pequeña ciudad situada al Sur de la República de México" (123), we see that we are dealing with a text that is grounded in a recognizable reality. The narrator goes on to describe the inhabitants of the town, particularly those in the household of don Antonio Ibánez where a robbery took place, and he or she reports with a minimum of interference the conversation that occurred between the police who investigated the crime and the women who witnessed it. Evita, one of the child characters in the story, is interrogated by the police along with a number of adults, but no more insight is given into the workings of her mind than to that of any other character. Evita has very little to say for herself, and the narrator observes, "Si algo vio la niña, no se supo nunca. Ella se empeñó en guardar silencio y fue inútil que los demás estuvieran pendientes de sus labios" (133). The other child character in the story, a servant girl named Lorenza, is completely mute. As Evita's mother puts it, "la pobre de Lorenza . . . se asustó tanto que perdió el habla" (135). Despite the supposed omniscience of the narrator, he or she seems unable or unwilling to penetrate the thoughts of the characters or to put forth any opinions about the events under narration. Instead, he or she merely sums up the way in which others interpret the crime, including a reiteration of the official police report:

> La única conclusión plausible era que aquellos extraños visitantes

> eran enemigos de don Antonio. ¿Y qué hacen los enemigos si no el mal? Durante varios días en Tiztla no se habló sino de los "enemigos." A medida que las lenguas los pulieron, se transformaron en enemigos cada vez más extraños, hasta que un día tomaron la forma de demonios. ¡Claro! Por eso la niña Evita nunca quiso decir lo que vio y Lorenza perdió el habla.
>
> El jefe de la policía redactó un acta en la cual explicaba detalladamente la visita noctura efectuada por los demonios en la casa de don Antonio Ibánez. El acta relataba todas las formas extravagantes que adoptaron los demonios esa noche memorable, como destruyeron un pabellón y un jardín y "la ronda del fuego infernal" que hicieron. La sirvienta Lorenza Varela perdió el habla a causa de lo que presenció esa noche, lo cual prueba que fue algo del otro mundo, ya que nunca se pudo saber qué fue lo que la hizo quedar muda. (136)

The interjection of fantasy here, unlike that found in the other stories, is supplied by the adult characters rather than by the children or the narrator. The narrator's distance from the event and the reluctance he or she shows to express an opinion confirms our initial impression that we are dealing with a voice that is impartial and reliable. We can see for ourselves from the summary provided for us that perfectly ordinary events have been transformed into supernatural ones through imagination, exaggeration, and gossiping tongues. The use of quotation marks to set off key expressions ("enemigos," "la ronda del fuego infernal") shows that they are the words of the characters in the story rather than the narrator's own. It also signals that the words are being used in an ironic way and that they should not be interpreted literally. In fact, an ironic reading of the entire passage is encouraged by the use of inappropriate discourse (the official language of a police report) for the narration of material borrowed from folklore (*demonios*), a technique that creates a humorous effect in the story and shows that this explanation should not be taken too seriously. Despite the presence of supernatural elements in the story, then, it is easy to read "El robo de Tiztla" up to this point in a text that is basically realistic in content and in tone. It portrays life in a small town in Mexico and focuses on the tendency of people there to create a dramatic event out of an ordinary occurrence.

In the final segment of the narrative, however, the story takes a turn in a different direction when the omniscient narrator suddenly begins to speak in the first person. This passage reads: "El misterio quedó encerrado en la mudez de Lorenza y en el silencio de Evita. Hoy, muchos años después, Evita, que soy yo, se decide a decir la verdad sobre el robo de Tiztla" (136). The discovery that the narrator is and has always been Eva opens the text to reinterpretation. Eva as an adult assumes the powers of an omniscient narrator in the first part of the tale in an attempt to objectively describe an event that occurred during her childhood. Not surprisingly, this objectivity brought her no closer to the truth than the other adult characters in the story. So long as she persisted in the role of a third-person narrator, she was forced to maintain a distance between herself and the child character, Evita. Her "omniscience" went no farther than the level of understanding reached by the adult characters in the tale, whose comprehension of events was finally reduced to absurdity by their blatant distortion of the facts. Only by recasting herself as the child, Evita, can the narrator uncover the truth because Evita is the only character in the story who possesses any degree of real knowledge. As the police commissioner correctly surmised many years before, "Esta mocosa sabe todo," (135) but we must wait until Evita decides to tell us what she knows.

The question naturally arises as to whether the narrator is trustworthy, since she has deceived us up to this point. However, the confessional tone of her remarks in the final segment is designed to draw us into the text and to make us feel that we are privy to secret information that others have long been denied. Furthermore, Evita seems prepared to carry out her promise to us: she explains that the robbery was the result of a childhood prank, that the thieves were not demons, but rather local boys hunting for nonexistent buried treasure, and that Lorenza was only pretending to be mute because she did not want anyone to suspect that she had played a part in luring the thieves to the house. In this way, the official "truth" created by adults and expressed in the police report is debunked and overshadowed by a second "truth" that seems more realistic and acceptable to us.

The truth is not as simple as it appears, however, since Eva adds an epilogue to the tale that once again pushes it into the realm of the fantastic. Speaking from the perspective of Evita, the child, she states: "Lorenza tenía una ventaja sobre mí: era hija de una bruja y su conocimiento del misterio era muy vasto" (137–38). This observation might be dismissed as childish fantasy if not for the adult Eva's firm support. Eva explains:

> Lorenza perdió el habla muchos meses, hasta que su mamá bajó de la cuadrilla donde vivía, en las cercanías de Chilapa. Mató a un

> conejo en el lugar en donde aparecieron los demonios que se llevaron la lengua de su hija y pronunció unas palabras mientras se llenaba las trenzas de ceniza. Desde entonces Lorenza pudo hablar con lengua de animal. Y con ella sigue hablando hasta ahora. (140)

As if she senses our reluctance to read this statement in a literal way, she quickly adds: "Y era verdad que su voz había cambiado. La lengua del conejo era demasiado chica y apenas le alcanzaba para hablar suspirando" (141). As in the other stories, the narrator's final statement does not actually close the text, but instead opens it up to multiple interpretations and the task of constructing "la verdad sobre el robo de Tiztla" remains in the hands of the reader.

On the surface, Garro's stories about children and their special vision of the world offer us a nostalgic, often humorous look at childhood and provide us with some insight into the workings of a child's mind. Beneath the surface, however, they transcend their subject matter and become complex, intricately woven studies of the conflicting ways in which human beings perceive reality. Garro attempts to redeem and give substance to a vision of the world that stands in opposition to that of mainstream society in order to subvert the notion that there is only one correct way to view reality. In order to realize this goal, a certain degree of duplicity must be used since we would most likely resist the attempt if it were carried out in a more straightforward way. Instead, we are misled time and time again in Garro's stories, and ultimately, we are left to find our own answers to the questions raised in the text. But by putting us in a position in which we ask questions about the experience of reading and examine the processes through which we grant authority or deny it to narrators, Garro has taken a step toward turning mainstream, patriarchal discursive practices inside out and creating a reverse discourse that speaks for those who are normally denied a voice.

Ocampo accomplishes a similar feat in her story, "El cuaderno," and uses a similar strategy to call our attention to phallocentric reading practices, but by casting an adult female in the role played by Garro's child characters, she dramatizes the way in which an omniscient narrative voice can marginalize women and make us turn a blind eye to the ways in which a woman's conception of reality might differ from a man's. Here, as in Garro's tales, tension is created through the juxtaposition of opposing ideas about what is real and possible. The protagonist, a simple, working-class pregnant woman named Ermelina, believes that she can determine the way her baby will look if she stares long enough at a given image. She borrows a notebook from her neighbor's child, which contains a picture of a blue-eyed, blond cherub; she commits the picture to memory; then, she takes a bus to the hospital where she promptly gives birth to the child. We are left behind in the apartment to chuckle at the note she leaves her husband, which reads: "El niño está por nacer, me voy a Maternidad, la sopa está lista, no hay más que calentarla para la hora de la comida, la figura que está en la hoja abierta de este cuaderno es igual a nuestro hijo, en cuanto la mires llévale a la señora Lucía que me lo ha prestado" (74–75). Up to this point in the narrative, the pregnant woman has been presented as a childlike, irrational being, and nothing has prepared us to think that the narrator might actually share her point of view. As in Garro's stories, the narrator has maintained a careful distance from the characters and, without clearly stating an opinion, has suggested that the women's ideas have no basis in reality. We imagine her husband's reaction to the note she has left and we laugh, believing that it is impossible for a woman to shape the physical image of her child by looking at a picture. The story ends, however, with the narrator confirming that this is, indeed, what happened: "Entre envoltorios de llantos y pañales, Ermelina reconoció la cara rosada pegada contra las lilas del cuaderno. La cara era quizá demasiado colorada, pero ella pensó que tenía el mismo color chillón que tienen los juguetes nuevos, para que no se decoloren de mano en mano" (76).

As was the case with Garro's stories, focalization in "El cuaderno" has gradually shifted from the eyes of an outside observer to those of Ermelina, thus making us see reality from her perspective and denying us access to any point of view that would contradict her impressions. It has been accomplished by duplicitous means, however, for if the narrator had begun the tale by establishing an obvious solidarity with the marginalized characters, our willingness to trust in the reliability of that narrator would have, no doubt, been diminished. With very little effort, the narrator manages to convince us in the early paragraphs of the text that Ermelina (and the other females in the story) are not to be taken seriously because the foundation on which their knowledge rests is faulty. We, in turn, are likely to dismiss the women's ideas as "female nonsense" simply because their thinking is not based on masculine reason and logic. To reverse this tendency, or to make a space in the text in which Ermelina's perspective can be presented with any degree of authority, can only be done through subversive means. We must first be shown what we want to see, so that we can identify the narrator as one who is reliable and trustworthy. Once we believe that the narrator is going to tell us the truth, we no longer ask questions about the basis of the authority on which the narrative rests. In this way, we can be led almost anywhere he or she wants to lead us. Only when our expectations are thwarted do we stop to examine how we have been taken in the wrong direction. We look more carefully at the narrator's words and try to see where he or she first began to trick us. If we continue to unravel the story all the way back to its beginning, we will ultimately end up with the question of why we were reluctant to see through Ermelina's eyes from the start. If her version of reality is the one that ultimately triumphs in the tale, why did we automatically suppose that a different vision of reality was more legitimate than hers? This question and others like it make us aware why women must often struggle to be heard and why so much literature written by women deals in one way or another with the need to deconstruct, decenter, or subvert the narrative process itself.

Jackson believes that fantastic fiction written by women has historically "constituted as much of a threat, in its own implicit way, to masculine culture as any explicit militancy against patriarchy's silencing and disempowering of women that these authors may have enacted on a social level. They are intimating a world, a consciousness, a reality, *larger* than the one that man has controlled" (*Miss Darrington,* xviii). She also notes that they are "attempting to find a language, a different literature, other than the one forged by men, to articulate senses and experiences which are frequently *beyond* words, beyond social definitions altogether" (*Miss Darrington,* xviii). These observations, while true, cannot be limited exclusively to works written by women; obviously, the fantastic is cultivated by both male and female writers, and regardless of the author's gender, it is a subversive type of literature that calls attention to the indeterminacy of man's relationship to a universe that he has so systematically attempted to order and bring under control. Whether the fantastic is more threatening when it issues from the pen of a woman is a question open to debate and merits further study. What is clear, however, is that women feel a strong attraction to the fantastic as a mode of expression precisely because it allows them to voice concerns about the way mainstream, patriarchal culture has traditionally limited their access to discursive power.

According to Jones, "The dominant discourse on authority silences those forms of expression linked metaphorically and symbolically to 'female' speech," since "this discourse is constructed on the basis of a conceptual myopia that normalizes authority as a disciplinary, commanding gaze. Such a discourse secures authority by opposing it to emotive connectedness or compassion" (120–21). It is perhaps not coincidental, then, that women writers turn to the fantastic in literature as a means of breaking those rules that not only define the basis of authority in our culture but also limit concepts such as possible, real, and true to that which has traditionally been visualized by men. Jones believes that "'female' hesitancy and other-oriented language patterns, considered as the marks of uncertainty or confusion, are derogated" in our patriarchal society (122), yet it is worth noting that the fantastic as a literary form validates language that gives rise to uncertainty, confusion, and hesitation as the very element that brings the genre into being. As feminists have shown us, "reason has been constructed as a masculine domain that is divorced from and deemed superior to the senses, emotion, and imagination" (Diamond and Quinby xvi). The fantastic deconstructs this domain and interrogates the limits that have been imposed not only on the way we think but also on the way we see, the way we use language, and the way we respond to literary texts. Clearly, the bonds between the fantastic, the questioning of patriarchal authority and the process by which it is granted to a speaker, the resistance to imposed order, rules, and limits, as well as the use of language to undermine the illusion that this imposed order is natural and normal are visible in the works we have examined here. This is not to suggest that women writers of the fantastic literally believe in the fantastic events they describe in their stories, nor should we assume that women in general accept the supernatural with the same ease as some of the characters in the narratives we have studied here. There is in this kind of fiction a notable desire to challenge the normalizing powers of patriarchal, mainstream literature, but to replace one system with another is merely to reinforce and promote the hierarchical thinking of the discursive system they wish to subvert. As Jackson has observed, the fantastic is a fiction dealing with an *extension* of the idea of what is possible or true. Women writers who attempt to extend the definitions to include experiences that have traditionally been ignored or overlooked by rational discursive systems do not promote one way of looking at the world over another. Instead, like some of the characters and narrators presented here, they explore the possibility that there may be multiple realities, multiple truths, and multiple interpretations of a single event, depending on the position from which one is looking and speaking.

7 / Cinematic Encounters with the Fantastic

Film criticism has tended to regard the fantastic as a broad category that encompasses horror, science fiction, and fantasy, with little attempt to differentiate between the various subgenres. Beneath this tendency lies the supposition that film, as a visual art, differs from the fantastic in literature and cannot be expected to produce the same kind of effect. Theorists like Todorov, Caillois, and Jackson have argued that the fantastic is born from hesitation or doubt on the reader's part about the nature of the story being told; he must vacillate between a natural and supernatural explanation. In literature, the fantastic element often exists outside of language because it resists representation and remains invisible or unnamed. It does not correspond to our known set of linguistic signs and signifiers, nor does it conform to our lived experiences. It exists in the minds of the characters as something that cannot be known or understood, and it enters the text through linguistic voids that encourage readers to fill them with their own imaginings. In cinema, the need for visual images to tell the story puts obstacles in the path of the filmmaker who wants to suggest the fantastic without explicitly encoding it into the text. Many films use fantasy to good effect, and technology has made it possible to create images on screen that have no basis in reality. But once the supernatural has been given concrete form on screen, most viewers recognize it as a cinematic device and it no longer provokes the frisson of hesitation and doubt that is sine qua non for the fantastic in fiction.

In *Cinema of the Fantastic*, for example, Steinbrunner and Goldblatt consider fantasy and the fantastic to be one in the same thing, and they describe it in a broad way to refer to any kind of film that can "express for audiences around the world man's fantastic speculations and nightmares" (1). They elaborate by saying, "The cinema of the fantastic . . . embodies the meanings of a highly varied group of adjectives—bizarre, poetic, unearthly, satanic, haunting, horrific, imaginary (although an individual movie may not be all of these). Its essence is fantasy, though not in the Disney sense, and it ranges from fairy tales to monster movies" (1). To illustrate the various forms that fantastic cinema might take, they choose for analysis fifteen films by German, French, and North American directors, ranging from Fritz Lang's *Metropolis* (1927) to Fred McLeod Wilcox's *Forbidden Planet* (1956). In addition to classic "horror" movies from Hollywood (*King Kong, The Black Cat, The Bride of Frankenstein*), they include a number of films inspired by fairy tales / folktales (*La Belle et la Bête, The Thief of Bagdad*), as well as several examples of science fiction (*Invasion of the Body Snatchers, The Thing*). Similar to the literary theorists who discussed the fantastic in the early 1970s, Steinbrunner and Goldblatt tend to limit their discussion of the fantastic to themes found in the films and to the sociohistorical context in which the films were produced.

More recent studies suggest that although film scholarship has become more sophisticated with regard to the discussion of specific works, there is still no general agreement among critics about how the term fantastic should be used with reference to film or what techniques are associated with it. To some degree, the interpretation of what constitutes the fantastic in a film is directly linked to the film under discussion, making the term applicable to everything from animated cartoons to science fiction. For example, films as diverse as *Star Trek* (Robert Wise, 1979), *Vertigo* (Alfred Hitchcock, 1958), *Brazil* (Terry Gilliam, 1985), and *The Ghost and Mrs. Muir* (Joseph Mankiewicz, 1947) have been discussed as examples of fantastic films, and while it is true that they all offer an alternate vision of what is "real" and "true," as the best fantastic fiction does, it is difficult to conceive of them as a single, unified genre because they vary a great deal in approach and handle the subject matter in vastly different ways.

Phillip Johansen has attempted to refine the use of the term to bring it more in line with the way literary theorists use it. For example, he links Kristin Thompson's concept of "cinematic excess" to Todorov's theory of the fantastic in his discussion of Ingmar Bergman's *The Magician*. He describes the "cinematic fantastic" as one where the film viewer is forced to make the same kind of decisions as Todorov's implied reader. Johansen believes that "excessive filmic elements evoke Todorov's 'fantastic' dilemma, which involves choosing between supernatural and 'explainable' rationale for experience," and he asserts that Todorov's ideas about the fantastic can prove useful in terms of understanding the complex nature of film codes (327). He acknowledges that the choices a viewer makes are slightly different than those outlined by Todorov, but they are equally important: "The 'reality' within Todorov's fantastic genre is now filmic reality. And like the reader of a 'fantastic' work, the film's spectator must decide whether or not an excessive object is truly subversive. That is, the spectator must decide if an object threatens existing narrative 'reality'" (328). Films that introduce elements that require us to reconstruct the existing world of the characters (what is presented in the film as "reality") through the introduction of ambiguous elements are the most effective in creating the fantastic effect.

In Latin America, where Hollywood films have generally dominated the market and created a taste for blockbuster hits, native-born filmmakers have tended to shy away from supernatural themes. One notable exception is the Mexican horror movies made throughout the 1950s and early 1960s on very low budgets with virtually unknown actors, largely to fill the needs of the drive-in movie audience in Mexico and in Spanish-speaking areas of the southwestern United States. Popular series featured the Aztec Mummy, vampire women, and zombies, usually matched against a foe like Santo (a popular masked wrestler), Samson, the Doctor of Doom, wrestling women, the human robot, the living head, or the invisible man. Although in recent years these films have acquired a kind of cult status among movie fans in the United States, in Latin America they are generally regarded as a chapter best omitted from the annals of filmmaking.

Only a handful of directors in Latin America have attempted to treat supernatural themes in a serious way. For example, film critic Roger Ebert calls the Chilean-born Alejandro Jodorowsky (who has made most of his films in Mexico) "a collision between Freud and Fellini." His films, such as *La montaña sagrada* (1973) and *Santa Sangre* (1989), are filled with phantasmagorical images and hallucinatory visions that may cause viewers to feel uncertain about the nature of what they are seeing on screen, but because the world of the characters is one where the bizarre is the norm, it is difficult to think of it as the world we know. Jodorowsky's work, like that of Luis Buñuel, is a poetic universe onto itself, rich in symbolic meaning but ultimately not fantastic, since it does not ask us to believe at any point that what we are watching represents the "real." Alfonso Arau's popular film, *Como agua para chocolate* (1992), also wanders into supernatural territory, but in tone and style it is more typical of what we think of as magical realism. The characters accept that the marvelous is part of their everyday lives and express little consternation when something that is seemingly impossible comes to pass. The magical qualities of food and love are woven into the plot as naturally as scenes portraying the violence of the Mexican revolution. *Santitos* (1999) by Mexican director Alejandro Springall is similar in the way it uses elements from popular culture, folklore, and Catholicism to substantiate the magical worldview of the characters. Daniel Greuner's *Sobrenatural* (1996) comes closer to the fantastic, for it deals with the possible existence of witchcraft and voodoo in modern Mexico City and presents the idea of the supernatural alongside growing proof that the film's protagonist, Dolores, is delusional. Nevertheless, the film lacks the kind of ambiguity that allows the fantastic to operate effectively in the text. All of the characters, including the psychiatrist who has been hired to cure Dolores, come to believe that they are dealing with a voodoo curse, and the final sequence, where we see Dolores's husband turned into a zombie, offers visual proof that we are dealing with a world where the supernatural is the norm. Guillermo del Toro is, without a doubt, the most famous director of horror films in Mexico, but it is important to note that most Mexican movie-goers are more familiar with his English-language films imported from Hollywood (*Mimic, Hellboy, Blade II*) than they are with his Spanish-language films (*Cronos, El espinazo del diablo, El laberinto del fauno*). Del Toro's films by and large follow Hollywood formulas, albeit with original twists and creative camerawork, and as in many popular horror films, there is little left to the imagination. Vampires, ghosts, monsters, mythical creatures, aliens, and mutants appear on screen and interact with human characters. The viewer feels suspense not because of the nature of the events he witnesses, but rather because he wants to know how the film's protagonist will escape danger and possible death at the hands of the supernatural menace. Although they are successful as horror films, they do not produce the reaction we associate with the fantastic in literature because for the time we are watching the film, there is no doubt that the supernatural exists in the world of the characters and we are supposed to accept this condition as part of the experience of watching the film.[1]

The Fantastic Films of Eliseo Subiela

The fantastic in film may produce fear, anxiety, or a thrill of excitement, but because it often takes a form that the viewer can almost immediately dismiss as unreal, it is unlikely that viewers will confuse fantastic worlds with their own. However, films that shy away from visual representation of the supernatural face the problem of how to insinuate without naming, without showing something that is outside the text and has no specific form. If the fantastic element exists nowhere outside of the characters' minds, the film veers into the genre of psychological thriller and is generally read in that light. While fiction writers face some of these same challenges, the filmmaker must consider additional factors due to the visual nature of the craft: How can viewers doubt what they see with their own eyes? Is it possible to see/ not see at the same time? Can the fantastic appear in a film without destroying the illusion that the film represents real human experiences and real human lives? Theories of the fantastic have most often discussed its relationship to written texts, but is it possible to extract some of the ideas expressed by theorists and apply them to a visual text? Johansen's discussion of Bergman's *The Magician* suggests that this is so, but how does the fantastic manifest itself in Latin American cinema?

Argentine director, Eliseo Subiela, has attempted to address these questions in films such as *No te mueras sin decirme adónde vas (Don't Die Without Telling Me Where You're Going)* (1995) and *Hombre mirando al sudeste (Man Facing Southeast)* (1986).[2] Known as the auteur of ambiguous, open-ended films that seamlessly weave possibly fantastic events into the fabric of everyday life, Subiela leaves viewers unsure about the meaning of what has unfolded on screen. Using cinematic techniques such as montage, overlapping editing, and crosscutting, he successfully creates structural tension between a world we recognize as real and one outside the boundaries of what we know as possible. His multifaceted, complex characters lead apparently normal lives, but may come from outer space, or return from the dead as spirits, or move objects with their minds, or construct the future through dreams. Whether they perform supernatural feats or merely believe they can is difficult to determine, since Subiela frequently uses point-of-view shots to limit our vision to what the characters see or imagine. He creates then reconfigures images of the supernatural by juxtaposing establishing shots that contain slightly different configurations of the characters and their surroundings. Visually, he presents the impossible as if it were possible, making the most unlikely events seem real by grounding them in the daily lives of the characters who are ordinary in almost every way. Given the narrative gaps in the films, it is difficult to say if what we have seen is the supernatural, a dream, a delusion, madness, or the literal representation of a poetic turn of phrase. The shifting boundaries between the real and dreamed, the lived and the imagined, the true and the invented keep viewers suspended between parallel worlds and allow hesitation and doubt to become an integral part of the text. As in the case of the best fantastic literature, the fantastic in Subiela's films emerges from the interstices between what we see, what we do not see, and what we imagine to be possible. They encourage multiple and open-ended interpretations of events portrayed on screen, but discourage monolithic readings of the film. Instead, we are left with the unsettling feeling that the supernatural and natural are overlapping and amorphous categories.

No te mueras sin decirme adonde vas is a good point of departure for an investigation into the techniques used by Subiela to create the fantastic in film because it deals with the relationship between film and life. It also questions the limits of human knowledge, the impact of technology, and the role of memory and dreams in the construction of lived experience. In the opening sequence of the film, for example, a North American inventor named William (James Murray) explains to his boss, Thomas Edison (Ricardo Fasan), that he is working on a machine that will be "un preservador de sueños." According to William, this device will provide:

> La posibilidad de imágenes que alivien, imágenes que liberen, imágenes que curen, imágenes que devuelvan la esperanza, la maravillosa posiblidad de miles de personas soñando el mismo sueño al mismo tiempo, la posibilidad de vencer la muerte. Esas imágenes van a estar ahí para siempre. Seres moviéndose, amándose, odiándose, metidos para siempre en una máquina, que podrá proyectarlos sobre una pantalla como una ventana por la que pueden echar a volar los sueños liberados, un preservador de sueños, para que no se esfumen cuando nos despertamos, cuando volvamos a la espantosa realidad.

This scene reminds viewers that what is normal and commonplace at the end of the twentieth century—in this case, cinema—was fantastic at the end of the nineteenth century when William first imagined the concept. Ten years before the Lumiére brothers would project the first moving images on a screen in Paris, William describes a device that is, as yet, unknown in New Jersey, where he works and lives. Edison, a visionary and dreamer in his own right, answers noncommittally, "Suena interesante, William, sigue trabajando y téngame informado." Shot in sepia tones with soft filters, the scene stands out visually from the rest of the film and serves as the framework for everything that follows. It presents the notion that there have always been people in the world who can believe in something that does not yet exist; they do not need to see in order to believe. True visionaries can see with their imagination.

The next scene shows that the device William invented, the movie camera, has come about just as he envisioned it, but ironically it does not protect him from "the horror of reality" or give him "a chance to beat death." Instead, it records the most painful moment of his life and preserves it for future generations. We now see a grainy, poorly preserved sepia print of a silent film, accompanied by piano music, in which William stands at the grave site of his beloved wife, Rachel (Mariana Arias). In the next shot, a close up of Rachel's photograph dollies out to become a medium long shot of the piano she once played, and then continues around and behind William, so that we see him staring at the photograph. Although the same piano music bridges this shot and the funeral scene, we understand now that it is a nondiegetic sound that triggers William's memory. It represents his dead wife, who was an accomplished pianist. The camera cuts to a close up of William's face, followed by a counter shot close up of Rachel's face in the photograph; an eye line match and careful framing create the illusion that they are looking at each other, even though we know that Rachel is dead. Unexpectedly, the next shot is a somewhat jarring but amusing moving picture from a zoetrope, a child's toy that is sometimes regarded as a primitive form of cinema. It is followed by a rapid cut to a medium long shot of William looking at the zoetrope, which dissolves into an extreme close up of William's eyes as he watches the images, then dissolves into another medium long shot of William asleep in his chair with the zoetrope in his hands. Finally, the camera dollies in to a close up of his sleeping face and then the shot fades out to white. Although the introductory scenes are very brief, they are extremely important for they plant the seeds for a fantastic reading of remainder of the film. It is never clear if what we see is William's dream, a film within a film, or if William has been reincarnated, as Rachel claims, and now occupies the body of the film's protagonist, Leopoldo (Darío Grandinetti). These early scenes also establish some of the important themes that the film will explore. Cinema, photographs, and sound recordings can serve as reminders of human experience, but cannot replace it. They preserve images, but not the essence of those we love. Man can master technology, but he cannot control life. These ideas are reinforced through the mise-en-scene: Rachel's photo and the sound of her piano suggest her presence, but at the same time signal her absence. The zoetrope is reminiscent of William's "dream preserver," but it also evokes a lost dream, the child that he never had. Much of the remaining film deals with the efforts of characters to recapture lost dreams and to recognize new ones when they present themselves.

The following sequence in the film begins with an extreme close up of hands threading film through a film projector. It is shot in color and has the texture and appearance of a film from the late twentieth century. It has no music, only the diegetic sound of the film running through the projector. A cut to a medium close up reveals the face of Leopoldo, a character we have not seen before, who is the film projectionist. As he makes the last connection to set the film in motion, the sound of Rachel's piano suddenly explodes in the silence and the screen fades to white, followed by the film's title and credits. The sound bridge of Rachel's piano music provides a clear link to the film's introduction, but just as important is Leopoldo's fascination with the mechanical gadgets and his connection to the movies. When William dreamed of cinema in 1885, he could not foresee what movies would be like in 1995, when Leopoldo projects films in a nearly empty movie theatre every night. Leopoldo, who inherited his job as projectionist from his father, is the last of a dying breed. The public no longer finds the world of movies fascinating and marvelous; in a world of computers, digitized video, Internet, and cell phones, a trip to the local movie theater is unnecessary and unappealing to most people. Leopoldo's boss feels compelled to sell the theater to an evangelical church, which attracts people though spectacles and promises of redemption, just as William imagined his "dream preserver" would do.

Another element that links Leopoldo to William is that he is also an inventor, and he is working on a device of his own which he calls the "recolector de sueños." Although his machine takes a different form, its purpose is essentially the same as that of William's invention. Leopoldo believes that he can record his dreams by connecting his head to a monitor while he sleeps, and that his dreams can be projected onto a television screen the next day so he can experience them while fully awake. His wife, Susana (Mónica Galán), is a practical woman who worries about how to pay the bills and calls his inventions "cachivaches inútiles." Leopoldo assures her his invention "puede revolucionar hasta el psicoanálisis," but Susana bursts into frustrated tears at her husband's folly. The lack of communication and understanding between Leopoldo and Susana has brought the marriage, after twenty years, to an emotional dead end. It stands in stark contrast to the deep love between William and Rachel, and it opens the doors to Leopoldo's encounter with the fantastic. Rachel first materializes in Leopoldo's dreams, and soon afterwards, she begins to appear during his waking hours as well. In fact, she becomes the living proof that his invention works, even though she takes spirit form and remains invisible to everyone but him. Rachel provides information from the world beyond about death, reincarnation, and Leopoldo's past lives so that the film advances using its own internal logic. For example, Leopoldo accepts that he is madly in love with a woman he has never met because Rachel convinces him that he is William reborn. Because he longs for love and understanding, he finds Rachel's explanation plausible; because he wants desperately to believe that his invention works, he feels sure that Rachel exists. Upon his first encounter with her, he admits, "Yo sé que es imposible que estés aquí. Pero te estoy viendo. No me importa que seas una halucinación. Quiero saber quién sos."

It is significant that the first scene between Rachel and Leopoldo takes place in the empty movie theater. This is a setting where fantastic images are projected on the screen as a matter of course. As Leopoldo looks from his projection booth to the main floor of the theater, he tells his boss, don Mario (Tincho Zabala), that he sees a woman there. When Mario goes down to investigate, we have a point-of-view shot from Leopoldo's perspective that shows Rachel standing behind Mario, yet Mario is gesturing to Leopoldo that the theater is empty. In the next shot, we see Leopoldo in the foreground and Rachel in deep focus, with Mario absent from the frame. This time, Rachel's piano music is audible, and we hear her voice for the first time. Leopoldo speaks to her and attempts to touch her, but his hand passes through her body as if it were air. Despite the look of incredulity on his face, he seems to accept the story she tells him when she explains she is a spirit who has come back in search of her great love, William, and in the next shot, we see Leopoldo on the phone in the theater lobby explaining to his friend, Oscar (Oscar Martinez), that "la mujer del sueño está aquí." During this shot, Leopoldo's point of view is maintained so that we see Rachel standing in the lobby as he talks on the phone. Then, as he returns to Rachel's side and continues his conversation with her, the camera cuts to a close up of don Mario, who is watching Leopoldo with a confused and worried expression on his face. Leopoldo looks back at Mario, and we see both Leopoldo and Rachel in the frame. However, as Leopoldo walks out of the frame, the point of view shifts and a high angle long shot reveals that Leopoldo is alone in the lobby. Leopoldo exits the theater, and the camera remains on don

Mario, who continues to look disconcerted; this conveys to viewers that Leopoldo is acting in a strange manner and throws doubt on Rachel's existence.

The next sequences in the film elaborate and expand on the techniques used previously to create a fantastic effect, allowing Rachel to appear and disappear mysteriously before our eyes, although the time she is on screen far outweighs the shots in which she is absent. These scenes provide her with an opportunity to explain and illustrate her experiences in the spirit world, which gives the film its own internal logic and blurs the boundaries between imagination, science, and metaphysics. Initially, Leopoldo seems torn between the belief that she is a hallucination and the desire to believe she is real. A medium long shot shows Leopoldo and Rachel standing together at a street corner, yet he does not speak to her or look at her. It seems, for a moment, that Leopoldo is no longer aware of her presence, yet a shift in point of view and a close up of Leopoldo's face in the next shot reveal great alarm. We see Rachel cross the street, floating through space, with complete disregard for the cars that are passing through her body. While her body is clearly visible on screen, special effects create the impression that other objects—cars—occupy the same space at the same time. Leopoldo's face expresses his disbelief and shock at seeing something he had previously believed impossible, but it also conveys fear and anxiety about her safety, as if she were a real woman. As he tries to reconcile what he sees with what he believes, Rachel experiences a similar kind of disjunction: for her, the achievements of the late twentieth century—neon lights, automobiles, tall buildings, modern shop windows, fashions, cinema—are completely outside her realm of knowledge; yet, they make up the setting in which she now finds herself. The shot/ counter shot arrangement of this street scene reminds us that many of our perceptions about reality depend on experiential knowledge, which is always limited.

A similar situation occurs when Leopoldo and Rachel arrive at Leopoldo's house and his wife, Susana, accuses him of talking to himself. She exclaims, "Uno de los dos está volviendo loco!" but it is clear that she thinks it is Leopoldo who has lost his grip on reality. As Susana serves dinner, we see Rachel in deep focus moving around the room, but Susana is completely unaware of her presence. Leopoldo appears distracted, but this is nothing new for his wife. They pass the evening in a normal way, and Leopoldo retires to his workshop where he connects himself again to the dream collector and dreams about William's life with Rachel. He sees William's death, Rachel's search for William after death, and his own childhood, when he intuitively felt a connection to a woman no longer present in his life. The dream sequence is filmed in sepia tones accompanied by the sound of Rachel's piano, which links it to his previous dream and also to William's movie. It advances the narrative that deals with William and Rachel, and it provides a strong contrast to Leopoldo's waking life, where he and his wife are mired in financial problems and boredom. When Leopoldo awakens, the film is once again in color, and Rachel is standing by the window, waiting for him. Only the shift in film style and use of color indicate that the dream has ended and we are once again seeing Leopoldo's "real" world. This, of course, is problematic, since Leopoldo's world is informed by the films he watches and his friend Oscar's science-fiction-based theories. One evening in the film projection room, he confronts Rachel by saying, "Podría ser toda una farsa, podría ser todo mentira. Podrías ser una agente terrestre, de otra planeta." Rachel laughs at Leopoldo's naive beliefs and reminds him that human beings are not able to conceive of everything that exists in the universe, but neither do things happen without reason. She explains that his perception of reality is shifting simply because he can see more clearly now; his dream collector has allowed him to free himself from a narrow, impoverished way of looking at things around him. One of the film's most tender and most unsettling moments follows this exchange, as Leopoldo leans forward to rest his head against Rachel's bosom. A shift in point of view and camera angle reveals that Leopoldo is alone, and he is embracing empty space. Romantic piano music conveys the intense emotion of the moment, and the screen fades to black, as if the scene were too private for viewers to share. It is a poignant visual representation of loss, Leopoldo's immense loneliness, and the lack of unconditional love in his life. It is also a turning point in the film, for Leopoldo never again doubts Rachel, and her presence on screen becomes more consistent, more solid, and more real. Viewers may opt to accept Leopoldo's point of view, to believe that Rachel exists only in Leopoldo's imagination, or interpret Leopoldo's experiences as part of a dream. Because of the way ambiguity is encoded into the filmic text, any of these readings are possible.

Structurally, Subiela uses a technique that is similar to what we find in some of the best fantastic fiction, a narrative frame that allows us to believe that the central story is a dream. While this interpretation is never forced, the possibility that the supernatural elements can be explained as a dream keeps the film from falling strictly into the category of fantasy. The final shot of the film's introductory sequence shows William asleep with a zoetrope in his hands. The closing shot of the film shows Leopoldo and Susana's young daughter (who may be the reincarnation of Rachel) playing with what seems to be the same zoetrope, one hundred years later and a continent away. It may be a simple coincidence, or it may signal that the child, like her parents, is a product of William's imagination. Later we learn that William was not able to father a child; it is not difficult to understand why he would dream about a loving family in the wake of his young wife's death. The film suggests that dreams may reveal the future one hopes for, or as psychoanalysis suggests, deep-rooted subconscious desires. Using this interpretation, Leopoldo, Susana, and their daughter do not exist yet, but represent the family William never had. They also represent future generations of moviegoers. Their displacement into the future symbolizes for William the widespread success of his invention and the transformation of millions of ordinary lives through his invention, cinema.

The relationship between dreams and reality is emphasized in a subplot of the film that deals with Susana's inability to have children. Using Leopoldo's dream collector, she visualizes the child who will later appear in the film's final scene. Upon waking, she denies that she dreamed of the child, but later, when she learns that she is pregnant, she recognizes that motherhood is something she longed for. Both she and Leopoldo accept the pregnancy as a "miracle," since there is no scientific explanation for her sudden fertility, but another miracle takes place simultaneously that is even more difficult to explain: Rachel's favorite locket materializes in Leopoldo's hand as Susana announces her good news. We then see Rachel moving into a white light to be reborn, and a cut to a close up of a crying newborn is accompanied by Rachel's voiceover, exclaiming "¡qué maravilloso! Tengo hambre, tengo frío, estoy viva." Leopoldo knows at once that the baby is Rachel, but he is confused by the idea that the woman who was his wife in another life is now his daughter. In a later scene, we see him delighting in the role of father and we understand that he is a changed man: he is happy, he and Susana have a warm and loving relationship, and Rachel is still with him in spirit. A point-of-view shot from the child's perspective shows Leopoldo performing extraordinary and magical feats for her entertainment. He produces butterflies from thin air and floats above the ground from joy. When he asks the baby, "¿Y ahora, qué voy a hacer con vos?" Rachel's voice answers, "Lo que has hecho siempre, quererme." This happy ending is something we associate with romantic comedies; it provides us with the "feel good" experience that many viewers want when they sit down to watch a film. However, the unusual circumstances behind the ending also leave us with a strong feeling of doubt and perhaps even discomfort, since they require us to embrace ideas that are far from conventional.

Along the same lines, the film calls attention to itself as a film by making the business of the movies a central theme that unites the characters on screen, yet it also relies heavily on techniques that filmmakers use to make viewers forget temporarily that what we are seeing is "only a movie." In most ways, Leopoldo is an ordinary man with ordinary problems. The setting of the film is a neighborhood in Buenos Aires, his home is middle class, and his life is routine. Point-of-view shots, close ups, and the effective use of music to create emotion allow viewers to see the world through Leopoldo's eyes and recognize similarities between it and the world they inhabit. As in the case of most fantastic fiction, the film starts out firmly grounded in a reality the viewers can accept as something like their own, and when supernatural elements begin to invade that reality, it produces moments of doubt and hesitation. Just as the film vacillates between representations of Rachel as visible/ invisible, it highlights then conceals the differences between film and real life. For example, soon after Leopoldo sees his father (Manuel Cruz) in a dream, he enters the movie theater and finds that he has walked back in time. The theater is full of people laughing in glee at a Nini Marshall film, and Leopoldo's father is at work in the projection booth. Leopoldo does not express much surprise at seeing his father, who has been dead for some time. Instead, he talks to him about his love for Rachel, which frightens him because he cannot understand it. He compares his life to a film by telling his father, "Amo a Rachel y es como estar enamorado de la actriz de una película. Si se apaga la proyección, sólo hay una pantalla en blanco." He tells his father that he is afraid because he cannot understand his feeling of happiness. His father advises, "No pienses, Leopoldo. La mente no hace más que crear abismos que sólo el corazón puede cruzar." This statement summarizes one of the pleasures viewers experience when they go to the movies: they can believe, so long as the film is projected against the screen, that anything is possible and emotions matter more than rational explanations. But once the film ends, viewers must make a conscious decision to hold on to the illusion or it will fade.

In Leopoldo's dream about his father, he discovers that films have the power to change people's lives, even though they may not understand the process behind it. We do not know what film Leopoldo is watching in the dream, but we see the audience completely caught up in the emotions portrayed on screen and a close up of Leopoldo's face shows that an emotional transformation is taking place in him as well. As he exits the theater, he notices that everyone around him is experiencing deep, life-changing feelings, and the speed of the film slows down to emphasize the importance of this revelation. Later, when Leopoldo returns home, Subiela uses the same technique of slow motion and dramatic music to draw a parallel between Leopoldo's rekindled love for Susana and the scene inside the movie theater: he suggests that Leopoldo is now seeing Susana with new eyes because of the emotions he uncovered while staring at the movie screen in his dream. As his relationship with Susana develops, he rediscovers feelings that had been buried for years. They extend beyond his personal home life; in the street and in the metro, he feels an overwhelming love for everyone and everything he sees. Unable to recognize the feeling of being in love again after so many years, he confesses to Rachel, "Tengo como una diarrea afectiva. Amo todo. Podría ser un sueño, pero la sensación es al revés; es como si estuviera saliendo de un sueño." Leopoldo's realization that he has not been living an authentic life marks a turning point in the film and puts the supernatural in a broader context: it gives way to the conventions of romance, where miracles are possible because of love. In the end, Leopoldo becomes a successful inventor and moves with his family to a beautiful home in the country. Leopoldo's friend, Oscar, who had lived with a robot as his only companion, reunites with his first love and is suddenly able to rise from his wheelchair and walk. Don Mario, the failed theater owner, gets a new lease on life when Leopoldo asks him to be his partner in the commercial production and distribution of the dream collector. Even Carlitos, the robot, finds a new companion, an electronic brain he can talk to, and Anita, the potted plant that Leopoldo carries with him everywhere in the film, is set free to grow in the garden with other plants. The transformation in the characters and their circumstances is more extraordinary than the fantastic events that led up to change, and their world, while still ordinary and recognizable as our own, is now filled with the magic that comes from feelings of profound happiness.

Hombre mirando al sudeste (Man Facing Southeast) (1986) is a much simpler film technically speaking, but it is complex in ideas and character development and has an ambiguous, open-ended structure that allows it to function well as a fantastic text. While some critics classify it as science fiction, others have tended to read the film as a metaphor for Argentina during the military dictatorship, stressing the parallelism between a mental hospital and a prison, patients and inmates, doctors and torturers. Rantes (Hugo Soto), the mental patient who claims to be from another planet, is a mysterious Christ-like figure who recalls the idealism of Argentina's liberal thinkers and symbolizes their resistance to oppression. Dr. Denis (Lorenzo Quinteros), an alienated and disillusioned psychiatrist, attempts to save Rantes, but ultimately is too weak to fight the system. Rather than lose his job at the hospital, he submits Rantes to treatment that he knows will harm the patient; Rantes's death and disappearance at the end of the film, like the death and disappearance of other patients, become statistics in official records that no one will bother to read. He leaves no trace behind to prove that he existed, and no one will ever know his true identity.

Rantes claims that he landed on earth near Junin, Argentina, but his spacecraft, if it exists, is never seen in the film. There is nothing about his physical appearance to suggest that he is from outer space, and he uses no visible forms of technology to communicate with his home planet. Instead, he merely stands in the hospital courtyard, facing southeast, where he claims he sends and receives transmissions. To classify the film as science fiction requires an enormous leap of faith, since most of the action revolves around the efforts of Dr. Denis and others to prove that Rantes is not an extraterrestrial but merely a "sick" young man. Only the mental patients believe that Rantes is from another planet, and it is, in fact, their testimony that provides an alternate ending for the film that allows it to enter the realm of the fantastic. Significantly, we never see Rantes's death on screen; instead, in a voiceover by Denis, the doctor explains that he was absent from the hospital on the day Rantes died. Rantes's body was immediately taken away and given to medical students for dissection before Denis could intervene. Denis had hoped to solve the mystery of Rantes's identity by examining his brain, but that option no longer exists. Rantes, for him, is simply a memory. The mental patients, however, say that Rantes was picked up by a spacecraft and taken back to his planet. The film closes with a shot of them gathered in the hospital yard, waiting for Rantes's spaceship to take them away. Although they are, technically speaking, eyewitnesses to Rantes's final day on earth, the doctor dismisses their story because he considers them insane. He substantiates and imposes the official version of truth on the narrative—that Rantes is dead—because death is the most logical ending for his patients. Rantes has been erased from the text, and viewers have no way of knowing what happened to him. Instead, we are left with two conflicting points of view, both flawed, both problematic, but both representing possibilities that have been suggested throughout the film. Because the film is structured to leave doubt about Rantes's identity and to call attention to the arbitrary nature of any attempt to limit the narration to a single, factual explanation, it allows for a fantastic reading of some of the events it portrays.

Rantes and the other mental patients construct the notion of interplanetary travel through their words and behavior, not through visible proof that such a phenomenon exists. It would be easy to discount their ideas altogether if it were not for some strange, even supernatural, elements in the film that resist a straightforward reading. For example, Rantes appears to have psychokinetic powers, but curiously, he does not use them to convince Dr. Denis that he is an extraterrestrial being. Instead, he quietly moves objects with his mind when he or others need or want something that is out of reach. The movement is as natural for him as reaching out with the hand, and he neither verbalizes nor acknowledges with facial expressions that anything out of the ordinary has occurred. In one case, he causes a radio to fall on the floor in order to distract the guard at the hospital, thus making it possible for him to escape unnoticed. In another scene, he observes a poor woman in a diner who does not have enough money to feed herself and her children. Rantes moves plates of food across the counter until they come to a stop in front of her. No words are spoken in the scene, and no one seems to notice, except the hungry woman. She locks eyes with Rantes, who nods to indicate that she should eat. When others in the restaurant realize that she has their food, Rantes creates a distraction with falling dishes, which gives the woman time to escape.

In the context of the film, these actions are not especially surprising, for Rantes constantly behaves in curious and unexpected ways, and he has a strange effect on the people around him. In one memorable scene, Rantes turns an ordinary concert in the park into a euphoric celebration of life: not only does his enthusiasm and joy infect those who are with him at the concert, but according to the mental patients, he also led them in a gleeful romp through the hospital hallways at the same time. Music bridges the shots of the hospital and the park, which are then juxtaposed through crosscutting to call attention to the similarities between the two groups of people. Both scenarios come to an abrupt end when the police arrive; Rantes must return to the mental hospital, the patients must return to their beds, Dr. Denis must return to his role of disinterested observer, and everyone must fall back into their normal routines. The magic of the earlier scene is lost, as Rantes is forcibly drugged until he falls into a catatonic state.

Viewers have been encouraged to identify with Dr. Denis during most of the film through point-of-view shots and voiceover narration; however, as Rantes grows weaker and more vulnerable, the doctor withdraws into his shell and distances himself from everyone around him. The physical decline in Rantes is paralleled by an emotional and moral decline in Denis, who continues to insist that psychiatry will help his patient, even when he sees the patient dying in front of his eyes. When Rantes begins taking antipsychotic drugs, his "delusions" of outer space disappear and he no longer is able to perform extraordinary feats. On the one hand, this confirms Denis's theory that Rantes is mentally ill; on the other hand, it suggests that Rantes's powers have been short-circuited by powerful drugs. The only thing that is clear to viewers is that Rantes has been silenced and brought under control by people who hold power over him.

It is more difficult to explain a secondary story line that involves Dr. Denis and the mysterious Beatriz (Inés Vernengo), a woman dubbed the Saint, who comes into his life via contact with Rantes. Beatriz first claims to be an evangelist who met Rantes when he was working in a small village with her church group. Later, Beatriz revises this story to tell Denis that she is, like Rantes, an agent from outer space, but she has been corrupted by contact with Earthlings and no longer wants to return to her home planet. Denis constructs yet a third identity for Beatriz, based on a photo he finds in her handbag. He conjectures that Beatriz is Rantes's sister and that they are both mentally ill. Although he feels a powerful sexual attraction to her, he reacts violently when she tells him she is an extraterrestrial. As in the case of Rantes, Beatriz's claim that she is from outer space is based on nothing but words. The only "proof" that she may not be human is a strange and inexplicable tendency to regurgitate a blue liquid from her mouth when she feels intense emotion. Yet, ironically, while Denis makes love to her, he fails to notice the blue drops that fall on his shirt. A close up of the drops reminds viewers that Rantes had talked about the blue liquid before, but Denis rejected it as nonsense. This shot is followed by a close up of Beatriz's face, where we see the liquid coming from the corner of her mouth, but significantly, there is no counter shot from the perspective of Denis to show that he sees her face. Later, when Beatriz confesses, "No soy lo que Ud. cree, doctor," Denis laughs at her insistence of using the formal "usted" with him after they have made love, but he does not pay attention to the urgency in her voice. An abrupt cut from a medium close up of their naked bodies entwined on the floor to a medium long shot of them fully dressed, sitting on separate sofas in tense poses suggests that the mood has changed suddenly. The sensual saxophone music that had been present in the love scene is gone, replaced by Beatriz's monologue as she explains her identity as a space alien to her lover. Although just minutes earlier Denis had declared, "Te quiero . . . soy feliz . . . pase lo que pase," he now shouts at her, "¡Andáte, loca de mierda!" As in the concert scene with Rantes, the happiness Denis felt was momentary and fragile; again he retreats into his shell and rejects words and behavior that do not conform to his ideas of "normal" human conduct. Significantly, he is not aware of anything supernatural happening around him, but he rejects Beatriz and Rantes because he considers them mad. Viewers, who have witnessed incidents that Denis has not, are in a position to understand that Denis's theories about the identity of Beatriz and Rantes are no more concrete than their assertions that they come from outer space. Both viewpoints are upheld in the film, although one takes it in the direction of psychological drama and the other takes it in the direction of science fiction. In the space between these two possibilities, there is room for the fantastic to take hold.

One final element in the film opens the door for a fantastic interpretation, and that is the photograph Denis finds in Beatriz's purse. In it, Beatriz and Rantes stand side by side, but one third of the photo has been torn away. The photo fascinates Denis because he assumes a third person was present in the photo, but he does not know who that person is. He uses the photo as "proof" that Rantes and Beatriz are human, and he speculates that the photo was taken at their family home when they were younger. But the missing part of the photo is a complete mystery and could just as well contain information that substantiates their story that they are from another planet. Denis sees what he wants to see in the photo, filling in gaps from his own life experience to construct an identity for Beatriz and Rantes. Throughout the film, Denis obsessively watches home movies of his former wife and children, where the illusion of a happy family is preserved on screen. He has become the missing father in his own family narrative, and he projects this interpretation onto the life story of Beatriz and Rantes, converting them into abandoned children like his own. The photo serves as a visual reminder to viewers that whenever we interpret the meaning of an image, we bring to it our own system of values and beliefs, as well as our own personal histories. What we accept as concrete proof is, sometimes, merely an idea that supports our own point of view. This idea detracts somewhat from Denis's authority as narrator and leaves room for viewers to question the logic behind his thinking. In this way, the film resists closure and invites an investigation into the contradictions inherent in all of the main characters.

Pastor Vega's Approach to the Fantastic

Las profecías de Amanda (The Prophesies of Amanda) (1999) by the Cuban director, Pastor Vega, addresses some of the same issues as Subiela's films, but uses a different technique. Vega mixes elements of a traditional bio-pic with a pseudo-documentary style to chronicle the life of Martha Estévez, a Habanera with legendary psychic abilities. Significantly, Vega does not reveal that the film is based on real facts until the closing credits, so as viewers watch the story unfold, they believe they are dealing with a fictional character named Amanda Fernández (played by Doren Granados/ Laura Flores/ Daisy Granados at different points in Amanda's life). In this way, Vega tests the limits of what we are willing to believe as part of a film versus what we can accept as "real facts," and he suggests that documentary films are no less manipulative and contrived than fictional ones.

Vega uses the technique of a film within a film to draw attention to the dramatic possibilities of daily life. While the film's editor, director, and producer argue about whether Amanda's life should follow the pattern of "la típica telenovela' or "una tragedia griega," the doctor (Marisela Berti) who is studying Amanda as a scientific experiment argues that the film cannot be made at all until her studies are complete. She insists that she must protect Amanda from the harmful effects of media attention, but it is clear that she is more interested in protecting her own scholarly reputation. Both the filmmaker and the doctor want to prove that Amanda's prophecies are accurate, but their reason for doing so is to enhance their careers, not to validate Amanda's perception of herself as a gifted seer. Narrative tension and a degree of doubt are inscribed into the film through counter voices in the media and the medical field, as well as people on the street who are interviewed for the documentary. Everyone has an opinion, whether they know Amanda or not, and for every individual who denies her powers, there is someone else who insists the powers are real.

The film takes an outwardly neutral position in terms of point of view and tone, as we might expect in a documentary film. We do not see Amanda through the eyes of any particular character, nor do we have access to her point of view in most shots. There are relatively few close ups to call attention to the characters' emotions, and only occasional scenes use shot/ counter shot editing that communicates thoughts and feelings that pass between characters. When Amanda is a young child, she is more often the object of others' gaze: teachers, school administrators, and psychologists, as well as her parents, stare at her in dismay when they realize that she is not like other children. Medium close ups show their reactions to her, but Amanda seldom returns their gaze, and we almost never see the world through her eyes. As Amanda grows older, she is more often shown in a medium long shot that shows her in relationship to her surroundings and other people. Many shots are in deep focus to remind us that Amanda is almost always surrounded by others, although she is usually the center of attention. This technique is important for the introduction of supernatural elements in the film, for when Amanda reads minds, predicts the future, or prophesies someone's fate, it takes place in the public realm and there are witnesses to her words and actions.

The mysterious and inexplicable element in the film, Amanda's ability to see and know things beyond the realm of ordinary human knowledge, does not take any particular visible form on screen. It exists primarily through words—Amanda's prophecies—and through the reaction of other characters to her words. Amanda claims that knowledge appears to her like a film she sees in her head. Often, as she speaks, the shot crosscuts to another setting, where we see the people she is describing in the situation she predicts. Although these scenes do not contain anything out of the ordinary, the uncanny similarity between what Amanda "sees" in her prophecies and what we see on the screen confirms that Amanda is accurate in her predictions and that she is telepathic. For example, when a distraught grandmother comes to Amanda to ask her to help cure an ailing granddaughter, we see the child in the hospital bed surrounded by worried doctors. Although Amanda does not know the woman or her granddaughter, she suggests the child's problem is caused by a neighbor with evil intentions who wants to break up the family home. A quick cut to a shot of the neighbor and the child's father sharing a complicit glance confirms that Amanda is on target. Amanda tells the woman how to cure her granddaughter with a spell, but she adds that it is also important to follow the doctors' orders, because "eso siempre ayuda." Later, we see the girl, fully recovered; both the mother and grandmother believe that Amanda has saved the girl's life, although there is no proof that Amanda's spell was more effective than the doctors' treatment. Their confidence in Amanda may be due to the fact that she gave them hope, assuring them that the girl would recover, whereas the doctors predicted that the child would die. But as former skeptics and nonbelievers, they are convincing witnesses to Amanda's psychic powers, for they can attest to her ability to penetrate the secret thoughts and intentions of complete strangers.

Equally important is the use of scientific experiments and psychological studies within the context of the film that allow viewers to see how the medical field approaches paranormal cases. Although carried out by professionals using standard testing, the examinations and studies ultimately prove whatever the doctor or psychologist want them to show. Results can be manipulated and interpreted in many different ways, depending on the expectations of the administrator of the test. For example, when Amanda is a young girl, results show that she is mildly retarded, unable to learn, and a negative influence on other children. This response comes in the wake of an unsettling prediction made by Amanda about the teacher's mother; she tells her, "Tu mamá se está quemando." In the next scene, we see the teacher rushing home to find that her mother has been injured in a fire and has been taken to the hospital. The pronouncement that Amanda is unfit to attend school is clearly a response to the teacher's emotional distress, but it becomes a pretext for Amanda's parents to isolate and mistreat her. Later, as a young adult, Amanda visits another psychologist to discuss her decision to leave a husband she does not love. The psychologist assures her, "Ni eres loca ni tonta ni nada de eso. ¿Qué me cuentas? Que tienes un don, es de la profecía. Hay un millón de cosas que nosotros los científicos no conocemos . . . no lo puedo explicar. A Juana de Arcos le pasó algo muy similar." His soothing words are clearly related to the sexual attraction he feels toward Amanda; a cut to the next shot reveals them in bed together making love. Many years later, another doctor becomes involved with Amanda when Amanda's husband dies exactly according to her predictions. The doctor carries out a number of tests to monitor Amanda's brain waves, to test her precognitive skills, and to determine if she is clairvoyant. She is able to produce impressive statistics based on her experiments, but she cannot explain Amanda's abilities, nor is she prepared to deal with Amanda as an equal when Amanda gives her psychic advice. While publicly claiming that Amanda's predictions are almost always correct, in private she complains that Amanda's prophesies about her have not come true. She asks Amanda to give a prognosis for her patients, but she attempts to control what Amanda says and scolds her for speaking too bluntly. Although the three doctors express different opinions about Amanda and react to her in different ways, all of them engage with her in a power struggle. Whether they deny, confirm, or ignore her psychic abilities, they all suggest that her lack of education and culture make her a second-class citizen, with fewer rights and privileges than they claim for themselves. Her ways of knowing are not like their own, and because her knowledge cannot be explained, they see her as a force that must be brought under control.

Many viewers will be reluctant to accept Amanda's prophecies as supernatural occurrences for the same reason. As a character, Amanda is developed with a mixture of pathos and humor that leaves us uncertain about how to read her frequent emotional outbursts. While she sometimes shows great compassion for others and helps them to lead better lives, she is more likely to rattle off her predictions in an offhand matter that makes others doubt her. For example, when the doctor asks her to diagnose the maladies of several patients, Amanda mentions cancer, a kidney transplant, and a magic spell cast by an unfaithful husband in the same tone of voice. Whereas the doctor accepts the first two predictions as real possibilities, she rejects the idea that magic could make her patient sick. When Amanda becomes agitated, she loses credibility in the doctor's eyes (and in the eyes of some viewers, perhaps) because she seems hysterical and irrational. Her outbursts, often punctuated by moments of song and dance, take away from the seriousness of the situation, but at the same time, they reveal a deep-seated frustration on the part of Amanda with figures of authority who have marginalized and mistreated her throughout her life.

While Amanda's prophecies do seem to be true a great deal of the time and she has an uncanny ability to read minds and learn information telepathically, she walks a fine line between wisdom and lunacy that makes it difficult for viewers to grasp the range of her power. In the film's closing sequence, Amanda finds herself in Old Havana where musicians, magicians, and con artists entertain the tourists. In this setting, magic is reduced to performance and mind reading is done for comic effect. Tourists applaud and slip money to performers who can read their secret thoughts. This stands in strong contrast to Amanda's beliefs: she has used her powers to help others and has never accepted money for her prophecies. She takes herself seriously and wants respect for her work. When a street performer shows her that he can read her mind, she gives him an enigmatic look that defies interpretation: whether she is embarrassed to realize her talents are not unique, or she understands that she is part of a much larger magical world is unclear. For viewers, the closing sequence simultaneously reframes Amanda's prophecies in a new context, suggesting that she is a kind of con artist like the street performers, while at the same time it affirms the existence of people like Amanda who have supernatural powers. Vega's film is an excellent example of how the fantastic in cinema does not have to rely on special effects, or even visual representation of the impossible. Instead, it suggests that the ordinary world around us is filled with magic and mystery, and that the inexplicable can and does happen in everyday life. The revelation that Amanda's story is based on the life of a real person solidifies that notion, and as the closing credits roll, Martha Estévez appears on screen in the place of the actresses who represented her in the film. The unexpected substitution of the real woman for her screen counterparts suggests that the events portrayed in the film also have some basis in reality, thus further blurring the line between fact and fiction.

As the opposition between truth and invention begins to break down in the closing shots of *Las profecías de Amanda*, Vega leaves us to ponder the limits of human knowledge and experience much in the same way Subiela does in his films. Although the two filmmakers take radically different approaches to the fantastic in terms of style and technique, they share a number of common themes and concerns that link their work to that of the finest writers of fantastic fiction in Latin America. Both filmmakers are attracted to the mysteries inherent in everyday life and portray eccentric but in many ways quite ordinary human beings whose lives are taken off course by the eruption of some supernatural phenomenon in their daily routine. Characters realize that their knowledge has been restricted by a too narrow view of life, and that there are experiences that defy any kind of rational explanation, other than what they conjecture or come to believe through their encounter with the fantastic. Out of step with those around them, they seek a more authentic way of being; some are successful, others less so, but all are changed by their experiences. Viewers are challenged to fill in gaps and interpret the significance of what they see, yet there are seldom straightforward answers to the questions that are raised. It is difficult to say whether events portrayed on screen are truly impossible or merely seem to be impossible; it is equally difficult to know what caused these events to happen or determine what they might mean. To doubt or to believe becomes conscious a choice that the characters and viewers alike must make, yet these states of mind are often shifting points on a continuum. Often the films lend themselves to psychological readings, and certainly they allow us to contemplate the complexities of the human mind, but they also resist closure by suggesting that scientific and medical explanations are no more valid than paranormal and metaphysical ones. They reveal the underpinnings of the system of reference we use to orient ourselves in life and call our attention to the ways in which we construct knowledge and interpret experience to prop up the beliefs we already possess.

Conclusion: Fantastic Literature in Spanish America in the Twenty-First Century

In the 1970s, Julio Cortázar urged Latin Americans to identify reality in their own terms and to leave room for the fantastic in their conception of the world. According to him, the fantastic assumes the important function of "taking us for a moment out of our habitual little boxes and showing us, although it might only be vicariously, that perhaps things do not end at the point where our mental habits fix them" (527). This observation links fantastic literature as a genre to the infinite possibilities of human imagination, and suggests that our mental habits can always benefit from occasional stretching and periodic transformation. Society's superstructure may push us to become "that obedient robot" that Cortázar warns us about, but the fantastic allows us to slip through the interstitial spaces to break down binary oppositions between fixed notions of the "real" and the "unreal." It encourages original thinking and leaves room for play in our thought processes, always pointing us toward what Cortázar calls "the latent possibility" of new frontiers (526). In the same decade, Ana María Barrenchea strongly contested Todorov's claim that the fantastic was "dead" in the twentieth century, pointing out that despite advancements in technology and science, there will always be something outside the realm of human knowledge that cannot be grasped in concrete terms and will inspire "imaginaciones fantásticas" (402). Because the fantastic element is born of language and has no actual existence outside the text, Barrenechea predicted that as fantastic literature became more sophisticated and complex, it would become more self-referential. She identified one of the main functions of the fantastic as the ability to turn literature inward on itself and interrogate the relationship between the language and the word it attempts to represent. Far from making the fantastic "un arte burgués," Barrenechea believed that the fantastic in Spanish America could be transformed into a vehicle with which to examine social problems. She noted that writers like Cortázar could open the genre to "otras posibilidades bajo el signo de lo social, siempre que lo fantástico sea una puesta en cuestión de un orden viejo que debe cambiar urgentemente" (403).

As a point of departure for a discussion of the nature of fantastic literature in Spanish America as we move into a new millennium, the comments of Cortázar and Barrenechea serve us well, for they remind us that the fantastic is not a fixed entity but one that shifts and slides in relationship to the way we think about the world around us. It is essentially a subversive form of discourse, for it uncovers and undermines the status quo and calls attention to the fact that very often what we believe is what we have been taught through an inherited set of cultural norms. It upsets power structures and gives a voice to those who have been traditionally marginalized or ignored. It questions the relationship between seeing and telling, between knowing and believing, and it makes us aware of how a given perspective can influence our reaction to what we read. It plays with our expectations as readers and helps us to understand our role in the interpretation of narrated events. Above all, it calls attention to the limitations and unreliability of language as a representational system, and it shows us that the gaps in a text can be as important as the words that make up the story.

One way to see how the fantastic might play out in Spanish America in the twenty-first century is to turn to a collection of fantastic stories by a master like Carlos Fuentes to see how the genre has changed over time in the hands of one writer. Fuentes began his literary career in 1954 with the publication of a collection of short stories, *Los días enmascarados*, in which "Chac Mool" and "Tlactocatzine del jardín de Flandes" stand out as key works in the development of fantastic literature in Mexico. Later, in 1962, with the publication of the novella, *Aura*, Fuentes returned to the fantastic and established himself as a master of the genre. Unlike romantic and modernist short stories, which often took place in exotic settings and dealt with strange characters, the stories of twentieth-century writers like Fuentes are based on the recognizable world of ordinary people and explore the mysterious and inexplicable elements that lie just below the surface of modern cities. They play with the reader's hesitation and doubt to suggest multiple levels of meaning in the narrative. Through language, they dig into the unknown parts of human experience: they question concepts such as individual identity, notions of time and space, the basis of human knowledge, but always from a point of departure that firmly establishes their connection to the real world.

So, has the fantastic outgrown its usefulness and appeal as many parts of Latin America rush toward modernization and development? Have technology and reality-based television replaced the importance of imagination? Has globalization truly created world citizens who no longer worry about where they come from or where they are going? What does the fantastic have to offer readers today? We can look to Fuentes for answers to these questions in his most recent collection of short stories, *Inquieta compañía*, published in 2004. Although Fuentes had not worked with the fantastic in more than four decades, he once again takes it up in this book to explore the interior world of the Mexican people, glimpsed among shadows and dreams, where the impossible can happen, but it may go unperceived. A look at the stories in the collection allows us to see how the fantastic has evolved, not only in Fuentes's work, but perhaps as a road map for future generations of writers, in order to arrive at a hypothesis of the nature of the fantastic in a postmodern world. *Inquieta compañía* touches on some of the same themes seen in earlier works, but it is not a simple case of recycled texts. Fuentes's technique as a writer has become more complex and subtle, the characters are more layered and ambiguous, and the narrative style is dense and rich. Ambiguity does not so much come out of the situation in which the characters find themselves, but rather from language itself. The stories in *Inquieta compañía* explore themes related to traditional fantastic literature—ghosts, witches, vampires—but all from a very modern point of view. Globalization, racism, hate and prejudice based on religious and ethnic differences, class conflict, imperialism, exploitation, and other social themes are extremely important in the tales, and they place us firmly in the twenty-first century, where the collision between Mexico's past and the future has created a narrow gap through which the fantastic can emerge.

In a 2002 interview, Fuentes explained how literature in Mexico has changed in the past fifty years; he claims:

> You have an absolute freedom in Mexican writing today in which you don't necessarily have to deal with the Mexican identity. You know why? Because we have an identity. . . . We know who we are. We know what it means to be a Mexican. Now the problem is to

> discover difference—not identity but difference: sexual difference, religious difference, political difference, moral differences, aesthetical differences. (n.p.)

Perhaps for this reason, Fuentes's focus in *Inquieta compañía* is the diverse forms that Mexican identity takes today and the difficulty Mexicans have in reconciling difference. It is a much more complex and richly layered treatment of identity than we have seen in earlier works, precisely because it attempts to explore the way Mexicans deal with the notion of self and otherness on a personal, national, and international level. For example, the first story of the collection takes place in Europe, but it deals indirectly with the problem of Mexican emigrant identity. "El amante del teatro" is Lorenzo (Larry) O'Shea, a Mexican national of Irish descent living in London. As in earlier works by Fuentes, the conflict between the Old World and the New World is very evident in the story, and Lorenzo suffers from moments of insecurity because he is a Latin living in an Anglo world. He is a man full of contradictions: he works as a technician in the movie industry, but he never goes to the movies. He feels proud of being Mexican, but he prefers to live in Europe. He believes that technology has taken the place of imagination and creativity in the modern world, but in the isolation of his apartment, he constructs imaginary worlds that stand in for reality. He falls in love with an unknown woman in the apartment facing his own, an actress who plays the role of Ophelia in *Hamlet*, but he hopes never to meet her in person because he fears that knowing the real woman would destroy the illusion of love he feels for her. At the end of the story, it is unclear what happens to him; perhaps he goes insane, perhaps he dies. If we are to believe what he says, he sacrifices his life trying to protect Ophelia from an insanely jealous Hamlet and now both he and his beloved are ghosts who inhabit the theater. The ambiguity of the story stems from the fact that Lorenzo, like all of the characters in the book, lives in absolute seclusion from the world and no one is witness to his actions. He directs his speech toward an imaginary public in hopes that someone will hear his voice.

The last story in the collection, "Vlad," is an inversion of the first, and it closes the collection by treating some of the same themes, but from the opposite perspective. Vlad is a Central European count living in Mexico City. Like Lorenzo, he feels displaced outside his native land, he lives in complete isolation from others, and he tries to avoid contact with the world around him. But while "the lover of theater" feels weak and ineffectual, Vlad is strong and powerful. Lorenzo becomes a victim, and Vlad is the victimizer. Vlad does not doubt himself and does not hesitate; he knows what he wants and he takes it. He is like the demented Hamlet from the first story: he abuses his power and enjoys cruel behavior. One of his victims is the narrator of the story, Yves Navarro, a Mexican of French origin, who loses his wife and daughter to Vlad. Yves is a man who closes his eyes so as to not see what is in front of him. From the beginning of the tale, the reader will suspect that Vlad is a vampire, but Yves insists on treating him as if he were a normal man. At the end of the story, when he can no longer deny Vlad's superhuman abilities, Yves understands that there is a danger even greater than that posed by the vampire: his sense of self has come apart at the seams. Through contact with Vlad, he sees that his life has been a lie, his wife does not love him, and she does not want the security and routine family life that Yves offers her. His wife and child prefer to run away with a vampire rather than continue living with him because they despise the dullness of their lives and no longer want to live as prisoners "del tedio cotidiano" (280). The great love that defined his existence does not exist, and his life no longer has meaning. It does not matter if the vampire kills him or not. The real horror is to feel alone and abandoned. In both stories, there is a disquieting mixture of eroticism and death, of physical attraction and dread. Love can save man, but it can also destroy him. Lorenzo and Yves suffer because they cannot find a way to fit into the world around them, Lorenzo because he is a foreigner in another land, and Yves because he allows a foreigner to dominate him in his own land. Although they are both sophisticated, cosmopolitan, intelligent, and rational men, they allow themselves to be overwhelmed by doubts and anxiety, and the buried emotions of previous generations return to make them feel insecure and defeated. There is no firm core to their being, and eventually, they dissolve into nothingness. Yves and Lorenzo are products of centuries of colonialism, of the imbalance of power between the Old World and the New, and of a modern world that is too impersonal, remote, and cruel. They do not know how to triumph because they do not know how to destroy other people.

Intolerance, prejudices, racism, and hate are other important themes in *Inquieta compañía*. "La gata de mi madre" emphasizes conflicts between races and classes in Mexico, both in the twenty-first century and at the time of Spanish conquest. The hate that doña Emérita Lizardi feels toward Lupe, her maid or "gata," is the distilled essence of generations of creoles who looked down on and abused indigenous people. Lupe is, for her, "una india patarrajada," (48), "huilita del pueblo," "putita" (49), "gatuperia tarada," "esclava de metate" (56), "Cleopatra de los nopales" (60). As a devout catholic, doña Emérita worships the Virgin of Guadalupe, but according to her, Juan Diego was a Spaniard, not an Indian, "porque a los indios no los hace santos ni Dios Todopoderoso" y "todos los santos son güeritos. Ya se lo dijo el Santo Padre" (67). When one day she believes that Lupe has been disrespectful to her, she falls down in a fit of rage and dies because she cannot bear the idea that an Indian would treat her in such a way. Her daughter, Leticia, believes that she is a more modern woman and less of a racist than her mother. She does not want the life her mother had, and for that reason, she chooses a dark-skinned man as her lover, "una versión totonaca de Benjamin Bratt" (54) who she met in Sanborns, but the relationship that develops between them is dark and dangerous. Leti's lover punishes her, tortures her, and turns her into a prisoner while he enjoys a sexual relationship with Lupe. Leti finds herself alone and helpless, on the verge of madness. The final irony of the story is that Leti's lover and Lupe are not Indians at all, but rather Jews who were burned alive by the Inquisition during Mexico's colonial period, and they have returned to the present to get revenge. They adopt the look of Indians as a disguise because they realize that hate, intolerance, and racism exist in many forms and are not limited to a single ethnic group. Now it is the turn of Leticia to pay for the crimes of generations of arrogant creoles. As in the other stories, we cannot know for sure if she is the victim of the fantastic, of madness, of frustrated sexual desire, or of solitude. She writes her story on loose-leaf paper that she throws into the street from between the bars of her window, but no one knows what goes on inside the house, where the doors are barred and the windows shuttered. The modern world outside continues on in its hurried rhythms, but Leti is condemned to live with the ghosts of the past.

"Calixta Brand" portrays another ethnic group that has contributed to the development of Mexican culture and that has suffered at the hands of the Spanish colonizers: the Arabs. In this story, the Arabic influence so visible in the city of Puebla and the surrounding area is an important backdrop against which modern Mexico's globalization can be examined. Calixta Brand is a North American who came to Cholula to study, but who ended up living in Mexico, married to a Mexican man. Her husband, Estéban, is the son of formerly wealthy hacienda owners, but he is also a modern businessman who works in the Volkswagon offices in Puebla. Miguel Aspe is an Arab, a student who works in Calixta's garden in the gloriously restored family estate in Huejotzingo. Far from being a traditional romantic triangle, the relationship between these three characters leads to an examination of the tensions between people of three very different ethnic groups. The initial attraction that Estéban felt for Calixta soon turns to hate; he thinks of her as "una pinche gringa" who makes him feel inferior simply because he lives at her side. For Estéban, Miguel represents the "Other" in every sense of the world. He is not only a potential rival but also a symbol of everything that is foreign in Mexico, of the mysterious and magical, of that which he cannot understand and cannot control. Through his contact with Calixta and Miguel, Estéban turns into a monster. He can no longer think clearly; he tortures himself with irrational ideas and humiliates and punishes his wife for imaginary crimes. Miguel is Calixta's guardian angel, figuratively and perhaps literally as well: Estéban begins to suspect that Miguel is a real angel, and the story ends when Estéban sees Miguel with the wings of an angel, flying toward heaven with Calixta in his arms. The story is a commentary about how cultural differences both stem from and lead to a breakdown in communication between people: for reasons that he cannot articulate, Estéban sees anyone who is different from him as a threat to the solidity of his world. This is a dangerous sentiment in a man whose livelihood depends on work with a foreign company. Globalization of Mexico's economy has provided him with a very comfortable life; he has been able to restore his family's estate thanks to the money he earns at Volkswagon, but it disturbs him deeply that he is expected to share his personal space with foreigners. Many would argue that Puebla is the most Spanish city in Mexico, and Estéban feels particularly proud of this fact. At the same time, the Moorish style of its architecture suggests the polymorphic nature of Spain's culture, which is a thorny problem for Estéban. His North American wife is another blemish on his creole image, and he is anxious to be rid of her. He wants to believe that he can construct rigid barriers between races and cultures, but he lives in a world where these frontiers no longer exist. Ironically, he fails to acknowledge that at some point in time his ancestors, the colonizers of Puebla, were also foreigners in Mexico, and that the colonial period, which he so greatly admires as an example of a time when Mexico was "pure," gave birth to the mestizo, or mixed race, that makes up Mexico today.

"La bella durmiente" is another story that shows the fantastic effects of globalization, and it also deals with the theme of foreigners living in Mexico. The action takes place in the vast desert region of Chihuahua, where a German engineer, who is an admirer of Kaiser Wilhelm, Pancho Villa, and Hitler, hides the body of Alberta Simmons, the sleeping beauty of the story's title. Alberta was a Mennonite who suffered persecution because of her religious beliefs, but she has at least two identities in the tale: she may have died in the concentration camps of Germany in 1945 along with her lover, Doktor Georg Reiter, who defied the Nazis in an attempt to save her, or she may be a North American who came to live in northern Mexico when she married Emil Baur, the German engineer, after World War II. Baur is rich, powerful, and eccentric: we never know why or how he does it, but he claims that he has devoted his life to keeping Alberta alive by giving her energy from his own body. The similarity between this story and *Aura* seems intentional: as in the earlier novella, Baur needs a young man who can help him with his experiments, and he finds the reincarnation of Georg Reiter in Dr. Jorge Caballero, a Mexican who has studied in Heidelberg. Jorge falls in love with Alberta, a very elderly woman who seems to be on the verge of death, and he transforms her into a young, beautiful, and sexually voracious young woman. But while *Aura* has a lyrical, romantic tone and, in spite of the fantastic elements, is primarily a love story that defies the passage of time, "La bella durmienta" has a colder and more impersonal tone. Baur's motivation is not romantic; he feels guilty because of what the Nazis did during the war and wants to revive Georg and Alberta as a way of proving that death is not a permanent condition. Each time he brings them back to life, he feels relieved because it is one less crime weighing on the shoulders of humanity. In the last fragment of the story, the tone changes abruptly, and there is a strong suggestion that Baur is insane and that his wife, Alberta, has been the innocent victim of his obsession. She tells us, "Eternamente sentada al lado de Emil Baur en la sala de la mansión del desierto, supe, una vez más, que mi propia voz no sería escuchada por mi marido. Yo sólo era el fantasma que servía de una voz a otros fantasmas" (210). The relationship between Emil, Alberta, and Jorge is a miniature version of what happened between Germany, the United States, and Mexico at the beginning of the twentieth century, when Mexico was a toy in the hands of two superpowers who hated each other. As Alberta explains in the early pages of the story, "Lo que los mexicanos le envidiaban a los gringos, se lo podían admirar a los alemanes" (166). Diplomatic relations between Mexico, the United States, and Germany were fragile in the early decades of the twentieth century, as foreign companies vied for the rights to natural resources and land use. The narrative ambiguity of the text reflects this political instability. There are moments when we do not know who is speaking in the text, who are the characters, or how to explain the circumstances they are living in. The fantastic effect is born from the doubt and hesitation that readers will experience when they try to interpret the meaning of what they are reading.

"La buena compañía" is perhaps the most traditional story in the collection because it contains almost all of the ingredients we associate with fantastic literature: an abandoned house, two mysterious and possibly insane old women, a young romantic nephew, and an incursion of inexplicable, possibly supernatural episodes into an ordinary world that we can recognize without hesitation as our own. Alejandro, or Alex, is a Mexican born in Paris who returns to Mexico City after the death of his mother. He goes to live with his two aunts, Serena y Zenaida, in a Porfirian-era mansion on Ribera de San Cosmé, where the elegance of the nineteenth century has given way to "la fealdad de las construcciones y la mediocridad de los comercios" where "La gente iba y venía, entraba a tiendas, compraba periódicos, se sentaba a comer en restoranes modestos" (112). There are two possible explanations for what happens in the story: the fantastic version is that Alejandro went to live with his aunts when he was a small child and died when he was run down by a streetcar; now he is a ghost and everything he believes he has done in the past fifteen years is an illusion. Another explanation is that the aunts are insane, and they are going to kill him so that a dead child who is buried in the basement of their house will have a companion. This perturbing and disquieting portrait of the Escandón family emphasizes the absolute seclusion in which they live. As in the other stories, fantastic elements occur without anyone in the outside world knowing about them. Behind the closed windows and doors, very strange things may happen, but the characters live as if they were in a vacuum. In the world's largest city, they live without human contact. They disappear from view without anyone noticing, and no one hears their voices. They all become ghosts in one way or another, solitary souls who do not leave their houses because in the outside world "Puede pasar . . . una desgracia" (96).

Ultimately, then, who is the "*inquieta compañía*" of the title of the collection of stories? As we might expect with traditional fantastic literature, we find repugnant images that inspire chills and reactions of fear or dread: rats and insects, bats, evil-looking cats, skeletons, cadavers, ghosts and vampires, hidden coffins in basements that smell of mold, secret tunnels, haunted houses, blood soup and poisoned sweets, acts of sadism, horrible tortures, nightmares, and madness. But the most disturbing creatures in the stories are the characters themselves, the human beings who feel pleasure when they commit cruel acts, who allow hate, racism, and intolerance to determine the nature of their existence.

Marriages fail, families are destroyed and break apart, prosperity and material wealth suffocate and kill hardworking people. With modern communication systems, improved transportation, and a tendency toward a globalized culture and economy, the world seems to be getting smaller, but human beings are more isolated than ever and each day understand each other less. History has taught them nothing; the world has not become a better place. The same problems exist, and people seem less prepared to deal with them. Nothing is secure; nothing has fixed meaning. The only element of hope is the ability of humans to fall in love, to love and be loved. The love of Alberta and Jorge, or the theater lover for his Ophelia, continues after death and suggests that life, after all, has significance. There is also the fragile but tangible possibility of forgiveness for some who begin to understand their errors. Typical of characters in fantastic literature when they are confronting the unknown, the characters of *Inquieta compañía* experience the transition from one century to another with hesitation and doubt. On the one hand, they appear to be following in the footsteps of previous generations and repeating the same errors; on the other, they are painfully aware that they are venturing into uncharted territory in a world where they feel increasingly isolated and alone. Similar to the modernist fantastic story at the end of the nineteenth century, these stories take the pulse of a world that does not know if it should move forward or back. As Sartre predicted in the 1950s, the "new" fantastic firmly establishes man at the center of a universe gone out of control, "a world in which these absurd manifestations appear as normal behavior" (61). Fuentes illustrates that even in a technologically advanced and scientifically grounded culture, the unknown still has the potential to unsettle the human spirit. By linking his literary explorations to social, economic, and political issues, he also shows us that the fantastic continues to be an effective tool for excavating the most disquieting aspects of human experience.

Whether the fantastic short story will continue to be cultivated by a new generation of writers is a question that only time can answer, but Fuentes's most recent exploration into the realm of the fantastic suggests that there is still a great deal of territory to explore. The possibilities of the fantastic in Latin American cinema are also great, as the films of Subiela and Vega illustrate. Regardless of the form it takes, the fantastic clearly still has the power to challenge our way of thinking. First, it undermines the notion that literature (or film) is a representation of the "real" world because it reminds us that we are part of the process of creating meaning when we read a text or see images on the screen. The fantastic can illuminate our understanding of psychological processes, especially when they go awry, and it also encourages us to think about how we acquire gendered identity. It makes us look at our attitudes toward the aging body and confront our fear of difference. It emphasizes the overlapping and often confusing boundaries between romantic love and the uncanny, between sexual desire and death or decay, between pain and pleasure. It illustrates the connection between our grasp of language and our notion of selfhood, and it shows what happens when one or both break down. In Latin America, the fantastic has taken on social meaning, especially in the way that it challenges the notion of history as a stable entity based on a series of chronological events. It makes us understand that writing, reading, and viewing are never neutral practices, but rather are always grounded in someone's perception of what is real, true, or possible. Because of its ability to play with our notions of time and space and to question fundamental ideas about individual, cultural, and national identity, the fantastic continues to be a rich vein that future generations of Spanish American writers and filmmakers can mine.

Notes

Introduction: The Fantastic as a Literary Genre

1. I prefer to use the word *fantasy* to refer to works of literature that deal with obviously invented worlds and supernatural beings, such as *The Lord of the Rings*, in which there is no pretense that the world of the text resembles our own. The marvelous is closely related to fantasy, in that it allows the existence of supernatural or otherworldly events and characters without the accompanying fear or anxiety that is associated with the fantastic. Myths, legends, and fairy tales are usually considered examples of the marvelous. The uncanny is a Freudian concept that refers to something that is both familiar and strange at the same time. In a literary text, the uncanny manifests itself as something that is mysterious and eerie but not necessarily inexplicable, since it comes into being through psychosis, dreams, or delusions. "The Sandman" by Hoffmann is often cited as an example of the uncanny. The absurd has its roots in French existentialism, which claims that humans are destined to fail in their search for meaning in life because life has no meaning. The fantastic, by contrast, suggests that there is meaning, but it lies beyond our reach. See Cornwell, for a full discussion of how the absurd is represented in literary texts. Many critics, including Cornwell, see Kafka as a writer linked to the absurd rather than the fantastic. The grotesque is often discussed in relation to the gothic in literature. The grotesque creates situations and characters that inspire both disgust and empathy in the reader, such as Frankenstein's monster, the Hunchback of Notre Dame, or the Phantom of the Opera. Most critics agree that the gothic appeared in European literature in the late eighteenth century along with romanticism, and representative works include Walpole's *The Castle of Otranto* and Radcliffe's *The Mysteries of Udolpho.* The gothic combines the sublime and beautiful with evil and terror, and it uses supernatural elements to create mystery or inspire fear. Generally in these texts, the supernatural element is explained in the end as something within the natural order (a dream, madness, a hoax, a hallucination). Lovecraft discusses gothic themes and formulas. For more on the gothic and the grotesque, see Punter.

2. There is disagreement about whether the term *realismo mágico* should be translated as magic realism or magical realism in English. I prefer the latter, as a nod to Angel Flores, who first popularized the term among North American critics. For me, magical realism is the same as *lo real maravilloso*, and Carpentier's ideas about it remain valid, regardless of what we call it. I favor interpretations of magical realism, like those offered by Mena, Irish, Ben-Ur, Alazraki, Chanady, and Angulo, where there is some attention to thematic content as well as style. I am also influenced by what writers associated with the genre, like García Márquez and Asturias, have said about it. They believe that magical realist fiction tends to filter reality through the myths and marginalized peoples of the Americas. While many critics argue that magical realism is a universal form of expression, my interest in it lies firmly in Spanish America. For a more universal approach, see Schroeder and also Warnes. Later in the Introduction, I will return to the subject of magical realism and its relationship to the fantastic.

3. Jesús Rodero, for example, uses terms like *la ficción científica, lo neofantástico, lo postfantástico*, and *el feminismo mágico* to classify types of fantastic stories in Latin America. Although he gives an excellent analysis of the stories, the subcategories he proposes bring us no closer to understanding the nature of the fantastic as a genre.

4. Sardiñas, for example, has recently edited an important volume of critical essays, *Teorías hispanoamericanas de la literatura fantástica*, which grew out of a 1999 conference held in Havana at the Casa de las Americas. It represents a major contribution to the field of fantastic studies, but it is largely unavailable to U.S. readers because of trade and travel restrictions between the United States and Cuba.

5. In a letter dated April 7, 1941, Caillois wrote to Victoria Ocampo: "He visto la Antología Borges-Adolfito-Silvina: es desconcertante desde cualquier punto de vista. Hasta ahora, Alemania era considerado el país por excelencia de la literatura fantástica: no hay, por decirlo así ningún alemán . . . en la Antología. ¿Tal vez un olvido? En cuanto a poner a Swedenborg, es increíble: nunca tuvo la intención de escribir literatura fantástica. Y si uno se ocupa de la literatura fantástica involuntaria, entonces puede empezarse con la Biblia y algunas otras obras del mismo tipo, bastante importantes. No encuentro tampoco muy correcto el haber puesto a M.L.D. y a Borges mismo. Por lo común, el que hace una antología evita incluirse en ella" (qtd. in Louis 416). As Louis observes, there is no writer in the anthology with the initials M.L.D., but most likely Caillois refers here to the Chilean author, María Luisa Bombal. It is interesting to note in the context of our discussion of European biases in fantastic criticism that Caillois appears unsettled by the inclusion of Spanish American writers to the exclusion of his German favorites, although he masks the comment in terms of poor taste.

6. Todorov believes that readers understand they are not to take allegorical and poetic language literally. Although two meanings are encoded into the allegorical text through language, the figurative meaning is privileged over the literal meaning because the reader understands that the purpose of the allegory is to teach a moral lesson. In a similar way, readers expect that poetry will use figurative language to convey a message; therefore, they do not hesitate between logical or supernatural explanation of what they read. Some critics see the fantastic and the allegorical as "structural playmates" (Siebers 38), but almost all critics agree that poetry has no place in the discussion of the fantastic. Fiction appears to be the genre that suits it best, and the short story is, in particular, the vehicle most often associated with the genre.

7. Swanson observes that the Boom of Latin American literature in the 1960s is

bound up with the idea of the New Novel, but both of these labels "seem loose and perhaps even misleading" (1). He argues that what we call *la nueva narrativa latinoamericana* is not really so new, that it stretches back into the early decades of the twentieth century, and there is no discernible end to it, even now, which makes it problematic to talk about post-Boom writing. For him, the short stories of Borges and Cortázar are important examples of *la nueva narrativa* and show that the idea of a Boom in the Spanish American novel merely represents a perceived break with tradition, a rejection of "the premises and formal structures of conventional realism" (2). Swanson insists, "This is all the more true in Latin America where fiction in the first half of the twentieth century was largely social realist in nature, attempting to pain authentically local or regional social, economic or geographic conditions. Generally, the 'new novelist' perceives realism as fundamentally flawed in its simplistic supposition that reality is essentially observable, comprehensible, and transferable to a written medium . . . and, more specifically, perceives Latin American social realism as misleading in its attempt to present its readers a socially or politically skewed or slanted vision of society as a mirror of reality" (3). In this way, the development of the fantastic short story in Spanish America is closely tied to the phenomenon that would later be called the Boom, and of the many fantastic stories studied here are not only precursors to the New Novel but actually part of a new trend in fiction. For an overview of the Boom, see King.

8. Vax's work originally appeared in French as *L'art et la littérature fantastiques* (Paris: Press Universitaires de France, 1960). I quote from the Spanish translation because in all likelihood this is the version most readers of Spanish American fantastic short stories will have seen.

9. Todorov does not offer a definition of what he means by implied reader, but the concept is discussed at length by Booth in *The Rhetoric of Fiction*. Booth's ideas about the "implied author," which he defines as the actual author's "second self," has a counterpart in the notion of the "implied reader" (138). This concept is at the heart of reader reception theory, although other terms have been proposed such as "addressee" and "narratee," with slightly different conceptualizations. Suleiman and Crosman claim that the implied reader "exists only in a given work and is co-extensive with it, so the latter differs from an actual reader in that he is created by the work and functions, in a sense, as the work's ideal interpreter" (8). Prince describes the kind of implied reader Todorov seems to have in mind when he writes about the "zero-degree narratee," who "knows narrative grammar, the rules, for example, that a minimal complete narrative sequence consists in the passage from a given situation to the inverse situation. He knows that the narrative possesses a temporal dimension and that it necessitates relations of causality. Finally, the zero-degree narratee possesses a sure memory, at least in regard to the events of the narrative about which he has been informed and the consequences that can be drawn from them" (10).

10. This is not to suggest there has been a failure on the part of critics to do excellent work on the fantastic. More than a dozen books and hundreds of scholarly articles have appeared in the past thirty years that provide insight into the nature of the genre and offer convincing textual analyses to illustrate their points. Still, in terms of the fundamental notions we have about the fantastic in literature, relatively little has changed since the 1970s and there is still marked disagreement about the meaning and use of the term. It is impossible to list here all of the important work that has

been done on the fantastic in recent decades, but in addition to the critics cited here, others who have been influential include Brooke-Rose, Apter, Schlobin, W.R. Irwin, König, Bravo, Cornwell, Armitt, Erdal Jordan, Risco, Dehennin, Arán, Alazraki, and von Mücke. In addition, Schroeder has contributed to the study of magical realism in Spanish America.

1 / Modernist Short Stories and the Fantastic

1. *Modernismo,* with reference to Spanish American writing, should not be confused with the English term modernism as it applies to North American and European writers. The two terms are used in different ways and identify trends that belong to two distinct cultural landscapes. Modernism in English refers to the generation of writers from around the beginning of World War I until the end of World War II, exemplified by figures such as Joyce, Eliot, Pound, Woolf, and Stein. They resemble more closely their Spanish American contemporaries such as Vallejo, Huidobro, and Borges (as a poet, early in his career), who are associated with the *vanguardista* movement in Spanish America. *Modernismo* in Spanish America occurs earlier, at the end of the nineteenth century and the beginning of the twentieth. Critics have traditionally framed it by the publication date of *Azul* in 1888 and Darió's death in 1916. Both *modernista* and modernist writers were concerned with the renovation of literary language, but they used very different methods to achieve this goal. When I speak about modernism here, I am of course referring to the Spanish American movement. Spanish American modernism is represented best by poetry, which has been the focus of most critical studies of the movement. In addition to the writers discussed in this chapter, other important figures are Martí, Gutiérrez Nájera, del Casal, and Asunción Silva.

2. Hahn identifies stories by Montalvo, Gorriti, Holmberg, Roa Bárcena, and R. Palma as examples of the romantic fantastic in Spanish America (*Fundadores del cuento).* Fuente del Pilar has compiled a similar anthology. Both critics situate the origins of the fantastic short story in Latin America in the second half of the nineteenth century, with the "second generation of Romantics" who were fascinated with "asuntos y motivos relacionados con la vida de ultratumba, con lo diabólico y con la inspiración artística" (Hahn, *Fundadores del cuento,* 11). Because modernist fantastic stories share this same thematic interest, they are often discussed in the same breath with romanticism, but it is important to note that they differ in two important ways from the earlier texts: modernists renovated language and narrative technique to make the fantastic a more self-conscious kind of literature, and they use standard themes of the fantastic to challenge notions of modernity.

3. Del George's comparative study of the fantastic in North and South America, for example, categorizes Spanish American stories like the ones studied here as "imitative of fantastic writers like Poe" (80). While Poe is, of course, an important influence on writers like Darío, Lugones, and Quiroga, I do not see the latter as imitators of a North American aesthetic. Del George notes that the Latin American modernists "followed Poe, who sought the cosmopolitan and universal, not the autochthonous experience" (80). The critic correctly points out that Spanish American modernists did not turn to their "heritage of pre-Colombian beliefs" as "source material for supernatural literature" (80), but there is no reason why they should. The cosmopolitanism of the writers is a reflection of their own urban environment, given that Buenos Aires, Havana, and Mexico City were undergoing a rapid process

of development and projected a cosmopolitan flare that rivaled or surpassed many cities in the United States.

4. Positivism was a system of philosophy elaborated around the middle of the nineteenth century by Auguste Comte, who recognized only concrete facts and observable phenomenon as the basis of knowledge. Although Comte was more interested in the relationship between phenomenon and the laws that govern them than the actual cause or origin of the phenomenon itself, the fine points of his arguments were often lost when they passed into general culture. His ideas were often blended with those of Herbert Spencer and the philosophy of social Darwinism. Positivism had great appeal in many parts of Latin America in the late nineteenth century because it coincided with a tremendous urge for progress and development and with the rise of capitalism and industrialization. Comte's view of science as the base upon which knowledge is built was widely accepted in Mexico and other Latin American countries as the solution to the "backwardness" that characterized so much of that region of the world. It overtly stood in contrast to native ways of being and thinking and aligned middle- and upper-class urban dwellers with Europeans rather than with their Indian or Afro-Hispanic countrymen. In Mexico, Porfirio Díaz's chief advisors were so influenced by Comte and his ideas that they adopted the name "científicos" for themselves, reflecting the notion that science or knowledge could be used in the service of the nation.

5. Iser's theories about the relationship between the reader and the text have important implications for the study of the fantastic, although he did not concern himself specifically with the fantastic as a genre. Fantastic short stories such as those examined here illustrate clearly the ideas developed by Iser and the practitioners of reader response theory, especially in terms of how the reader is called on to complete the meaning of the text through interpretation. Iser's idea of the implied reader of a text is particularly useful in the analysis of fantastic stories, since it enables us to discuss the creation of specific effects through the manipulation of language and viewpoint. Just as importantly, the reader response approach does not insist on a single, stabilized interpretation of the text immune to cultural shifts, but rather recognizes that there is always a degree of subjectivity in the way people read. Such a view is helpful for a discussion of the fantastic, since it accommodates a kind of literature that relies on the reader's uncertainty and doubt to achieve a particular effect. In short, reflective of Iser's concerns, the fantastic teaches readers that they must think in order to understand, but it does not tell them *what* to think.

6. Angel Rama's influential book, *La ciudad letrada*, launched numerous investigations and debates about the role of the intellectual elite in Latin America, specifically in relationship to the great metropolises that were their centers of power. Central to his study is the question of what control writers and intellectuals had in governing and structuring the way the real city in Latin America was imagined and understood. Moraña, Dabove, Franco (*Decline and Fall*), and de la Campa have followed this line of investigation. Fantastic literature at the end of the nineteenth and beginning of the twentieth centuries often used the archetypal man of letters as a character or narrator, but rather than prop up ideas associated with positivism and emerging capitalism and industrialization, the fantastic tended to debunk the claims of the literary and scientific elite. In this way, it offered a countervoice to the official discourse of nation-building projects like those of Porfirio Díaz's *científicos*.

7. One of the genres most cultivated by romantic short story writers was the literary

legend, sometimes known as the *tradición*. The subject matter generally came from popular, oral sources and tended to focus on characters and incidents from pre-Colombian or colonial times. These short fictional works provided readers with a nostalgic look back, often as a means of comparing and contrasting "old" Latin America with the "new." Although many of them contained magical or marvelous elements, they are not, properly speaking, fantastic because it is understood from the outset that readers are not dealing with their own recognizable world in the text. Ricardo Palma's *tradición*, "El alacrán de Fray Gómez," is a good example of a romantic legend about a priest who has supernatural experiences, and Darío's tale initially seems to be following that model.

8. Readers who are very familiar with Christian imagery might understand the title of the story sooner, but for others, "Verónica" makes sense only upon the irruption of the fantastic in the text: the inexplicable appearance of Christ's face as an artifact in the friar's room links the story to the Bible, where a woman named Veronica discovers the miraculous image of Christ on a cloth she used to wipe his brow on the road to Calvary. The name Veronica derives from Latin and means "true icon"; for early Christians, Veronica's cloth was important proof of Christ's divine presence. But Darío seems to ask between the lines of his story, if we accept Veronica's icon as true, does that mean that Fray Tomás's icon is also true? If it is true, is it the result of a miracle, or are miracles the product of scientific knowledge? The discomfort or doubt such questions can generate is one important way in which the story differs from romantic legends.

9. Ocasio, for example, speaks of Quiroga as "a remarkable literary figure for his innovations in the Latin American short story of the early twentieth century," and he notes Quiroga's influence on Borges and Cortázar (58). Most critics who study Quiroga's work approach him as a *criollista,* or regional writer, and give more attention to stories, such as "A la deriva," "La gallina degollada," and "El hombre muerto," in a realist or psychological vein. His jungle stories, like "Anaconda" and "Juan Darien," have also received considerable attention because of the way he mixes the magical and the real, leading some critics to think of him as a precursor to magical realist writers like García Márquez. Little attention has been given to Quiroga's fantastic stories, however, perhaps because their thematic links to romanticism have led critics to dismiss them as throwbacks to an earlier age.

2 / The Fantastic as an Interrogation of Literary Practices

1. Borges acknowledges the existence of his double, the implied author who appears in so much of his work, in the 1960 essay "Borges y yo," but the idea is present in his earlier fiction. In stories such as the ones studied here, there is an intentional blurring of identities between Borges (the real author), the implied author, and the narrator. At times, all seem to be speaking as Borges, and the effect of the story depends to some degree on this confusion.

2. For more on "Pierre Menard, autor del Quijote," see Balderston, Dapía ("Pierre Menard"), Nallim, Aguilar, Gracia, and Castillo. These essays explore the philosophical underpinnings of Borges's story, including their relationship to the work of Fritz Mauthner and epistemological skepticism. Balderston looks at the parallelism between Borges's fictional Menard and the French writer Paul Valéry. He also situates the story in its sociohistorical context, pointing out that in Europe Hitler's

armies were overrunning neighboring countries; in Spain, Franco was crushing the last remnants of Republican resistance; and industrialized nations like Japan and the United States "were producing those new weapons that Don Quixote so despised" (38). Balderston believes that the "arms and letters debate" taking place in the world at that time is inscribed into Borges's story. As he puts it, "Who but Menard would have had the bravura to cast the question in those terms?" (38). Balderston refutes claims that Borges is an "escapist" writer and insists, instead, that all kinds of writing are linked epistemologically to the real world that spawned them.

3. For other readings of "El milagro secreto," see Quackenbush, Alvarez, Montes Capó, Waldegaray, and Sustaita. Balderston also looks at the story and its relationship to historical events in 1939, specifically Hitler's invasion of Czechoslovakia. For Balderston, the story is about "ways to escape from a circular nightmare. For the author of that nightmare was Adolf Hitler" (68).

4. In some ways, Tlön appears to be like Middle Earth or Narnia in English literature. As an invented place, it has obvious roots in the fantasy genre, but the way that Borges frames his story situates it more firmly in the realm of the fantastic. He is not merely describing a magical place; he asserts that it invades and usurps the "real" world at the end of the story, contrary to the expectations of his audience.

5. "Tlön, Uqbar, Orbis Tertius" appeared in the first edition of the *Antología de literatura fantástica*, edited by Borges, Ocampo, and Bioy Casares in 1940. The postscript in which Borges explains the appearance of objects from Tlön is dated 1947. Readers in 1940 could see at first glance that Borges was playing one of his famous games, referring to a future point in time and to events that had not happened yet. In later editions of the *Antología de literatura fantástica*, however, the irony of the postscript date is lost on readers who are unfamiliar with the original publication date of the story. The fantastic effect is greater as a result because the postscript seems to refer to real events that happened after Borges completed the original story.

6. For other treatments of the story, see Graff, Lunsford, Dapía ("This is Not a Universe "), and Tofts. These articles examine the philosophical roots of the story from an epistemological or phenomenological perspective, but they do not discuss it as an example of the fantastic. De Costa looks at humor in the story. Other articles that deal with Borges's ideas about literature include Boulter, Brown, Alonso, and Toro. These articles explore the connection between Borges's fiction writing and his critical essays on literature, and they also explain in what sense his work can be considered within the framework of postmodern theory. Although they do not make specific reference to "Tlön," they illustrate ideas that are present in the story.

7. For other approaches to "Continuidad de los parques," see Titler, Lagmanovich, Filinich, Lunn and Albrecht, and Zavala. These critics focus on the use of different levels of narration in the text, but they do not discuss it specifically as a fantastic story.

3 / Reclaiming History: Fantastic Journeys in Time and Space

1. The theme of the double is evident in all of the stories examined here, but because I have chosen to focus on how the texts rewrite history, I will not go into depth about the use of doubles. Essentially, the double in "La noche boca arriba" is a result of time travel or the splitting of time into two halves that make up the whole of the individual's experience. It does not appear to be related to the psychological split that is so often associated with the double in literature of the uncanny. I address the theme

of the double in Chapter 4 as it relates to the fantastic and the construction of gendered identity. For discussions of the double in Cortázar's fiction, see Kerr, Tyler, and Carmosino.

2. For other discussions of "La noche boca arriba," see Amícola, Co, Serra, and Antolín. While these critics pay attention to the use of dreams in the story or the blurring of reality and fantasy, they do not discuss the story specifically as an example of the fantastic, nor do they relate it to historical context.

3. See Cypess, for a fascinating discussion of how "La culpa es de los tlaxcaltecas" reworks the Malinche story. Petrea offers an analysis of the story's feminist overtones, and Dowling studies the importance of eroticism in Garro's work.

4. Other scholars who have looked at "Chac Mool" as an example of the fantastic include Gutierrez Mouat and Tyler. Arlington considers how Fuentes deals with issues of identity and religious syncretism. Valverde examines the treatment of masculinity in the story.

5. A number of scholars have looked at the treatment of doubles in this and other stories by Borges, including Gyurko, J. Irwin, Smith, and Dubnick. For additional discussion of "El sur" and the way it relates to national or individual identity, see Conde, Saona, Tedio, and González Casanovas.

4 / Psychoanalytic Readings of the Fantastic

1. Throughout this chapter, the word Other, when capitalized, refers to Jacques Lacan's conception of the term as he has described it in his many essays on subjectivity. Lacan's language is slippery and often vague, which has led to many debates about the meaning of the terms he has used. He does not provide neat definitions or tidy summaries of his complex thought, which makes it difficult to quote him in passing. Any attempt to define or summarize runs the risk of oversimplification or misrepresentation of Lacan's idea. However, within the narrow confines of this study, Other can be understood to mean "that which always insinuates itself between the individual and the objects of 'his' desire; which traverses those objects and makes them unstable; and which makes desire insatiable by continuously moving its target" (Bowie 83). In terms of the construction of the human subject, "The Other is the ultimate signifier of everyone the subject is not, as well as everything the subject does not have. For Lacan, the discovery of the Other parallels the acquisition of the abilities to speak and to distinguish between *I* and *you*, which are tantamount to the acquisition of social identity" (*Columbia Dictionary*, 216). In the stories examined here, the female characters are often doubles of the male characters, but not in a way that manifests itself purely on the thematic level. Because the male narrators are attempting to carve out a gendered subject position from which they can tell the story, the female characters are pushed into the role of Other, representing not only difference but also danger. This treatment of female characters in fiction is much in keeping with Simone de Beauvoir's discussion of women as Other in *The Second Sex*. De Beauvoir's discussion of female Otherness is not incompatible with Lacan's more abstract use of the term, and it adds nuances to the reading of the stories to consider how the two concepts overlap.

2. Lacan does not use the term Desire to mean sexual desire, although that may be one manifestation of it. In a Lacanian sense, Desire "is directed toward the fantasy constructions that govern the endless search for a satisfactory object in the world" (*Columbia Dictionary*, 78). Lacan speaks of Desire as "that which is thus given to the

Other to fill, and which is strictly that which it does not have, since it, too, lacks being" (263). I capitalize the word Desire in this chapter to indicate that I am following Lacan's broader understanding of it. In these specific stories, Desire is a mechanism that brings the fantastic into being in the texts. Its inability to be pinned down in language or to be contained in a single object creates a chain of signifiers that shift and morph into the unrecognizable (and unspeakable). It is this similarity to the language of the fantastic that makes psychoanalytic readings of the stories possible.

3. Lacan speaks of three registers or orders that mediate human development, the Real, the Imaginary, and the Symbolic. The Real is the most elusive, since it remains outside of speech and language. It should not be confused with "reality," which is (in Lacan's view) a subjective perception of that which surrounds us. The Imaginary refers to our ability to perceive and interpret images: "Human beings exist in the Imaginary from their earliest years, when experience is dominated by visual and spatial relationships, the most important of which is the relationship to the image of one's own body that Lacan described in the concept of the Mirror Stage" (*Columbia Dictionary,* 151). Entry into the Symbolic order parallels what Freud described as the Oedipus Complex. In Lacan's conception of the process, it is the Mirror Stage that marks "a kind of primary alienation, the opening of an unbridgeable gap between the child and her or his own self-image, which will be a feature of all of her or his future relationships" (*Columbia Dictionary,* 189). Entry into the Symbolic order marks an entry into "language itself and the entire realm of culture, conceived as a symbol system structured on the model of language" (*Columbia Dictionary,* 299). Although the Imaginary and the Symbolic often seem to be in opposition to one another, they are interconnected and cannot exist one without the other. All three orders are part of human consciousness, according to Lacan. In the stories under examination here, the focus is clearly on how the Symbolic order places demands on individuals to line up in binary opposition to each other following socially approved codes of gendered identity. The blurring of gender difference or the inability to perceive or acknowledge it leads to trouble, since it destabilizes the position from which the male narrator speaks.

4. Lacan speaks of the Name of the Father, the Phallic Order, and the Law of the Father, as interrelated concepts. While he acknowledges the role of the actual father in the formation of an individual subject, he insists that the Law of the Father is more abstract and consists of a set of societal laws that mediate the subject's relationship to himself and others. The Law of the Father teaches us that there is some normative way of organizing and structuring society, and that it is entrusted to the Phallus (the imaginary and symbolic functions of the male organ, associated with power and dominance in a patriarchal culture). Recognition of the Phallus as a signifier of sexual difference (and lack) is crucial for entry into the Symbolic Order, but it also sets into motion Desire, which is, in the simplest terms, a longing to return to an imaginary and undifferentiated state of wholeness.

5 / The Fantastic and the Conventions of Gothic Romance

1. Because gothic romances in the twentieth century have become mass-marketed commodities aimed chiefly at female readers, it is all the more important to look at the ideas they express about female sexuality. Modleski, for example, reads them as an expression of female paranoia related to marriage.

2. I use *desire* here in the Freudian sense of it as an instinctual libidinal drive.

Lacan conceives of it in more complex terms that have led some theorists to question whether female subjects can ever claim agency as a desiring subject.

3. In Chapter 4, male characters attempted to identify with female doubles. Here, no gender lines are crossed: Felipe's double is General Llorente; Aura's double is Consuelo. Although the effect is still supernatural, it is not as psychologically traumatic because gendered identity is never questioned.

7 / Cinematic Encounters with the Fantastic

1. Juan Padron's animated film, *Vampiros en la Habana* (1985), is a tongue-in-cheek treatment of the horror genre. He strips the genre of its fear-inducing potential by portraying Cuban vampires as friendly and fun-loving characters who speak in popular slang, hang out on street corners, dress in fashionable clothes, and listen to Cuban jazz. It is one of the most original approaches to vampire films in Latin America, but because it is an animated feature film, it should be excluded from our discussion of what makes a film fantastic. Cartoons do not pretend to represent "reality," which is one of the vital components of the fantastic.

2. I have excluded other Subiela films from the discussion because they can more appropriately be called "fantasies." *Pequeños milagros* (1997) and *El lado oscuro del corazón* (1992), for example, present the marvelous as a normal part of the world of the characters. People fly, they transform themselves into fairies, they carry out extraordinary feats in a routine manner. The films are constructed in poetic and allegorical language, which gives them a magical tone without linking them to a world audiences perceive as "real."

Bibliography

Agosín, Marjorie. "María Luisa Bombal o el lenguaje alucinado." *Symposium: A Quarterly Journal in Modern Literatures* 48.4 (winter 1995): 251–56.

Aguilar, Jesús. "Can Pierre Menard be the author of Don Quixote?" *Variaciones Borges: Journal of the Jorge Luis Borges Center for Studies & Documentation* 8 (1999): 166–77.

Alazraki, Jaime. *En busca del unicornio: Los cuentos de Julio Cortázar. Elementos para una poética de lo neofantástico*. Madrid: Gredos, 1983.

———. "Neofantastic Literature—A Structuralist Answer." *The Analysis of Literary Texts: Current Trends in Methodology*. Ed. Randolph Pope. Ypsilanti, MI: Bilingual Press, 1980. 286–90.

———. "Para una revalidación del concepto realismo mágico en la literatura hispanoamericana." *Homenaje a Andrés Iduarte*. Ed. Alazraki et al. Clear Creek, IN: The American Hispanist, 1976. 9–21.

———, ed. *Teorías de lo fantástico*. Madrid: Arcos, 2001.

Alegría, Fernando. "Alejo Carpentier: realismo mágico." *Humanitas* 1 (1960): 345–72.

Alonso, Carlos J. "Borges y la teoría." *MLN* 120 (2005): 437–56.

Alvarez, Nicolás. "El discurso narrativo y la historia de 'El milagro secreto' de Jorge Luis Borges." *Círculo: Publicación del Círculo de Cultura Panamericano* 24 (1995): 74–79.

Amícola, José. "'La noche boca arriba' como encrucijada literaria." *Revista Iberoamericana* 63.180 (July 1997): 459–64.

Anderson Imbert, Enrique. *Los cuentos fantásticos de Rubén Darío*. Cambridge, MA: Harvard University Press: 1967.

———. "Literatura fantástica, realismo mágico y lo real maravilloso." *Otros mundos otros fuegos. Fantasía y realismo mágico en Iberoamérica*. Ed. D. Yates. East Lansing: Latin American Studies Center of Michigan State University, 1975. 39–44.

Angulo, Maria Elena. *Magic Realism: Social Context and Discourse*. New York: Garland, 1995.

Antolín, Francisco. "'La noche boca arriba' de Cortázar: Oposición de paradigmas." *Explicación de textos literarios* 9.2 (1981): 147–51.

Apter, T.E. *Fantasy Literature: An Approach to Reality*. Bloomington: Indiana University Press, 1982.

Aran, Pampa. *El fantástico literario: aportes teóricos*. Madrid: Tauro, 1999.

Araújo, Helena. "Geografía de lo fantástico en la escritura femenina latinoamericana." *Boletín Cultural y Bibliográfico* 32.38 (1995): 14–48.

Arlington, Melvin S. "The God Made Flesh: Some Observations on Syncretism and Identity in 'Chac Mool.'" *Interpretaciones a la obra de Carlos Fuentes: Un gigante de las letras hispanoamericanas*. Ed. Ana María López de Hernández. Madrid: Beramar, 1990. 235–41.

Armitt, Lucie. *Contemporary Women's Fiction and the Fantastic*. New York: St. Martin's Press, 2000.

———. *Theorizing the Fantastic*. London: Arnold, 1996.

Asturias, Miguel Angel. "Hearing the Scream." *Atlas: A Window on the World* 14.6 (Dec. 1967): 47–62.

Balderston, Daniel. *Out of Context: Historical Reference and the Representation of Reality in Borges*. Durham, NC: Duke University Press, 1993.

Barcía, Pedro Luis, ed. *Leopoldo Lugones: Cuentos Fantásticos*. Madrid: Castalia, 1987.

Barchino Pérez, Matías. "La criaturas del tiempo: Los últimos cuentos de miedo de Carlos Fuentes." *Anales de Literatura Hispanoamericana* 34 (2005): 29–41.

Barrenechea, Ana María. "Ensayo de una tipología de la literatura fantástica." *Revista Iberoamericana* 38.80 (July-Sept. 1972): 391–403.

Barthes, Roland. "The Death of the Author." *Image, Music, Text*. Trans. Stephen Heath. New York: Hill and Wang, 1977. 142–48.

Beauvoir, Simone de. *The Second Sex*. Trans. H.M. Parshley. New York: Alfred A. Knopf, 1952.

Belevan, Harry. *Teoría de lo fantástico: Apuntes para una dinámica de la literatura de expresión fantástica*. Barcelona: Anagrama, 1976.

Belsey, Catherine. *Critical Practice*. London: Methuen, 1980.

Ben-Ur, Lorraine Elena. "El realismo mágico en la crítica hispanoamericana." *Journal of Spanish Studies Twentieth-Century* 4.3 (winter 1976): 149–63.

Berger, John. *Ways of Seeing*. Harmondsworth, England: Penguin, 1972.

Bioy Casares, Adolfo. "En memoria de Paulina." *La trama celeste*. Buenos Aires: Sur, 1967. 11–26.

———. "On Fantastic Literature." *TriQuarterly* 25 (1972): 222–30.

———. "Prólogo." *Antología de la literatura fantástica*. Ed. Jorge Luis Borges, Silvina Ocampo, and Adolfo Bioy Casares. Buenos Aires: Ed. Sudamericana, 1940. 7–14.

Booth, Wayne. *The Rhetoric of Fiction*. Chicago: University of Chicago Press, 1983.

Borges, Jorge Luis. "El milagro secreto." *Ficciones*. Madrid: Ed. Alianza, 1995. 173–83.

———. "Pierre Menard, Autor del *Quijote*." *Ficciones*. Madrid: Ed. Alianza, 1995. 41–55.

———. "El sur." *Ficciones*. Madrid: Ed. Alianza, 1995. 205–16.

———. "Tlón, Uqbar, Orbis Tertius." *Ficciones*. Madrid: Ed. Alianza, 1995. 13–40.

Bombal, María Luisa. *La última niebla. La amortajada*. Barcelona: Seix Barral, 1994.

Boulter, Jonathan Stuart. "Partial Glimpses of the Infinite: Borges and the Simulacrum." *Hispanic Review* 69.3 (summer 2001): 355–77.

Bové, Paul A. "Discourse." *Critical Terms for Literary Study*. Ed. Lentricchia and McLaughlin. Chicago: University of Chicago Press, 1990. 50–65.

Bowie, Malcolm. *Lacan*. Cambridge, MA: Harvard University Press, 1991.

Bravo, Victor. *Magias y maravillas en el continente literario: para un deslinde del realismo mágico y lo real maravilloso*. Caracas: Ed. Bello, 1988.

———. *Los poderes de la ficción: para una interpretación de la litertura fantástica*. Caracas: Monte Avila, 1987.

Brooke-Rose, Christine. *A Rhetoric of the Unreal: Studies in Narrative and Structure, Especially of the Fantastic*. Cambridge: Cambridge University Press, 1981.

Brown, J. Andrew. "Borges's Scientific Discipline." *Hispanic Review* 72.4 (autumn 2004): 505–22.

Bush, Andrew. "Reintroduction to Fantastic Literature: A Latin American Reply." *Papers in Romance* 2, Supplement 1 (July 1980): 85–90.

Caillois, Roger. "The Fantastic." Trans. Will McLendon. *Forum* 2.2 (May 1958): 51–55.

Calderón Bird, Raúl. "Lo fantástico en dos libros de Elena Garro." *Signos: Literarios y Lingüisticos* 2.2 (July-Dec. 2000): 111–22.

Callan, Richard. "The Jungian Basis of Carlos Fuentes' *Aura*." *Kentucky Romance Quarterly* 18 (1971): 65–75.

Campa, Román de la. *Latin Americanism*. Minneapolis: University of Minnesota Press, 1999.

Carillo, Emilio. *El cuento fantástico*. Buenos Aires: Editorial Nova, 1968.

Carmosino, Roger B. "El doble manifiesto y el doble impacto en cuatro relatos de Julio

Cortázar." *South Eastern Latin Americanist* 37.3 (winter 1994): 1–10.

———. "Forma y funciones del doble en tres cuentos de Cortázar: 'La noche boca arriba,'
'Las armas secretas,' y 'El otro cielo.'" *Texto crítico* 2.2 (Jan. 1996): 83–92.

Carpentier, Alejo. "De lo real maravilloso Americano." *Tientos y diferencias.* Mexico: UNAM, 1964. (First published as "Prólogo" to the novel, *El reino de este mundo*, 1949.)

Castellanos Ronzón, Carlos. "Reflexiones sobre el tiempo lógico en *Aura*." *Texto Crítico* 5:9 (July-Dec. 2001): 197–214.

Castillo, Jorge Luis. "Pierre Menard and the School of the Skeptics." *Hispanic Review* 71 (summer 2003): 415–28.

Chanady, Amaryll Beatrice. *Magical Realism and The Fantastic: Resolved Versus Unresolved Antinomy.* New York: Garland, 1985.

Chodorow, Nancy J. *Femininities, Masculinities, Sexualities: Freud and Beyond.* Lexington: University of Kentucky Press, 1994.

Clark, Maria B. "Usurping Difference in the Feminine Fantastic from the Riverplate." *Studies in Twentieth-Century Literature* 20.1 (winter 1996): 235–49.

Co, Francisca. "El soñador en 'La noche boca arriba.'" *Visión de la narrativa hispánica. Ensayos.* Ed. Juan Cruz Mendizábal and Juan Fernández Jiménez. Indiana: Dept. of Spanish and Classical Languages, Indiana University of Pennsylvania, 1999. 31–36.

Cócaro, Nicolás. *Cuentos fantásticos argentinos.* Buenos Aires: Emece, 1960 (reprinted 1996 and 2000).

Coates, Paul. *The Double and the Other: Identity as Ideology in Post-Romantic Fiction.* London: MacMillan Press, 1988.

Collette, Marianella. "La fase del espejo, lo simbólico y lo imaginario en la novela *Aura*, de Carlos Fuentes." *Revista Canadiense de Estudios Hispánicos* 19.2 (winter 1995): 281–98.

Columbia Dictionary of Modern Literary and Cultural Criticism. Ed. Joseph Childers and Gary Hentzl. New York: Columbia University Press, 1995.

Conde, Susana. "Un personaje en busca de su identidad: El yo, la nación y la narración en 'El Sur.' *Borges*." Ed. Alberto C. Revah. Buenos Aires: Biblioteca del Congreso de la Nación, 1997. 43–58.

Corona, Ignacio. "Contesting the Lettered City: Cultural Mediation and Communicative Strategies in the Contemporary Chronicle in Mexico." *Latin American Literature and Mass Media.* Ed. Edmundo Paz-Soldán and Debra A. Castillo. New York: Garland, 2001. 193–206.

Cornwell, Neil. *The Absurd in Literature.* Manchester, England: Manchester University Press, 2006.

———. *The Literary Fantastic: From Gothic to Postmodernism.* New York: Harvester Wheatsheaf, 1990.

Cortázar, Julio. "Casa tomada." *Relatos.* Buenos Aires: Ed. Sudamericana, 1970. 413–20.

———. "La continuidad de los parques." *Relatos.* Buenos Aires: Ed. Sudamericana, 1970. 312–14.

———. "La noche boca arriba." *Relatos.* Buenos Aires: Ed. Sudamericana, 1970. 72–82.

———. "The Present State of Fiction in Latin America." Trans. Margery A. Safir. *Books Abroad* 80.8 (summer 1976): 522–32.

Creech, James. "'Chasing After Advances': Diderot's Article 'Encyclopedia.'" *Yale French Studies* 63 (1982): 185–97.

Cypess, Sandra Messinger. "The Figure of La Malinche in the Texts of Elena Garro." *A Different Reality. Studies on the Work of Elena Garro.* Ed. Anita Stoll. Lewisburg: Bucknell University Press, 1990. 117–35.

Dabove, Juan Pablo. *Nightmares of the Lettered City: Banditry and Literature in Latin America, 1816–1929.* Pittsburgh, PA: University of Pittsburgh Press, 2007.

Dapía, Silvia G. "Pierre Menard: Autor del Quijote." *Romance Languages Annual* 5 (1993): 376–80.

———. "'This Is Not a Universe': An Approach to Borges's 'Tlön, Uqbar, Orbis Tertius." *Chasqui: Revista de Literatura Latinoamericana* 26.2 (1997): 94–107.

Darío, Ruben. "El caso de la señorita Amelia." *Cuentos Fantásticos.* Ed. José Olivio Jiménez. Madrid: Alianza, 1976. 43–49.

———. "Verónica." *Cuentos Fantásticos.* Ed. José Olivio Jiménez. Madrid: Alianza, 1976. 51–55.

De Costa, René. *Humor in Borges.* Detroit, MI: Wayne State University Press, 2000.

Dehennin, Elsa. "Acercamiento a una narrativa de lo imposible." *Homenaje a Ana Maria Barrenechea*, Ed. Lía Schwartz Lerner, Isaías Lerner et al. Madrid: Castalia, 1984. 385–96.

———. *Del realismo español al fantástico hispanoamericano: Estudios de narratología.* Geneva, Switzerland: Droz, 1996.

Del George, Dana. *The Supernatural in Short Fiction of the Americas: The Other World in the New World.* Westport, CT: Greenwood Press, 2001.

D'Haen, Theo L. "Magical Realism and Postmodernism: Decentering Privileged Centers." *Magical Realism: Theory, History, Community.* Ed. Parkinson Zamora and Faris. Chapel Hill, NC: Duke University Press, 1995. 191–208.

Deutsch, Helene. *The Psychology of Women.* New York: Grune and Stratton, 1945.

Diamond, Irene, and Lee Quinby, eds. *Feminism & Foucault: Reflections of Resistance.* Boston: Northeastern University Press, 1988.

Dowling, Lee H. "The Erotic Dimension of Elena Garro's 'La culpa es de los tlaxcaltecas.'" *Chasqui: Revista de la literatura latinoamericana* 28.2 (Nov. 1999): 31–59.

Dubnick, Heather L. "Mirrors and Fatherhood: Doubling, mise en abime, and the Uncanny in the Fictions of Jorge Luis Borges." *Romance Notes* 44.1 (fall 2003): 69–81.

Duncan, Cynthia. "Carlos Fuentes' 'Chac Mool' and Todorov's Theory of the Fantastic. A Case for the Twentieth Century." *Hispanic Journal* 8.1 (fall 1986): 125–33.

———. "La culpa es de los tlaxcaltecas: A reevaluation of Mexico's Past Through Myth." *Critica hispánica* 7.2 (1985): 121–27.

———. "Reading Power: Some Observations on the Construction of Meaning and Authority in María Luisa Bombal's *La última niebla*." *Revista Hispánica Moderna* 51.2 (Dec. 1998): 304–16.

Eagleton, Terry. *Literary Theory: An Introduction*. Minneapolis: University of Minnesota Press, 1983.

———. *Text, Ideology, Realism*. Baltimore, MD: Johns Hopkins University, Press, 1980.

Ebert, Roger. Rev of *Santa Sangre*, dir. Alejandro Jodorowsky. *Chicago Sun Times*, June 27, 1990. http://rogerebert.suntimes.com.

Erdal Jordan, Mary. *La narrativa fantástica. Evolución del género y su relación con las concepciones del lenguaje*. Madrid: Vervuert/ Iberoamericana, 1998.

Faris, Wendy B. "Scheherazde's Children: Magical Realism and Postmodern Fiction." *Magical Realism: Theory, History, Community*. Ed. Parkinson Zamora and Faris. Chapel Hill, NC: Duke University Press, 1995. 163–90.

Fausto-Sterling, Anne. "Menopause: The Storm Before the Calm." *Feminist Theory and the Body*. Ed. Janet Price and Margrit Shildrick. New York: Routledge, 1999. 169–78.

Filinich, María Isabel. "'Continuidad de los parques': Lo continuo y lo discontinuo." *Hispamerica: Revista de Literatura* 25.73 (April 1996): 113–19.

Fleming, Leonor, ed. *Horacio Quiroga. Cuentos*. Madrid: Cátedra, 1999.

Flores, Angel. "Magical Realism in Spanish American Fiction." *Hispania* 37.2 (May 1955): 187–92.

Foucault, Michel. *The Archaeology of Knowledge*. Trans. A.M. Sheridan Smith. New York: Pantheon, 1972.

Franco, Jean. *The Decline and Fall of the Lettered City: Latin America in the Cold War*. Cambridge, MA: Harvard University Press, 2002.

———. "The Nation as Imagined Community." *The New Historicism*. Ed. Aram H. Veeser. New York: Routledge, 1989. 204–12

Freud, Sigmund. "The Uncanny." *The Standard Edition of the Complete Psychological Works of Sigmund Freud*. Trans. and ed. James Strachey in collaboration with Anna Freud. Vox. XVII. London: Hogarth Press, 1955. 219–52.

Fuente del Pilar, José Javier, ed. *Antología del cuento fantástico hispanoamericano del siglo XIX*. Madrid: Miraguana Ediciones, 2003.

Fuentes, Carlos. *Aura*. Mexico: Biblioteca Era, 1993.

———. "Chac Mool." *Los días enmascarados*. Mexico: Los Presentes, 1954. 7–28.

———. *Inquieta compañía*. Mexico: Alfaguara, 2004.

———. "On Reading and Writing Myself: How I Wrote *Aura*." *World Literature Today: A Literary Quarterly of the University of Oklahoma* 57 (1983): 531–39.

———. Radio interview with Bob Edwards, *NPR Morning Edition*, May 21, 2002.

García Canclini, Néstor. *Culturas híbridas: Estrategias para entrar y salir de la modernidad*. Buenos Aires: Editorial Paidós, 2001.

García Márquez, Gabriel. Interview with Fernández Brasso. *Gabriel García Márquez: Una conversación infinita*. Madrid: Azur, 1969.

Garro, Elena. "La culpa es de los tlaxcaltecas." *La Semana de colores*. Xalapa, Mexico: Univeridad Veracruzana, 1964. 9–33.

———. "El duende." *La Semana de colores*. Xalapa, Mexico: Univeridad Veracruzana, 1964. 145–57.

———. "El robo de Tiztla." *La Semana de colores*. Xalapa, Mexico: Univeridad Veracruzana, 1964. 123–41.

———. "La semana de colores." *La Semana de colores*. Xalapa, Mexico: Univeridad Veracruzana, 1964. 76–96.

Geary, Robert F. *The Supernatural in Gothic Fiction: Horror, Belief, and Literary Change*. Lewiston, ID: Edwin Mellen, 1992.

González, José Luis. "Cuatro cuestiones: literatura realista y literatura fantástica." *Mexico en la Cultura*, Suplemento *Novedades* 336 (Aug. 28, 1955): 3.

González, José Ramón. "Estrategias discursivas y relato fantástico: Sobre 'La culpa es de los tlaxcaltecas' de Elena Garro." *La Torre: Revista de la Universidad de Puerto Rico* 5.20 (Oct. 1991): 475–88.

González Casanovas, Roberto J. "Borges's Argentinian South: Legend, Fiction, and Myth in 'El Sur.'" *West Virginia University Philological Papers* 37 (1991): 151–57.

Gracia, Jorge J.E. "Borges's 'Pierre Menard': Philosophy or Literature?" *The Journal of Aesthetics and Art Criticism* 59 (winter 2001): 45–57.

Graff, Gerald. "Interpretation on Tlön: A Response to Stanley Fish." *New Literary History* 17.1 (autumn 1985): 109–17.

Guerra Cunningham, Lucía. "La marginalidad subversiva del deseo en *La última niebla* de María Luisa Bombal." *Hispamérica: Revista de Literatura* 21.62 (Aug. 1992): 53–63.

Gutierrez Mouat, Ricardo. "Carlos Fuentes y el relato fantástico." *Modern Language Studies* 15.1 (winter 1985): 39–49.

Gyurko, Lanin A. "Borges and the Theme of the Double." *Ibero-Amerikanisches Archiv* 2.3 (1976): 193–226.

Haggerty, George. "The Horrors of Catholicism: Religion and Sexuality in Gothic Fiction." *Romanticism on the Net: An Electronic Journal Devoted to Romantic Studies* 36–37 (2004) (electronic publication).

Hahn, Oscar. *El cuento fantástico hispanoamericano en el siglo XIX*. Mexico: Premia Ed., 1978.

———. *Fundadores del cuento fantástico hispanoamericano*. Santiago, Chile: Ed. Andrés Bello, 1998.

———. "Trayectoria del cuento fantástico hispanoamericano." *Mester* 19.2 (fall 1990): 34–45.

Hutcheon, Linda. *A Poetics of Postmodernism: History, Theory, Fiction*. New York: Routledge, 1988.

Irish, James. "Magical Realism: A Search for Caribbean and Latin American Roots." *Literary Half Yearly* (University of Mysore) 2.2 (1970): 127–39.

Irwin, John T. "Double You, Double V: Borges and Poe in the Labyrinth." *Crítica Hispánica* 15.2 (fall 1993): 85–94.

Irwin, W.R. *The Game of the Impossible. A Rhetoric of Fantasy*. Urbana: University of Illinois Press, 1976.

Iser, Wolfgang. *The Act of Reading: A Theory of Aesthetic Response*. Baltimore, MD: Johns Hopkins University Press, 1978.

Jackson, Rosemary. *Fantasy, the Literature of Subversion*. London: Methuen, 1981.

———. "Introduction." *What Did Miss Darrington See? An Anthology of Feminist Supernatural Fiction*. Ed. Jessica Amanda Salmonson. New York: The Feminist Press at the CUNY, 1989. xv-xxxv.

Johansen, Phillip. "The Cinematic Fantastic." *Arachne: An Interdisciplinary Journal of the Humanities* 2.2 (1995): 325–36.

Johnson, Barbara. "Writing." *Critical Terms for Literary Study*. Ed. Lentricchia and McLaughlin. Chicago: University of Chicago Press, 1990. 39–49.

Jones, Kathleen B. "On Authority: Or Why Women Are Not Entitled to Speak." *Feminism & Foucault: Reflections of Resistance*. Ed. Diamond and Quinby. Boston: Northeastern University Press, 1988. 119–33.

Kaplan, Marina E. "'Tlön, Uqbar, Orbis Tertius' y 'Urn Burial.'" *Comparative Literature* 36.4 (autumn 1984): 328–42.

Keppler, C.F. *The Literature of the Second Self*. Tucson: University of Arizona Press, 1972.

Kerr, Lucille. "El individuo y el otro. Crítica a los cuentos de Julio Cortázar." *Revista Iberoamericana* 39 (1973): 693–95.

King, John. "The Boom of the Latin American Novel." *The Cambridge Companion to the Latin American Novel*. Ed. Efraín Kistal. Cambridge: Cambridge University Press, 2005. 59–80.

Klein, Melanie. *Love, Guilt, and Reparation*. New York: Delta, 1975.

Klingenberg, Patricia Nisbet. *Fantasies of the Feminine: The Short Stories of Silvina Ocampo*. Lewiston, IL: Bucknell University Press, 1999.

———. "The Feminine 'I': Silvina Ocampo's Fantasies of the Subject. *RLA: Romance Languages Annual* 1 (1989): 488–94.

———. "The Mad Double in the Stories of Silvina Ocampo." *Latin American Literary Review* 16.32 (July-Dec. 1988): 29–40.

———. "The Twisted Mirror: The Fantastic Stories of Silvina Ocampo." *Letras Femeninas* 13.1–2 (spring-autumn 1987): 67–78.

———. “The Grotesque in Silvina Ocampo’s Short Stories.” *Letras femeninas* 10.1 (spring 1984): 23–26.

König, Irmtrud. *La formación de la narrativa fantástica hispanoamericana en la época moderna*. Frankfurt: Verlag Peter Lang, 1984.

Lacan, Jacques. *Feminine Sexuality*. Ed. and trans. Juliet Mitchell and Jacqueline Rose. New York: W.W. Norton, 1982.

Lagmanovich, David. “Estrategias del cuento breve en Cortázar: Un paso por ‘Continuidad de los parques.’” *Explicación de Textos Literarios* 17.1–2 (1988): 177–85.

Leal, Luis. *Breve historia del cuento mexicano*. México: Ediciones de Andrea, 1956.

———. “El realismo mágico en la literatura hispanoamericana.” *Cuadernos americanos* 15 (1967): 230–35.

Lentricchia, Frank, and Thomas McLaughlin. *Critical Terms for Literary Study*. Chicago: University of Chicago Press, 1990.

Lockert, Lucia Fox. “Silvina Ocampo’s Fantastic Short Stories.” *Monographic Review/Revista Monográfica* 4: 221–29.

López Castaño, Oscar. “La alucinación como forma de vida en *La última niebla*.” *Linguistica y Literatura* 13.21 (Jan.-June 1992): 84–94.

Louis, Annick. “Definiendo un género, *La antología de la literatura fantástica* de Silvina Ocampo, Adolfo Bioy Casares y Jorge Luis Borges.” *Nueva Revista de Filología Hispánica* 49.2 (2001): 409–37.

Lovecraft, Howard Phillips. *Supernatural Horror in Literature*. New York: Dover, 1973.

Lugones, Leopoldo. “Viola Acherontia.” *Las fuerzas extrañas*. Ed. Arturo García Ramos. Madrid: Cátedra, 1996. 121–29.

———. “Yzur.” *Las fuerzas extrañas*. Ed. Arturo García Ramos. Madrid: Cátedra, 1996. 133–44.

Lunn, Patricia V., and Jane W. Albrecht. “The Grammar of Technique: Inside ‘Continuidad de los parques.’” *Hispania* 80.2 (May 1997): 227–33.

Lunsford, Kern L. “Jorge Luis Borges’s ‘Tlön, Uqbar, Orbis Tertius’: Epistemology and History; Language and Literary Creation.” *Cincinnati Romance Review* 8 (1989): 101–9.

Martin, Wallace. *Recent Theories of Narrative*. Ithaca, NY: Cornell University Press, 1986.

Martínez Morales, José Luis. “*Aura*, y el espectro de la transgression.” *Palabra y el Hombre: Revista de la Universidad Veracruzana* 123 (July-Sept. 2002): 99–109.

Massé, Michelle A. *In the Name of Love. Women, Masochism, and the Gothic*. Ithaca, NY: Cornell University Press, 1992.

Meehan, Thomas. “Los niños perversos en los cuentos de Silvina Ocampo.” *Hispanic Literatures, 4th Annual Conference*, 1978. Indiana University of Pennsylvania, 1979: 57–68.

Meléndez, Gabriel. "Lo fantástico en los cuentos de José Emilio Pacheco." *Confluencia* 4.1 (fall 1988): 97–107.

Mena, Lucila Inés. "Fantasía y realismo mágico." *Otros mundos otros fuegos. Fantasía y realismo mágico en Iberoamérica*. Ed. D. Yates. East Lansing: Latin American Studies Center of Michigan State University, 1975. 63–68.

Méndez Rodenas, Adriana. "El lenguaje de los sueños en *La última niebla*: La metáfora del Eros." *Revista Iberoamericana* 60: 168–69.

Merino, Blanca. "Fantasía y realidad en *Aura* de Carlos Fuentes." *Literatura Mexicana* 2.1 (1991): 135–47.

Modleski, Tania. *Loving with a Vengeance. Mass-produced Fantasies for Women*. New York: Routledge, 1990.

Moers, Ellen. *Literary Women*. New York: Doubleday, 1976.

Molloy, Sylvia. "Simplicidad inquietante en los relatos de Silvina Ocampo." *Lexis* 2.2 (1978): 241–51.

Monet-Viera, Molly. "Strange Forces: Occultism and the Inauguration of the Fantastic Genre in Latin America." *Romance Studies* 19.2 (Dec. 2001): 123–34.

Montes Capó, Cristián. "Temporalidad y existencia en 'El milagro secreto' de Jorge Luis Borges." *Taller de Letras* 32 (May 2003): 53–66.

Mora Valcárcel, Carmen de. "La literatura fantástica argentina en los años veinte: Leopoldo Lugones." *Río de la Plata: Culturas* 4–6 (1987): 207–14.

Morales, Ana Maria, and José Miguel Sardiñas. "Bibliografía sobre literatura fantástica." *Signos: Literarios y Lingüísticos* 2.2 (July-Dec. 2000): 181–212.

———. "Las fronteras de lo fantástico," Sardiñas, 241–54.

Moraña, Mabel. *Crítica impura: Estudios de literatura y cultura latinoamericanos*. Madrid: Iberoamericana, 2004.

Muñoz-Basols, Javier. "La recreación del género gótico a través de la percepción sensorial: La construcción de la hipotiposis en *Aura* de Carlos Fuentes." *Atenea* 23.2 (Dec. 2003): 73–85.

Nance, Kimberly A. "Contradictory Instructions: Folklore, Precepts and Ideologies of Reading in the Latin American Fantastic." *Confluencia: Revista Hispánica de Cultura y Literatura* 17.1 (fall 2001): 7–18.

Noguera, Rubén. "The Fantastic in the Stories of Julio Cortázar." *Revista de Estudios Hispánicos* 21 (1994): 221–34.

Ocampo, Silvina. *La furia y otros cuentos*. Buenos Aires: Sur, 1959.

Ocasio, Rafael. *Literature of Latin America*. Westport, CT: Greenwood Press, 2004.

Olea Franco, Rafael. *En el reino fantástico de los aparecidos: Roa Bárcena, Fuentes y Pacheco*. Mexico City: El Colegio de México, 2004.

———. "Literatura fantástica y nacionalismo: De *Los días enmascarados* a *Aura*." *Literatura Mexicana* 17.1 (2006): 113–26.

Olivio Jiménez, José. "Prólogo," *Cuentos fantásticos*, Rubén Darío. Madrid: Alianza, 1976. 7–23.

Orphee, Elvira. "Su demonio privado." *Su demonio preferido*. Buenos Aires: Emece, 1973. 61–87.

Ostrov, Andrea. "*La última niebla*: La locura de una mujer razonable: Lectura de la novel de María Luisa Bombal." *Acta Literaria* 19 (1994): 39–48.

Ostrowski, Witold. "The Fantastic and the Realistic in Literature." *Zagadnienia Radzajow Literackich* 9.16 (1966): 54–71.

Pacheco, José Emilio. "La fiesta brava." *El principio del placer*. Mexico: Joaquín Mortiz, 1972. 77–113.

Parkinson Zamora, Lois, and Wendy B. Faris, Eds. *Magical Realism: Theory, History, Community*. Chapel Hill, NC: Duke University Press, 1995.

Paz-Soldán, Edmundo, and Debra A. Castillo, eds. *Latin American Literature and Mass Media*. New York: Garland, 2001.

Pérez, Genaro J. "La configuración de elementos góticos en 'Constancia,'" *Aura* y 'Tlactocatzine, del jardín de Flandes' de Carlos Fuentes." *Hispania* 80.1 (Mar. 1997): 9–20.

Petrea, Mariana. "De la conquista histórica a la conquista personal: Perspectiva ficcional feminista de la identidad mexicana y mexicoamericana." *Alba de América: Revista literaria* 17.32 (Mar. 1999): 163–71.

Plank, William G. "The Imaginary: Synthesis of Fantasy and Reality." *The Scope of the Fantastic— Theory, Technique, Major Authors*. Ed. Robert A. Collins and Howard D. Pearce. Westport, CT: Greenwood Press, 1980. 77–82.

Porro, Juana. "La literatura fantástica como un saber para enseñar." *Signos: Literarios y Lingüísticos* 2.2 (July-Dec. 2000): 171–78.

Prince, Gerald. "Introduction to the Narratee." *Reader Response Criticism: From Formalism to Post-Structuralism*. Ed. Jane P. Tomkins. Baltimore, MD: Johns Hopkins University Press, 1980. 7–25. (Originally appeared in *Poetique* 14 [1973]: 178–96.)

Punter, David, Ed. *A Companion to the Gothic*. Oxford: Blackwell, 2000.

Quackenbush, L. Howard. "Borges' Tragedy." *Hispanofila* 31.2 (Jan. 1988): 77–86.

Quiroga, Horacio. "El almohadón de pluma." *Cuentos de amor, de locura y de muerte*. Buenos Aires: Losada, 1973. 55–59.

———. "El vampiro." *Relatos fantásticos hispanoamericanos: Antología*. Ed. José Miguel Sardiñas and Ana María Morales. Havana: Casa de las Américas, 2003. 181–207.

Rabkin, Eric. *The Fantastic in Literature*. Princeton, NJ: Princeton University Press, 1976.

Rama, Angel. *La ciudad letrada*. Hanover, NH: Ediciones del Norte, 1984.

Rank, Otto. *The Double: A Psychoanalytic Study*. New York: Meridan Books, 1979.

Risco, Antonio. *Literatura fantástica de la lengua española*. Madrid: Altea, Taurus, Alfaguara, 1987.

———. "Notas para un estudio de la literatura fantástica hispánica del siglo XX." *Monographic Review/ Revista Monográfica* 3.1–2 (1987): 58–70.

Rodero, Jesús. *La edad de la incertidumbre: Un estudio del cuento fantástico del siglo XX en Latinoamérica.* New York: Peter Lang, 2006.

Rodríguez-Luis, Julio. *The Contemporary Praxis of the Fantastic: Borges and Cortázar.* New York: Garland, 1991.

Rodriguez Monegal, Emir. "Borges: Una teoría de la literatura fantástica." *Revista Iberoamericana* 42.9 (Apr.-June 1976): 177–89.

———. "Realismo mágico versus literatura fantástica: un diálogo de sordos." *Otros mundos otros fuegos. Fantasía y realismo mágico en Iberoamérica.* Ed. D. Yates. East Lansing: Latin American Studies Center of Michigan State University, 1975. 25–37.

Roh, Franz. "Magic Realism: Post-Expressionism." Trans. Wendy B. Faris. *Magical Realism: Theory, History, Community.* Ed. Parkinson Zamora and Faris. Chapel Hill, NC: Duke University Press, 1995. 15–31.

Rottensteiner, Franz. *The Fantasy Book.* New York: Macmillan, 1978.

Ruthven, K.K. *Feminist Literary Studies.* Cambridge: Cambridge University Press, 1990.

Salgado, María A. "Rubén Darío's Short Stories: Autobiography, Fantasy and the Fantastic." *The Dark Fantastic.* Ed. C.W. Sullivan III. Westport, CT: Greenwood Press, 1997. 1–21.

Sandner, David, ed. *Fantastic Literature: A Critical Reader.* Westport, CT: Praeger, 2004.

———. "Theorizing the Fantastic: Editing Fantastic Literature: A Critical Reader and the Six Stages of Fantasy Criticism." *Journal of the Fantastic in the Arts* 16.4 (63) (winter 2006): 277–301.

Sanmartín Ortí, Pau. "*Aura*: Análisis de lo fantástico en la obra de Carlos Fuentes." *Líneas actuales de investigación literaria: Estudios de la literatura hispánica*, Ed. Verónica Arenas Lozano, Josefa Badía Herrera et al. Valencia, Spain: Universitat de Valencia, 2004. 699–708.

Saona, Margarita. "Borges, 'El sur' y la nación imaginada." *Inti: Revista de Literatura Hispánica* 55–56 (spring-autumn 2002): 139–48.

Sardiñas, José Miguel, ed. *Relatos fantásticos hispanoamericanos.* Havana: Casa de las Américas, 2003.

———, ed. *Teorías hispanoamericanas de la literatura fantástica.* Havana: Casa de las Americas, 2007.

Sartre, Jean Paul. "Aminadab: of the Fantastic Considered as a Language." *Literary and Philosophical Essays.* Trans. Annette Michelson. London: Rider and Co., 1955. 56–72.

Scari, Robert M. "Horacio Quiroga y los fenómenos parapsicológicos." *Cuadernos Hispanoamericanos* 397 (July 1983): 123–32.

Schlobin, Roger, ed. *The Aesthetics of Fantasy Literature.* Notre Dame, IN: University of Notre Dame Press, 1982.

Schroeder, Shannin. *Rediscovering Magical Realism in the Americas*. Westport, CT: Praeger Press, 2004.

Serra, Edelweis. "Conjunción de la realidad y fantasía en 'La noche boca arriba.'" *Otros mundos otros fuegos. Fantasía y realismo mágico en Iberoamérica*. Ed. D. Yates. East Lansing: Latin American Studies Center of Michigan State University, 1975. 121–27.

Sharman, Adam. *Tradition and Modernity in Spanish American Literature: From Darío to Carpentier*. New York: Palgrave Macmillan, 2006.

Shaw, Donald L. "The Presence of Myth in Borges, Carpentier, Asturias, Rulfo and García Márquez." *A Companion to Magical Realism*. Ed. Stephen M. Hart and Wen- Chin Ouyang. Woodbridge, England: Tamesis, 2005. 46–54.

Sieber, Sharon L. "Time, Simultaneity, and the Fantastic in the Narrative of Jorge Luis Borges." *Romance Quarterly* 51.3 (summer 2004): 200–11.

Siebers, Tobin. "Balzac and the Literature of Belief." *L'ésprit créateur* 28.3 (fall 1988): 37–47.

Smith, April Kendziora. "The 'Other' in Borges, Borges in Others." *Perspectives on Contemporary Literature* 12 (1986): 104–12.

Stavans, Ilán, ed. *Rubén Darío. Selected Writings*. New York: Penguin Books, 2005.

Steinbrunner, Chris, and Burt Goldblatt. *Cinema of the Fantastic*. New York: Galahad, 1972.

Stoll, Anita K. ed. *A Different Reality: Studies on the Work of Elena Garro*. Lewisburg: Bucknell University Press, 1990.

Subiela, Eliseo. *No te mueras sin decirme adónde vas*. INCASS and Artear S.A., 1995.

———. *Hombre mirando al sudeste*. Cinequanon and Transeuropa S.A., 1986.

Suleiman, Susan R., and Inge Crosman, eds. *The Reader in the Text: Essays on Audience and Interpretation*. Princeton, NJ: Princeton University Press, 1980. 3–45.

Swanson, Philip. *The New Novel in Latin America*. Manchester, England: Manchester University Press, 1995.

Tedio, Guillermo. "Borges y 'El Sur.' Entre gauchos y compadritos." *Espéculo: Revista de estudios literarios* 14 (Mar.-June 2000) (electronic publication, no pagination).

Titler, Jonathan. "La continuidad en 'Continuidad de los parques.'" *Crítica Hispánica* 6.2 (1984): 167–74.

Todorov, Tzvetan. *The Fantastic: A Structural Approach to a Literary Genre*. New York: Cornell University Press, 1975. (Originally published in French as *Introduction a la litterature fantastique*. Paris: Ed. du Seuil, 1970.)

Tofts, Darren. "The World Will be Tlön: Mapping the Fantastic onto the Virtual." *Postmodern Culture* 13.2 (Jan. 2003) (electronic journal, no pagination).

Toro, Alfonso de. "Jorge Luis Borges o la literatura del deseo: Descentración-simulación del canón y estrategias postmodernas." *Taller de Letras* 39 (2006): 101–26.

Tolliver, Joyce. "Otro modo de ver: The Gaze in *La última niebla*." *Revista Canadiense de Estudios Hispánicos* 17.1 (fall 1992): 105–21.

Trovatto, Barbara. "Los espacios antagónicos en *La última niebla* de María Luisa Bombal." *Cuaderno Internacional de Estudios Hispánicos y Lingüística* 1.1 (spring 2001): 69–74.

Tyler, Joseph. "Chac Mool. A Journey into the Fantastic." *Hispanic Journal* 10.2 (spring 1989): 177–83.

———. "Speculum, spectrum y otras reflexiones alucinantes sobre el doble en Julio Cortázar." *Semiosis: Seminario de Semiótica, Teoría, Análisis* 2.4 (July-Dec. 2006): 49–57.

Uslar Pietri, Arturo. *Letras y hombres de Venezuela*. Mexico: Fondo de Cultura Económica, 1948.

Valverde, César. "Pasado soterrado y masculinidad perdida en 'La muñeca reina' y 'Chac Mool.'" *Hispanic Journal* 23.2 (fall 2002): 67–78.

Vax, Louis. *Arte y literatura fantásticas*. Trans. Juan Merino. Buenos Aires: Ed. Universitaria de Buenos Aires, 1965. (Originally published in French as *L'art et la litterature fantastiques*. Paris: Presses Universitaires de France, 1960.)

Veeser, H. Aram, ed. *The New Historicism*. New York: Routledge, 1989.

Vega, Pastor. *Las profecías de Amanda*. Havana: ICAIC, 1999.

Veirave, Alfredo. "'El almohadón de plumas': Lo ficticio y lo real." *Aproximaciones a Horacio Quiroga*, Ed. Angel Flores. Caracas, Venezuela: Monte Avila, 1976. 209–14.

Verani, Hugo J. *José Emilio Pacheco ante la crítica*. Xalapa, Mexico: Universidad Veracruzana, 1987.

Veres, Luis. *Los reyes y el laberinto. Sobre Borges, Lugones, y otros ensayos*. Valencia, Spain: Generalitat Valenciana, 2007.

Von Mücke, Dorothea E. *The Seduction of the Occult and the Rise of the Fantastic Tale*. Stanford, CA: Stanford University Press, 2003.

Waldegaray, Marta Inés. "'La otra muerte' y 'El milagro secreto': Relaciones entre literatura e historia." *Variaciones Borges: Journal of the Jorge Luis Borges Center for Studies and Documentation* 17 (2004): 187–97.

Warner, Marina. *Fantastic Metamorphoses, Other Worlds: Ways of Telling the Self*. Oxford: Oxford University Press, 2002.

Warnes, Christopher. *Magical Realism and the Postcolonial Novel: Between Faith and Irreverence*. New York: Palgrave Macmillan, 2009.

Woodyard, Kathleen. "Performing Age, Performing Gender." *NWSA Journal* 18 (1990): 162–89.

Yates, Donald, ed. *Otros mundos otros fuegos: Fantasía y realismo mágico en Iberoamérica*. East Lansing: Latin American Studies Center of Michigan State University, 1975.

Zavala, Lauro. "Continuaciones para 'Continuidad de los parques' de Julio Cortázar." *Texto Crítico* 8.14 (Jan.-June 2004): 99–107.

Index

About the Author

Cynthia Duncan is Associate Professor of Hispanic Studies at the University of Washington, Tacoma.